Life is a Pilgrimage

Selected Omega Publications titles

The Call of the Dervish
by Pir Vilayat Inayat Khan

The Complete Sayings of Hazrat Inayat Khan
by Hazrat Inayat Khan

Introducing Spirituality into Counseling and Therapy
by Pir Vilayat Inayat Khan

The Message in Our Time;The Life and Teachings of
Sufi Master Pir-o-Murshid Inayat Khan
by Pir Vilayat Inayat Khan

The Music of Life; The Inner Nature and Effects of Sound
by Hazrat Inayat Khan

Song of the Prophets; The Unity of Religious Ideals
by Hazrat Inayat Khan

Spy Princess; The Life of Noor Inayat Khan
by Shrabani Basu

That Which Transpires Behind That Which Appears
by Pir Vilayat Inayat Khan

We Rubies Four
The Memoirs of Claire Ray Harper
(Khairunisa Inayat Khan)
by Claire Ray Harper and David Ray Harper

For a complete listing of Omega titles see
www.omegapub.com

Life is a Pilgrimage

Pir Vilayat Inayat Khan

Omega Publications
New Lebanon, New York

Published by
OMEGA PUBLICATIONS, INC.
New Lebanon, New York
www.omegapub.com

Editing and interior design by Green Lion Press
Cover photo of Pir Vilayat Inayat Khan courtesy of the
Sufi Order International
Cover design by Yasodhara Sandra Lillydahl

This edition is printed on acid-free paper that meets ANSI standard X39-48.

Printed and bound in the United States of America

Inayat Khan, Pir Vilayat (1916–2004)
Life is a Pilgrimage
Includes editorial note, introduction, index, biographical note
ISBN 978-0930872-81-6
1.Sufism I. Title
Library of Congress Control Number: 2011937535

Table of Contents

Editorial Note

Life is a Pilgrimage is based on a series of letters Pir Vilayat wrote for distribution to his mureeds, or initiated students, over the years 1983–2004.

He wrote from airplanes and airports, from his meditation "pod" at the Abode of the Message, from retreats. He called the series *Keeping in Touch* (KIT). These missives were forwarded to the Sufi Order Secretariat, which xeroxed them and mailed them out to mureeds on the KIT list.

The frequency of the letters varied. During some periods they came monthly; at other periods they were sporadic. In the last years of his life they became much less frequent, and sometimes KIT messages were folded into other communications from the Secretariat.*

These writings were often topical, addressing whatever was on his mind at the moment or whatever he thought might be on the minds of his mureeds. They typically presupposed familiarity with his style or teaching and with themes and even phrases that he often used in his teaching. The writing style was generally informal: colloquial, elliptical, unedited, and full of free associations. The writing was sometimes hasty, ideas tumbling over one another as they poured from his lively, original mind. It was what, these days, would probably be an online "blog."

*Exact dating and tracking is sometimes difficult. The writings were typically undated; once separated from their postmarked envelope and filed, the date of writing or promulgation was no longer evident. Nor did the Secretariat keep any detailed records. These messages were seen at the time as ephemeral, the sharings of the moment.

And yet there was brilliance, poetry, depth of insight, rich veins of precious and inspired teachings in these ephemeral missives.

It seemed to some mureeds a shame that they should be lost, or scattered, surviving only as tattered sheets stuck in a folder. Those who had read these little essays the first time around wanted to revisit and savor them. Newer mureeds who in some cases had never met Pir Vilayat wanted to see this side of him. And then there is the world of seekers, scholars, and other readers who might be inspired, delighted, and energized by his wisdom and personality as they come through in these letters, were they made available.

In short, the dormant trove of KITs called out for a properly edited and organized, well designed and produced book.

Omega Publications negotiated with Pir Zia Inayat-Khan, the copyright holder of Pir Vilayat's writings. We gained permission to reproduce the KITs and a contract was signed.

Yasodhara Sandra Lillydahl began working from her personal collection of papers, organizing the KITs by theme, eliminating redundancies and duplications, and doing other initial editing. She created a full organized text, with an introductory prologue taken from one KIT, eleven chapters representing eleven themes, and an afterword consisting of Pir Vilayat's final message to his mureeds before his death (not one of the original KIT series).

At that point she passed a scanned and OCR'd electronic form of her text on to me for copy-editing and preparation for publication.

My editing process required getting out the OCR and other errors introduced when the texts were scanned and converted to electronic form. Then misspellings, typos, and other outright errors already present in the original KITs were corrected. This was a demanding but comparatively straightforward process.

Then it required taking the informal and colloquial, unedited flow of Pir Vilayat's words as they tumbled from his fingers into his computer and, as it were, brush their hair and re-button their buttons to make them presentable to a broader audience. This editing phase was a critical and very delicate matter.

Places where Pir Vilayat began a sentence making one point and shifted to another point mid-sentence, such that the sentence seemed to contradict itself leaving the reader baffled, had to be broken up or the missing transition indicated. These transitions may have been naturally supplied by mureeds who had heard him speak at greater length about both points and perhaps even supplying just that transition on remembered occasions. But for a new audience, one that might include people who had never met Pir Vilayat or been exposed to his teachings, it would very likely look incoherent or confused.

Similarly, what was to be done with certain favorite words and pet phrases Pir Vilayat always used, familiar to his mureeds and, indeed, beloved of them, which in fact were archaic usages no longer having the original meaning, or cognates from French or other languages not having the same meaning in English, or outright malapropisms? There was no confusion for mureeds who had spent hundreds of hours sitting at his feet and listening to tapes, and who now scarcely connected with the other meanings when hearing those words from him. But a new audience would be stopped short, or led to a wrong understanding.

This editing could only be done by someone who knew Pir Vilayat's teaching deeply over many decades, who could recognize what he had in mind and what he was intending behind the rich overlapping tumble of words. But it also had to be someone who had sufficient mastery of language to present it clearly and unconfusingly with the lightest possible touch, so that Pir Vilayat's words, and his voice, and his characteristic flavor and personality, still sang off the page.

Here again what was needed was someone so tuned into Pir Vilayat's spirit, and so committed to preserving that voice, that the corrections would be made without compromise of what the most dedicated mureed knew and loved.

A delicate job indeed! And a demanding and time-consuming one. But one that needed to be done right so that these great treasures of Pir Vilayat's teachings should shine with their deep wisdom and his unique spirit both for those who knew and loved him and for those who may just be discovering him.

I believe I brought the required experience, attunement, skills, and dedication to the task. I took it on as a sacred service and gift of love to Pir Vilayat for all that he gave to me in my own spiritual realization and in gratitude for the amazing being that he was, a blessing and a miracle in my life.

We further acknowledge Jelaluddin Howard Fisher, who did the book design and typesetting, and also patiently implemented all the editing corrections.

Vajra Nurhakika Dana Densmore

Foreword

Following the words of Pir Vilayat is like soaring through the galaxies—the vast expanse of outer space and the luminous inner worlds. On this astral journey we meet the saints and masters of all traditions as we leap and dance between science, philosophy, and religion. All the while his words draw us onward toward greater heights of awareness and freedom.

In this volume we encounter Pir Vilayat's thoughts and teachings on many subjects. We hear his words and read his writings, the fruit of decades of spiritual practice, meditation, and teaching. And we witness as he, like the conductor of some grand cosmic symphony, draws together a hundred voices—mystics, astrophysicists, and thinkers from every era of history and every branch of learning. And yet throughout there is a single call, expressed in a line of Euler, "the pull of the future is stronger than the push of the past."

As we read, we find that Pir Vilayat's thoughts are constantly moving forward, transforming and expanding toward a future filled with new possibilities. In fact nothing in his universe remains still. Through his teachings, the philosophies of the past are resurrected into new living forms that can travel and evolve with us as we inquire into emerging questions on the expanding frontiers of our own human experience.

Pir Vilayat recognizes that we must each travel through the entire human drama. He unveils the pain and tragedy that he has found in his own life. But he also shows how suffering can be transmuted into joy, freeing us from the painful limitations of our own being. He invites us to search and strive for the Divine. And in so doing we discover that our searching and striving, our own spiritual journey, is the Divine itself. As Hazrat Inayat Khan states, "It is not by self-realization that one realizes God, it is by God-realization that one realizes self."

As his son, I witnessed Pir Vilayat in the final weeks of his life. Even confined to his hospital bed, nothing was over. Every day he began new writing projects. He contemplated recent satellite images of space. He was excited to talk with each and every visitor. And his eyes twinkled as he imagined what the future would hold for all of us.

The world will continue to grow and change. And so will we. Whether or not we choose, we will be transformed a thousand times. Will we participate consciously and purposefully in our own unfoldment? Will we acknowledge our own role in the future of the planet? Whether we turn inward or outward, we are immersed in the Divine, a great tidal current pulling us forever onward.

Mirza Inayat Khan
September, 2011

Introduction

The Universel—The Spirituality of the Future

Following is an attempt to explore how our vision of the spirituality of the future, the Universel, opens new perspectives in our quest for awakening. The spiritual itinerary of Pir-o-Murshid Inayat Khan led him to branch out from the traditional transmission of his Sufi predecessors into an even more encompassing span, as found amongst the more liberal Sufis nurtured in the Chishti Order in India. He incorporated this broad outreach in the interfaith Universal Worship service, but he clearly anticipated that the message for our time could not be a syncretistic collation of the bountiful gifts of the great world religions in their diversity. The original insight of the religious pioneers—patriarchs, rishis, prophets, masters, saints, women dervishes—has often been distorted or paraphrased by the transmission of their pupils and interpreters, and by the "institutionalization" of spirituality. Their dogmas or methods of meditation at first sight appear as conflicting. When, however, these doctrines and faiths are rethought and updated in the perspectives opening up to us in our day and age, and more particularly in a projected vision of the future, we can appreciate their congruity in their complementarity. This is the task that Pir-o-Murshid Inayat Khan initiated and that we are invited to pursue in the Universel. The Sufi transmission remains the seed embedded in this splendid flowering of spirituality which he baptized as the Universal Message—the Universel, announcing the millennium.

We need first to meet a preliminary which calls our attention: owning to the reality of pain is our compelling concern. I hear a call from the Earth—the Message answers the call by the voice of the heart.

In what way can awakening meet that plea? This is what we are venturing to explore.

First, let us list a few typical cases of pain:

(i) Physical pain: cancer, AIDS, arthritis, acute nerve pains, all bodily pains.

(ii) Psychological distress: having been abused, humiliated, snubbed, derided, having been treated unjustly, repressed by the ego of a person—particularly in a marital relationship, let down, abandoned by spouse or partner, experiencing unreciprocated love, a feeling of inadequacy, a poor self image, a sense of failure, pathological disturbances, loss at the death of a dear one, having a retarded child, drugged teenagers, imprisonment, or being tortured.

(iii) At the soul level: feeling suffocated by the limitations in one's understanding, failure to see meaningfulness in life, or in one's own life, feeling trapped by conditions that seem to preclude enlightenment, being disheartened, disgusted by the profanity and the grossness in the psychological environment—a desperate need for the sacred.

The question before us is what solace, what remedy (if any), what help can the new vistas in spirituality, meditation, and awakening offer? Simple escape from prevailing conditions cannot offer meaningfulness and joy.

It evidences a lack of appreciation of the invaluable legacy of the great civilizations from which we benefit: Beethoven's Ninth Symphony, the Chaconne of Bach, Notre Dame of Paris, Persepolis, Rembrandt, Shakespeare; the technologies—TV, the computer; the achievements of mountaineers; outer space exploration; the exploits of the minds of mathematicians, physicists, psychologists; the dedication of welfare workers, rescue workers, valor in battle; the exploits in the mind of rishis, physicists, the divine power of dervishes. The ascetic's "desirelessness" would not bring the universe to that degree of sophisticated flowering. It will, however, free us from the constraint of our personal perspective. It fosters detachment, freedom, and provides a psychological analgesic against anguish due to our dependence upon environmental conditions that wreak confinement and stress. It is certainly a refuge when we are stymied by psychological overstress that has become intolerable; and therefore a useful rescue *vade mecum* in our psychological first aid chest.

In Buddhism, the crucial step leading to awakening is letting go of the launching platform. Obviously, to awaken from the perspective of the way things appear to the cosmic thinking behind it, one needs to downplay the commonplace perspective to highlight the perspective of the meaningfulness underpinning it, but does that entail discarding all the bounties of the inheritance of our civilizations that are essential features of our psyche? To eschew doing just this, we need to effect a transmutation of suffering in our psyche so as to carry them aloft in our flight above existential conditions. Beethoven's optimism in the victory of good over evil, Brahms' conversion of pain into joy, the glorification of the sacred that inspired the builders of the Chartres Cathedral, Mother Teresa's compassion, and the courage of firemen and rescue operators represent the quintessence of the symphonies or the monuments in stone. The culmination of the thinking of the whole cosmos at its leading edge is incorporated right into the electronics and hardware of the rocket hurtling across sidereal space, carrying the quintessence of human ingenuity nurtured on Planet Earth beyond the telluric orb of matter.

What help does awakening "beyond life" (as in *samadhi*) provide us to find a solution to suffering? Significantly, this feat of stepping out of the commonplace into a cosmic outreach and transcendent overarching dimension that motivated the Hindu rishis and Buddhists is precisely what sparked the genius of creative people to explore a psychological space beyond the middle range.

Here indifference is countered by enthusiasm. These outstanding achievements of human initiative and strenuous toil are, for the Sufis, the many-splendored outbursts of the nostalgia of the universe, breaking through each of the fragments of itself (including us humans) as it evolves (as we evolve). Pir-o-Murshid Inayat Khan beckons us to use that driving force, while being cautioned by the way this force can become deviated in us. Selfishness and greed can corrupt us in our striving to improve our human conditions and in our personal involvement in existential circumstances, rather than our honoring a concern to share in building a beautiful world of beautiful people. He therefore urges us to orient that force with a wise, masterful will.

Creativity is sparked by the personalization of the driving emotion of the whole universe, customized by our diverse uniqueness, in the context of the problems that arise when the individuated wills of the fragments of the universe affirm their individual idiosyncrasies and conflict, causing joy and pain. Creativity, born out of the human drama, peaks in the cosmic celebration signaling itself to us, and sometimes erupting within that very drama when it inspires us to reach beyond our differences out of love and understanding for the sacredness of the human spirit. Thus the divine creativity is carried further through the human being; and, spurred by suffering, it proves healing.

It is our passion for our ideal that fosters our creativity. Our artwork is our own personality. The beauty is that we can make it what we wish. Our thoughts, emotions, and realizations—especially if recurrent—shape our personality and even our face.

At this time, we are challenged to balance our need for freedom and our sense of fulfillment from being of service by involving ourselves with people and circumstances out of love and responsibility, sharing the joys and pains together, and through this discovering the meaningfulness which we were seeking "beyond the beyond" right in the drama and power of life in the world. Religious tenets need to be updated by virtue of our present day concern for realism. This is why Pir-o-Murshid Inayat Khan does not say "give up the world," but "loosen the ties," thereby honoring your need for freedom within constraining circumstances while at the same time taking responsibility. For him, awakening is achieved by downplaying the commonplace perspective while highlighting a perspective where you see what is enacted behind the apparent scenario, not simply dismissing the physical world or psychological circumstances as *maya* or illusion. This is awakening in life rather than beyond life.

Applying the theory of *maya* at the psychological level, according to Patanjali's Yoga Sutras, shows that distress can result from a faulty assessment of our problems and from our deceptive self image. But being cautioned against "what is not" is not sufficient. We wish to know "what is." This is where Sufism holds a complementary rather than contradictory view about *maya*. What is enacted in our problems that we may fail to grasp—albeit blurred by our faulty assessment—is signaling to us by dint of those very problems. Let us consider our problems as clues leading to grasping what the issues are at a cosmic scale, rather than entrapping ourselves in our personal bias. Follow the clue by shifting consciousness to the antipodal vantage point to that of the personal pole of our being. Identify with the deathless and impersonal pole of our being, which is co-extensive with that of all beings—what is sometimes meant by the word God.

This validation of life is in some way connected with an evolutionary trend in the notion of God, no more "up there," transcendent or out of reach, but as the universe, including ourselves.

This breakthrough in the concept of God represents freedom from the theological conditioning of our minds.

Pir-o-Murshid Inayat Khan was announcing the spirituality of the millennium. He called it the "Message of Spiritual Liberty," liberated from many of the hackneyed views of the past. Notice also that it is a collective awakening, rather than a personal one, therefore something that is happening to humanity as we evolve.

This may serve as a clue to what is meant by the "Universel." It now becomes clear that on that last day when Pir-o-Murshid Inayat Khan was with his mureeds in Suresnes, France before departing for India where he met his death, he was announcing the next step: the Universel, beyond all "isms." The temple of the Universel could not just be a building in stone, a housing for the celebration of the unity of religious ideals, but a temple made of people—people who, through the power of prayer, are announcing the spiritual message for the future: the liberated message of spiritual liberty.

The solution to the problem of the day is that the consciousness of humanity may be awakened to the divinity of the human being.

> **O Thou who art the maker, moulder and builder of the Universe, build with Thine own hands the Universel, our temple, for Thy divine Message of love, harmony and beauty.**
>
> **Pir-o-Murshid Inayat Khan**

Chapter 1

The Call of the Heart

A Millennium Message
December 2000

Although the threshold leading into the Millennium does not correspond to a significant astrological conjunction, nor to the actual birth of Christ, we have created that quantum leap in our minds: therefore it has an important significance if we will take heed of what it is telling us. Its message is this: the future is not there for us to enter into—we create it. The collective thinking of the Planet is beckoning and warning us to change.

When one turns a new page, particularly a new chapter, one needs to let go of the previous page even though it is still in the book. However in real life, the past itself has changed. From your car window, the landscape you left behind may still linger in your mind, but from the overview of a helicopter you can see that it has changed—a car may cross the road. Interestingly, our memory is gifted with the faculty of extracting the gist of the experience of the past. The task for our mind is now to interfuse the insight gained by the legacy of the past with the prospects of the future.

Our motto for the Millennium is, in the words of Euler, "the pull of the future is stronger than the push of the past." Since we create the future, it is our New Year resolutions, actually: our New Millennium resolutions—our pledges that will open the door to change.

Our soul-searching concerning the spoliation of our beautiful planet, crime, vulgarity, point to the challenge before us. To trigger change, there is first work to do with ourselves: rise above resentment. The tour de force is to love people who make it difficult to love them without capitulating to their domination and thereby abandoning our values. It is our sense of the sacred that is the door out of the imbroglio—glorification lifts us above our selfishness and greed and invests us with spiritual authority.

A new spirituality is emerging out of the religions of the past, free from dogmas, prescriptions, gurus, and the institutionalization of religions. It is calling upon us to take responsibility, honor our values, celebrate the marvel of life and realize the privilege of participating in the cosmic celebration right in the middle of the drama of humanity.

You may recognize this vision for the future of spirituality. It is the Universel—the message for the Millennium of spiritual freedom, honoring the divinity of the human status, mastery through accomplishment.

It carries a heartening energy: re-enchantment.

Global Thinking

It would be a truism to say that Planet Earth, and we as the decision-making members of the planetary population, are right in the midst of a revolution. For the evolutionary thrust of which we are the beneficiaries to advance, the status quo has inevitably to break down; our concern is whether a radical breakthrough will outweigh the breakdown, or whether the breakdown will reach a point of no return. Clearly we and we only have the answer in our hands. But who are we? I hope I am not making too judgmental a statement by saying that only a very small portion of the population of the Planet are prepared to prioritize the interest of the whole over their greed, failing to see that the well being of the whole does reflect upon the living standard of the individual.

The troubling increase in crime, violence, vulgarity, lack of charity, sacrilege, abuse, and the ruthless exploitation of the environment is an indication that a growing portion of humanity is in trouble. Moreover we have the bigotry of fundamentalists, and perhaps a large majority of well-meaning people are still into their personal thing, not having the foggiest sense of what the global perspective could possibly mean! We have the irresponsible population explosion. On the other hand, we have the few whose intuition gives them some clues as to what measures we need to take to avert a catastrophe.

Paradoxically, the very technology which is destroying the environment could be harnessed to save it. But our way of thinking and more so our values are the determining factors. We have not grown on a par with the potentialities that, like the apprentice sorcerer, we have unleashed. It is really a matter of both consciousness and conscience. Vested interests have sabotaged technological breakthroughs that could have helped. There is also simply a habit-forming complacency, and sectarianism. Sometimes one wonders how things could ever change for the better. Yet indeed we never cease to be amazed by the dramatic upheavals in our day and age. This being so, there is hope.

The evolutionary forward thrust has not reached its culmination in Homo sapiens such as we are at present. Looking back gives us some clues as to how we could improve. Species progress through an increase in the scope of their consciousness. Whereas the tree is locked in the immediate environment, the awareness, the thinking of pioneers amongst us encompasses the galaxies. Thinking big will get us out of the rut. Global consciousness means understand ing that we are all in this together; that the well-being of the whole promotes our personal interest.

There seem to be two issues: promoting global awareness and thwarting the abusers. Granted, the media have alerted people throughout the globe of the hazards we are running into; yet the people and industries simply go on abusing the Planet and other people as though they had not been warned. This cuts right into the political field where religious parochialism has caused the death of thousands of innocent people and wreaked havoc on the environment. In many areas, advocating tolerance in the interest of a global religious vision would be interpreted as treason. How can we reach a global sense of the unity of the human family if we cling to our divisions?

To advance we must not, like the wife of Lot, look back, which risks sclerosed thinking. It is a positive vision of the way the future could be, the way we could make the future, that will propel us forward.

It takes courage to let go of all that one has built up over the years without any guarantee that a new light will dawn upon one's horizon. But we find ourselves sometimes confronted with the choice between situations which progress gradually like a bud unfurls, or where things remain at a standstill and run the chance of reversing into decay, or again where nature proceeds by leaps and bounds. There are situations which one cannot change in their outer circumstances, but will change by one's changing oneself, or by a new way of handling them. In exceptional cases and perhaps the most meaningful, there is no slow transition from one perspective to the other—the transit is sudden. Here lies the difference between the moment of time where there is an overlap between past and future, and the instant where there is a sudden and irreversible break of continuity.

The holistic paradigm has revolutionized science, but in our commonplace thinking, most people still think in categories. If you think holistically, you are not a fraction of the totality, but a relatively permanent expression of that totality in its wholeness, which is potentially present in you. Should we apply this way of thinking to our relationship with the environment, we would not think of it as something one can exploit without spoiling one's very underpinning from right under one's feet.

The revolution in the thinking at the prow of the evolutionary advance has moreover changed our way of looking at causality. Instead of the simplistic view, it is now understood that each wave in the ocean is not simply the result of the previous one. The whole ocean rises as each wave, and each wave is interjected back into the ocean. The whole ocean then arises as each *new* wave. Generalizing, we realize the implications of our interventions not only in the hardware, but also the software of the universe. Also we see how intervening in one area of the psycho-ecosystem affects every other area. Therefore our free-wheeling into the future must integrate a greater compass and complexity than ever before. We need to shift between several vantage points. By integrating the know-how of creative thinkers, consciousness at the leading edge is becoming stereoscopic.

To network with those who are not in the race, we even need to integrate old ideas into the wider web of new ideas rather than rejecting the old like a baby being thrown out with the bathwater. We will even need to find common ground between thinking in the reductionist way and the holistic way. We will even need to account for further dimensions of time in our understanding of causal inference, for example including a transcendental vector of time to the simplistic process of becoming, as illustrated in Jung's synchronicity. We will be learning to see how the "everywhere and always" manifests in the forward march of becoming. If we hoist our vantage point from the commonplace narrow range in the act of self transcendence, we will grasp things in a wider context. This is where some of the skills of meditation are proving useful to people.

The whole universe has contributed to the way humanity thinks today; if the Planet had no

intelligence, it could not have intelligent beings on it. The collective working of many minds as one single idea, and the activity of the whole world in a certain direction are governed by the intelligence of the Planet.

Pir-o-Murshid Inayat Khan

Our way of considering the cosmos and the Planet Earth in particular, has taken a quantum leap. Instead of looking at the stars as viewed from Planet Earth, we are now able to imagine how Planet Earth looks as viewed from the stars. This has surreptitiously revolutionized our way of considering our Planet, which in turn revolutionizes our way of seeing ourselves. We imagine outer space to be "out there," but has it ever occurred to you that actually Planet Earth is in outer space? It all depends on how you look at it. Since we can now see our live cells in powerful microscopes, our whole perception of the fabric of our body has undergone a dramatic change. Instead of dismissing our bodies as other than ourselves, we are beginning to honor the involvement of our innate sense of meaningfulness with the very fabric of our bodiness.

In the realm of psychology, by the same token, we realize that our sense of personal inadequacy or our pessimistic judgment in our assessment of a situation is due to our mind's having got entrapped in a way of thinking from which we failed to see a way out. Yes, one can get trapped in one's thinking and ascribe the prison to one's fate. The bind is in the mind.

More than ever, people find themselves willy-nilly enrolled in the inexorable machinery constructed generation after generations, conditioning them and robbing them of their creativity. At what cost our modern efficiency! People suffer from the total lack of opportunity to harness their creative urge as was the case before arts and crafts were replaced by machined standardization—now computerized.

Our experiments with political institutions have proven how crucial freedom is to promote progress—in fact freedom from conformity generates creativity. On the other hand, there is nothing in the world more abused than freedom. We see its consequences in the decadence, vulgarity, slovenliness and permissiveness of our modern societies. There is no accounting for taste!

One could define creativity as the act of exploring uncharted regions of the mind, while grasping a correspondence between the mental constructs thus gleaned and forms or configurations or scenarios in the fabric of matter. Creativity is a congruent conjunction between the timeless and the transient, the heavenly and the earthly. It is a sudden sense of meaningfulness that sparks our innovative faculty. What we mean by our sense of meaningfulness is our mind's ability to click when it grasps a correspondence between two thoughts which had hitherto appeared unrelated. To be creative rather than just fanciful, one's vision needs to click with the possibility of its actual realization at the existential level.

The grasp of congruence sparks our being with delight because it gives us a sense of thinking in sync with the thinking of the universe, and of feeling in resonance with the emotion of the cosmos, and hence makes us aware of our holistic connectiveness with the totality which we call God, not just at the physical level but at all levels.

I Have a Dream

December 2001. This letter responds to international events following the terrorist attacks on the United States in September 11, 2001.

Martin Luther King:

We cannot walk alone. As we walk, we must make the pledge that we shall march ahead. We cannot turn back. This is our hope.... With this faith

> **we will be able to hew out the mountain of despair. With this faith, we will be able to work together, to pray together, to struggle together, to go to jail together, to stand up for freedom together.... This will be the day when all God's children will be able to sing with a new meaning "My country, 'tis of thee, Sweet land of liberty, Of thee I sing. Land where my fathers died...." When we let freedom ring, when we let it ring from every village, from every state, and every city, we will be able to speed up that day when all of God's children, black men and white men, Jews and Gentiles,** [may I add Jews and Arabs?] **Protestants and Catholics, will be able to join hands and sing in the words of the old Negro spiritual: "Free at last! Free at last! Thank God Almighty, we are free at last!"**

I had a dream. My hopes suffered a tragic setback—maybe yours have, too. Our hearts have been devastated: people killing each other, blowing themselves up, revenge, torture, leaving a trail of misery, of despair, the hordes of displaced refugees, contempt for human dignity.

Yet I still have a dream—a dream of peace. Is it likewise with you? Do you still hold that dream? Is it okay to dream wishful thinking? They call it ineffective, utopist.

Utopia was the dream of Thomas More and the title of his book published in 1516. His Utopia was an imaginary island that might serve as a model for human communities, governed by an ideally perfect social and political system. It reflects earlier idyllic political models, for example Plato's Republic. Also J. S. Bach described his music as a model for a human commonwealth: "each theme enjoying a range of freedom but each limiting its freedom in the interest of the whole." He added: "such is the harmony governing the motion of the stars."

Perchance dreams do come true. We call it a miracle because it defies logic. But in mathematics, one chance in a million or even in a billion is still not illogical—just not very probable, but for the heroes, not to be dismissed.

It is never in your pocket, but it lures you ever forward into breaking new ground—opening new horizons. This is the stuff with which the spirit of heroes is made. It challenges one to defy those admittedly reasonable words: "unpractical," "not feasible," "it doesn't work," "it cannot possibly work." The answer is, "What if it could? What if my assessment is wrong? What if what is judged impossible is possible? What if my belief, and your belief, and that of many other people makes what seems impossible possible?" Belief is an unaccountable force. However it can also operate as misconstrued and misleading obscurantism. Hence Hazrat Inayat Khan's injunction: *Shatter your ideal on the rock of truth.*

As a soul evolves from stage to stage, it must break the former belief in order to establish the later, and this breaking of the belief is called by Sufis *Tark*, which means abandonment.

He who fights his nature for his ideal is a saint; he who subjects his ideal to his realization of truth is the master (*Gayan*).

One needs to distinguish between belief and faith. Belief is based upon a holy scripture or the injunction of a believer, sometimes factual evidence; whereas faith is a kind of gut feeling, not based on evidence, a sense that everything makes sense ultimately and that there is splendor behind the existential, awry universe. This conviction overrides the proof of the contrary. It belongs to a higher knowledge. It is what Hazrat Inayat Khan calls "the reason behind reason."

Blind idealism can lead to the kind of intolerance that begets violence, persecution, cruelty, even torture (as evidenced in the Spanish inquisition), and in our day in the 11th of September massacre. The challenge is to give the minimum ethical decency priority over one's impulse to pursue one's belief at the cost of human suffering. In the hierarchy of ideals, the paramount value is the truth.

It comes by rising above all that hinders one's faith in truth: the abandoning of the worldly ideal, the abandonment of the heavenly ideal, the abandoning of the divine ideal, and even the abandoning of abandonment. This brings the seer to the shores of the ultimate truth.

Hazrat Inayat Khan:
The Way of Illumination (private papers)

Surprising words that aver their pertinence in the present world situation! Yes, as one becomes more aware, one's erstwhile ideal concedes its inadequacy. Here is proof that one has progressed. This is the dark night of the mind of St. John of the Cross. One easily confuses ideal with ideology (for example: Nazi ideology, Communist ideology, racist ideology). Ideology begets hatred with its inevitable follow-up of conflict, war, misery, poverty, uprooted refugees, disruption of the fruits of efforts of dedicated people, disruption of civilizations built sometimes over eons of time.

The present world conflict is triggered by a tug of war. On one side, the ideology fostering material profit and profiteering, sustained by ever more sophisticated technology, which has the disadvantage of opening the door to ruthless, insensitive greed (affluence while people are sleeping in the streets), manipulation, perjury, ego games, power games, a degeneration in standards in morals, a pursuit of ugliness in art, slovenliness, facetiousness, vulgarity, crime, lack of self respect.

On the other side, we find a more traditional ideology that upholds age-hallowed standards of dignity, that criticizes what is considered a moral decadence, and condemns depravity, sacrilege of the sacredness of religious transmissions. Among those adhering to the latter ideology, some adopt extreme, bigoted, inflexible attitudes called fanaticism, and feel threatened by the established holders of power, spoiling it for those loyal to the prescriptions of their religion.

Is there a way of reconciling these seeming irreconcilables?

Sufism teaches that spiritual progress and material progress are concomitant and that there can be no genuine or lasting progress until the spiritual quality is adopted.

When dominated and repressed by the holders of power, when frustration reaches a point of uncontrollable emotion of desperation, it can explode, culminating in horrendous destructive acts such as the 11th of September outrage, triggering a spiraling vicious circle of retaliation. A dignified solution looms obviously at hand for those who see the counter-productiveness of hotheaded retribution.

The nations of today stand in the quest of their own national benefit regardless of other nations. This has made the world a battlefield of continual struggle where life has become chaos.

Can you now hear the voice of despair? Can we measure how great must be the degree of frustration and anger for young men to offer their lives for freedom from oppression? Where there is suffering, where there is misery, penury, if the oppressed feel that their grievances will not be heard or heeded, they will resort to terrorism to exercise pressure for their cause. Aggression is triggered by fear, frustration, suffering. True, it is counterproductive. This very aggression puts the wrench in the wheels of conflict resolution. The end does not justify the means; violence proves in the end to defeat its purpose, playing into the vicious circle of violence. There is here a misconstruction that needs to be unmasked on both sides. The communications breakdown is sparked by a lack of trust. Mutual trust is gained painstakingly by the ongoing experience of working together, as Martin Luther King said. If one discounts one's memory of history, one easily stumbles into a Catch 22. The killings by the oppressed who feel maligned by a contempt of human rights is considered as terrorism, whereas killing the new terrorists by those comfortably and legally established who owe their position of power by themselves having resorted initially to terrorism is accepted as a legal act by dint of invoking the righteousness of their antiterrorist claim against the terror that they themselves triggered in the first place. There is no doubt that the human factor here is the criterion: respect for human dignity.

Much as the counterproductive vicious circle of conflict in which the world is engaged seems inevitable, it is difficult to realize that the solution is right at hand. One has difficulty in seeing how it could work. Resort to force is shortsighted; it will never solve problems in the long run.

Christ says this clearly. To St. Peter who sought to protect him from Judas's betrayal:

He who lives by the sword will perish by the sword.

Indeed, of what use would it have been if St. Peter had attacked Judas?

Yet one needs to take precautions to protect innocent people so that the 11th of September outrage could not be repeated. Pir o Murshid Inayat Khan advocates:

Avoid the harm done by the enemy by taking precautions, facing it with strength.

He warns, however, that the strength of intervention should be resorted to

...only if one is sure that kindness and forgiveness will have no power whatever over the hard heart of the enemy, but on the other hand will make it worse.

Could one forgive the terrorists who committed such a monstrous crime on September 11th? Innocent people as hostages in hijacked planes turned into live bombs—innocent people fleeing the flames by jumping out the windows to their death! We can never forget this. Could one forgive Hitler or Stalin, and many, many heartless brutal beings? Could anyone have converted Hitler or Stalin by nonviolence? By forgiving them? They would have scoffed at our naiveté! Of course one cannot force one's forgiveness upon a person who does not recognize that he is guilty.

If we had not countered Nazism with strength, we in Europe would be living under a ruthless dictatorship with the ensuing damage to the values of our civilizations achieved at the cost of so much dedication, sacrifice and ingenuity.

Christ intervened with violence in the temple against the profanation of the sacred.

Yet the secret of breaking the pattern of the vicious circle of retribution and escalating retaliation is to bravely and trustingly opt for the reverse: kindness, forgiveness, but joined with authority. One needs to take precautions to ensure, to prevent, that outrages to decent behavior do not reoccur, causing further victims "only if one is sure that kindness and forgiveness will have no power whatever over the hard heart of the enemy, but on the other hand will make it worse." [Hazrat Inayat Khan]

On the other hand, in some cases the way of kindness will disarm the opponent if we listen to their grievance and take heed of them, as Gandhi said: "The objective should not be to punish the opponent or to inflict injury upon him. We must make him feel that in us he has a friend. It is a means to secure the cooperation of the opponent consistent with truth and justice."

Forgiveness is difficult and obstructed by those who fail to believe in a peaceful solution. It requires implicit trust that this solution can prove effective.

Hazrat Inayat Khan says "Forgive the enemy and forget his enmity if he truly wishes it. And take the first step in establishing friendship instead of holding in one's mind the pain of the past."

This is my dream, my faith, the policy I have arrived at dealing with my frustrations, and my ultimate trust in the basic need of humans for peace and harmony which is disrupted when grievances are not dealt with and hatred and violence are aroused: the belief that there is a way of understanding, of kindness and mutual trust, of respect for human dignity and love. Do you believe this too? I believe that if one overcomes that psychological layer of resentment, one will uncover that core of the goodness that lies in wait in the depth of the human soul, the divinity in the human being.

My faith is that with shared endeavor we can make what seems impossible possible. I hear that many kindred spirits think this way. Together we can build a force of peace in a disrupted and wounded world. It starts in our personal lives and snowballs in society at large at a global scale. Forgiveness starts by getting into the consciousness, the *conscience* of the "other" (the "other oneself"), where one sees his or her grievances, resentment, and struggle for self esteem. Forgiveness is sparked by understanding, by withholding one's condemning. One hopes that one's love and forgiveness will defuse the resentment of those whom one has offended, and who have offended one. I realize that it is difficult if one has been abused. How far can one go? One needs to trust that eventually, in the long run, our trust in shared forgiveness will spread far and wide to build a beautiful world of beautiful people.

The story goes that there was an old man called St. Nicholas, trekking through the snow in Northern reaches, whose joy was giving. He gave presents to children so that as they grew up they might themselves give presents to people in the form of kindness and generosity. That present is love.

"We are tested in our love," says Hazrat Pir-o-Murshid Inayat Khan. This giving love can be very difficult if it is to a person who has harmed one, and more so if to a person who has hurt someone whom one loves. So we are tested in the utmost. It is the message of Christ whose birth we celebrate at the solstice when light begins to increase carrying a message of hope.

This is my wish for the New Year: Hope—faith in the power of love.

A Christmas Message

May my Christmas message reach you from my pod in the middle of the woods at the Abode of the Message. May it be a joyous one, and may the New Year open up exciting new perspectives, and may your life be blessed by making room for the divine presence.

Christmastide evidences our attunement to the seasonal cycles of Planet Earth. We, just like the plants, go through a threshold state of soul-searching, lying low in anticipation of the rebirth of life when the light tide changes and daylight wins over the dark night. There is anxiety before the unknown. As we hear echoes of alarmist presages of an escalation of belligerent conflicts, we, of course, interrogate ourselves as to the wisdom of meeting a threat with a show of strength. Throughout the globe, there have been demonstrations of public opinion against the use of nuclear weapons that could lead us to the point of no return by igniting the world arsenals. A demonstration of the absurdity of giving vent to warring instincts was to be found in the First World War when, on Christmas Eve, soldiers on either side of the line dropped their guns and played cards.

On the other hand, we are told how naive it is to assume that by disarming ourselves we will stay the hand of any potential violator of a gentlemen's peace pledge simply by being less threatening. Truly, when threatened, animals become more aggressive. But there are always the ones who will attack covetously or maliciously. Animals will hold each other at bay by threatening displays, but it takes only a little inadvertency to lose one's nerve and the truce is lost. Then things escalate beyond control.

The threat parade becomes absurdly self-defeating when, for example, in order to save one's own side, one enters into a situation in which everything is inevitably blown up, which is the sardonic paradox of our time. On the other hand, nonviolence would prove self-defeating, for example, in the hypothetical event of a Nazi holding one hundred hostages at gunpoint, given that one were placed before the choice of either shooting him and saving the hostages or observing nonviolence and letting the hostages be sacrificed. Does not our sense of honour and chivalry call upon us to protect the victims of wanton violence? How can one do this without retaliating in violence?

Is there a way out of this dilemma? How could one become a warrior of peace? Remember Bernard Shaw's challenge: "Dare you wage war upon war?" Gandhi's nonviolence was not quietist, as the historic raid on the Dharasana Salt Works showed. The marchers were mown down mercilessly by the troops, yet kept on advancing to the extent that the conscience of the masses of Britons at home was stirred and nauseated. This resulted in India's freedom.

Christ's "turn the other cheek" is not passivity; it requires valor. Pilate carried the power of Rome behind him while Jesus stood in front of him on the bench of the accused, in the consciousness of the divine sovereignty suffering from the limitation of the existential condition, yet still sovereign. Pilate did everything he could to browbeat Jesus, who had previously been tortured. Finally, Pilate was so impressed with Jesus' composure that when requested to have the plaque announcing "Jesus King of the Jews" removed, he refused, saying "It has been written." Such is the power of God-consciousness.

An application of this disarming valor is to be found in the case of the Admiral in the Indian Navy who went out unarmed to face a raging mob of sailors and persuaded them to turn back by dint of his masterful sovereignty. The mad elephant can only be controlled by the *madhzub*—the dervish who is gifted with the sovereignty resulting from God-consciousness. When unsure of the strength of our being, we resort to the force of arms. In so doing, we will never plug in to our own resourcefulness. Consequently, we neglect to fall upon our real inner power. We have no idea as to the extent of the power we represent jointly. The forces of goodwill in the universe are immensely more powerful and numerous than the individuals who flout the dignity of the human person and his or her right to self expression and justice. But we are not as well organized as they are, and are bickering in our own party disputes rather than linking together while respecting each other's idiosyncrasies. This latter is networking—networking for peace in the consciousness of our joint power in the name of the spiritual government of the world.

May this be our motto for the New Year, for the message of Christmas is goodwill in gratitude for the return of light after the threatening increase in darkness. The rejoicing celebrating the changing of the light tide at Christmastime acquires a new relevance at Easter. A few days before, Jesus had enjoined upon his disciples to stand by him through the night until the light started dawning. "Did you watch with me?"

May every day of the New Year be a Christmas day for you. I am by your side in loyalty in our mutual dedication.

Suffering

Since time immemorial beautiful beings have dedicated their lives towards coming to the succor of those in distress in body, mind and soul. In search for a solution to suffering, Buddha renounced his palace. While many have renounced personal well being out of a feeling of compassion, many more have caused untold suffering to others in ruthless pursuance of personal interests, out of greed or crass disregard for the ordeal that millions are enduring now. Most people find their place somewhere between these two extremes. Is there any way of allaying the psychological affliction attendant upon illness and death, starvation, penury, failure, abandonment, injustice, and, moreover, the nagging, often unconscious fear that these arouse?

While recognizing the reality of the dire physical pain endured by many, sometimes beyond the normal limits of human endurance, our recourse is to call upon the influence of mind over body, first by recognizing the impact upon body functions of our attitude towards psychological trauma. Resentment, remorse, self pity, envy, hatred, frustration, anger, addiction, and co-dependence alter physiological functions, mediated by the endocrine glands affecting digestion, blood pressure, the lymph glands, the immune system, neurotransmitters, and the replication of the DNA by the RNA. A large body of research is being carried out at present to determine which psychological syndrome affects which hormone secretion, and which hormone affects which body function. But we can explore methods of dealing with the psychological trauma.

Reciprocally, since the bodily afflictions and the prospect of death arouse psychological attitudes, one would need to investigate how best to deal with these. No doubt these attitudes involve our sense of identity and how our sense of identity is related to our body. Buddha's solution: of not identifying with the body or even the personality may well yield concrete results by dis-identifying with the seat of the pain or despair, but it does go counter to our involvement with the existential reality and all its implications with regard to accomplishment, building a better world, fostering a way of life, providing a practical underpinning for the development of culture, human relationships, etc. Besides owing to the momentous developments of science (for example we can now see the live body cell in action), we have developed in our time a healthy respect for the privilege of involving ourselves with the fabric of the universe in our intimate relationship with our own bodiness. We are also our bodies;

our bodies have accrued to us from the universe and have become part of our being, as have our personalities.

A way of looking at ourselves that takes into account the emerging paradigms of science (and indeed confirms Hindu, Buddhist and Sufi mystics' experience) would be to not envision ourselves as discrete entities, but rather realize that we are a cross between a vortex which is coextensive and isomorphic with the nature of the whole universe, and a temporarily stable but evolving sub-whole that is a continuity in change.

Undoubtedly we are inexorably drawn into the process of becoming, which means entropy. But we also have the ability of intercepting the arrow of time vertically, as it were, by our incentive and inventiveness which then will enrich the flow, like a tributary to a river which then will be drawn into the flow. Moreover we have the ability to escape the entropy by resurrecting.

This updated sense of identity involves, then, two views. The first one is that we expand—and here, to find fulfillment, we need to concentrate upon radiating rather than disintegrating. The second is that we transmute—that is, we extract the quintessence of our being from its underpinning, as in distillation in Alchemy. An application of the scientific principle according to which information is built on the expenditure of energy, and that matter is a state of energy, would mean in practice that we would strive to make the best of the energy that is our body to foster realization, wisdom, and enlightenment, to be of service, and to contribute to the well being of the physical and social environment. What is more, both energy and its state as matter exist in various degrees of subtlety versus grossness, and nature takes care of the transmutation of both. The photon evidences a degree of rarefaction or sublimation above the electron, and the electrons of our body stuff get transmuted into photons before and after death. The state of energy is defined by its frequency, hence the distinction that contemplatives make between pure spirit acting as a catalyst, and the grosser states of energy.

If anything is gained by the existential condition, then the relatively stable sub-wholes must be assured. But for there to be evolution, they must communicate to the environment the know-how gained through experience by expanding, and to the software programmed by the mind of the universe by resurrecting.

The Sufi outlook adds a whole further perspective, suggesting we look at ourselves from the divine vantage point as an expression or derivative of the divine nature. So long as we start with our personal vantage point, we will have difficulty in transcendence; but if we proceed in the opposite direction, we will glean a whole different sense of identity, one which will see dissolution and reinstatement in the context of the thinking of the universe.

The Sufis call this *uns*, enjoying the intimacy of the proximity of the King, by being invited to share in the strategy at the court of the King. May I also add: and the Queen.

Suffering and Joy

Are you harboring suffering somewhere deep within you, yet smiling? Do you feel wronged by someone, although you bear no grudge? Do you conceal in your unconscious an uncanny notion that life (fate?) has been hard on you, yet voice gratitude for all that life has brought you? Do you harbor a feeling of unfulfillment for not having accomplished what you would have wished to in your life? Yet do you experience bewonderment at the great achievements of our civilizations? Do you feel sorry for yourself for the sacrifice you have taken upon yourself to help someone, while withholding any smidgen of resentment toward the beneficiary of your munificence?

Are you pining in your being, locked in the dilemma of unrequited love, but rejoice in his or her happiness? Or are you frustrated from being with your loved one, through the prevailing circumstances while you welcome your rival open-heartedly? Are you aware that while you feel sorry for a dear one who has died, you are really sorry for your loss, while the deceased has found release from pain? Do you suffer from loneliness yet prove the bright spirit of the party? Do you long to be alone, yet give your whole-hearted solicitation to your guests? Can you rejoice in the good luck of your friends while you are desolate and abandoned? Can you commiserate with the depression of another without slipping in that despondent mood? Do you have the tenacity to persevere in an unsuccessful enterprise on your hunch that it will eventually prove itself? Can you hang on to the last shreds of the rope of hope when everything collapses around you?

Can you maintain your composure in the midst of turbulence. keep your wits in an emergency? Can you honor your faith in the divine meaningfulness behind the cosmic software while faced with proof of the contrary? Can you see some mitigating grace in the hearts of those who have let you down? Can you love the people you criticize and guard people's pride at your detriment? Can you brave being maligned while feeling precarious in your self esteem? Can you listen to the woeful plaints of the unfortunate while straining on the lead to get on with your concerns? Can you cater for people's pain while yours is far greater? Can you live with unbearable guilt compulsively present, yet keep your spirit high? Can you give joy to people around you while your heart is bursting with grief? Can you jubilate in the cosmic celebration, glorifying God while in your moment of need feeling abandoned?

Here lies the challenge of life—of your life. Life avers itself to be a battle for the victory of alacrity against suffering, which at the extreme is jubilation against despair. The wager is inestimable—the triumph, and the tragedy! Winning or losing are in the balance. One needs to know where the ultimate issues of one's life lie, where one is being challenged.

Getting away from suffering proves illusory. It will stick to you on the luxury yacht or in the desert, or in the underground caves or on the mountain top or amid the laughter of the comedy show or in your sleep or upon awakening. Or under tranquilizers, surreptitiously concealed in the unconscious, it will sometimes erupt furiously, irrationally, unquellable. It will turn your reveling sour when you face it, and mar your quest for entertainment to get away from it. The opiate of distraction will wear thin. Can you fight tears with laughter? Can one transmute suffering into joy? Or is it more realistic to be able to live with suffering, whilst simultaneously exulting in joy?

But the cruelty of some knows no bounds—concentration camps, murder—unbelievable! What a tour-de-force to make good the scars! Is there a cure? Engaging headlong in creativity has sometimes proven a wonderful palliative, particularly if the work of art sparkles with joy. Suffering like all emotions is a psychic energy that can be put to good use. Ultimately only in acts of service is there a way out—by serving other suffering beings, alleviating pain wherever possible, even if such help only gives a scant relief to the victim. Noticing another's suffering offsets one's pondering upon one's own. Self pity can harden one's heart, nurture spite, and mask one's sensitivity to another's plight. In contrast, love directed toward fellow beings melts one's heart, ridding it of rancor, and so acts therapeutically.

Look around you—world wide. Wherever you go, what do you see? Is it people suffering, people having fun, sometimes oblivious that it was at the cost of much suffering by those who made this well-being possible; people struggling to stave off starvation, some dying of starvation, others more fortunate, surviving marginally; others opulent; the lazy, the inefficient, the mixed-up ones, the smart, the venturesome, the tycoons, the stalwart, the timorous, the opportunists, the traitors, the facetious, the playboys, the sadists, the criminals, the despots or simply the ruthless or the greedy or the selfish, the oppressed under despotism, the heroes, the activists, the handicapped, the mentally ill, those who have lost the last grains of self esteem, the homeless wandering the streets, sleeping in appalling conditions where life has become an ordeal, the patients in bodily pain and anxiety about death, the dedicated ones, social workers, environmentalists, medical practitioners, teachers, healers, therapists, consolers, those who administer the solace of faith to the broken spirits, the saintly, the bigoted, the sanctimonious, the jesters and buffoons who are sometimes more successful at fighting suffering with joy, and despondency with good humor, the artists, the mystics, the scientists, and last but not least numerically, the good God-fearing honest-to-goodness living middle range. What a drama we are involved in! Or rather how much are we aware of what is going on, and to what extent are we actively involved in it? What are the issues being enacted? Or do we pass it all by, pursuing our own trips?

What is the degree of your involvement? That is precisely the measure of your mettle. What are your motivations to do what you are doing on Planet Earth?

What contribution does spirituality have to offer to these vital problems? Genuine spirituality evokes awareness and enhanced sensitivity, and therefore compassion for all beings, because the thought of God raises one above and beyond one's personal self concern or limited perspective. I am obviously not referring here to dogmatism or fundamentalism or belief systems. Rather the reference is to genuine spiritual emotion found amongst the mystics and sages who inspire one to rise above one's selfishness by awakening the greatest of all powers: love.

Service

The ordeal of the fire triggers the heroism in the fireman. The suffering of the patient calls for the compassion of the nurse and the skill of the doctor. The agony of the dying in the streets of Calcutta produces a Mother Teresa. The budding genius of the child calls for the teacher to facilitate it. The helplessness of the destitute calls for food banks and night shelters. The despair of the broken psyche calls for the dedicated priest or the psychotherapist. One species may call to be serviced by another as the trees dying in the rain forests tax the skill of the ecologist to service them, or the endangered species call for the biologist to perpetuate their presence on the planet. This is the meaning of service.

The whole Planet calls out to be served and serviced, but it is being more exploited than served. There was a time when we humans took it for granted that it was our prerogative to control the planet. Leadership is not controlling but releasing potentialities, facilitating them and coordinating them. The reward is accessory. When the reward becomes the objective, there is exploitation.

The trouble is that we feel our generosity runs counter to what we believe to be our most dire needs, or more so, those of our families. Moreover, we rightly are afraid that once we get ourselves involved in helping others, we shall be drawn further and further into sacrificing our own needs, since the demands appear to be much greater than we had at first suspected. In order to help others, one needs to hoist oneself in a position where one can help, but one needs to tithe some of one's gain into lending a helping hand to those who cannot fend for themselves. In India's Ajmer and Rishikesh, one may find that as soon as one metes out a few rupees or chapattis, one is harassed by a solicitous crowd who may even tear one's clothes to pieces to grab what they can, so great is their hunger. Consequently, many prefer not starting this in the first place. Some even argue that one is simply perpetuating their misery by giving a pittance which could never answer their needs. Nature has a way of stemming the population explosion by pruning it at the cost of starvation.

Then there is the burnout of overstressing oneself by sheer zeal. The danger lurks in self pity that might very well brook unconscious resentment for the person one is helping. One refuses to admit this to one's conscious mind, but it may cause ponderous soul searchings and internal conflicts. Therefore, the cutting off point between stress and overstress must be clearly evaluated to avoid being self-defeating and counterproductive. This is where wisdom regarding balance in life proves to be a saving grace.

One should be wary of the personal satisfaction of helping, as witnessed in a number of do-gooders and philanthropists. It escalates patronization. People feel indebted to one's generosity as if strings are attached to one's beneficence, and it culminates in sheer crass egotism. St. Vincent de Paul, who created hospitals for the poor in France, once said that those whom you have benefited nurture an unconscious resentment against you for the dependence in which you have placed them. Is the answer in anonymous, impersonal service? Institutional welfare with all its positive side has proven its inadequacy in dealing with the roots of human problems by merely providing palliatives.

The problem is deeper than just providing food and shelter to the homeless. Behind their inability to cope are a broken self image, low self esteem, abysmal loneliness and dejection. The real issue is helping people to convince themselves that they can do something useful by giving them a chance to find an activity that is not too challenging, yet moderately rewarding. The public services do not know how to meet that problem, nor can this be institutionalized. The trouble with an impersonal system is first, that it lends itself to terrible abuses, and secondly it tends to take away personal incentive and effort by making people rely on the system rather than explore their own resourcefulness.

It is only under stress that one's latent resourcefulness is discovered and actuated. We are living at a time when an increasing section of the public is pushed out of the active sector because of their inability to cope with the growing demands for technological skills. They do not stand a chance competing with highly skilled people. The dejected ones are the victims of our relentless progress into automation and eventually, computing robotology.

Our affluence has created a demand and in turn, that demand is creating a supply. More and more people are sensitive to this call and are willing to help. In fact, if most people were aware of the extent of the despair of other people, they would do something about it. It is not fulfilling to simply pursue one's personal advantage in life. Most evolved people need to serve a purpose beyond their own personal one in which the potentialities in their being attain fruition.

Reflections on Noor's Birthday

Noor Inayat Khan (1914–1944) was the older sister of Pir Vilayat Inayat Khan. She volunteered for British SOE resistance service in World War II. Under the code name "Madeleine," Noor became the first woman wireless transmitter in occupied France. Betrayed to the Gestapo, she was executed in Dachau concentration camp in 1944.

Today is my sister Noor's birthday, and her memory is stronger than ever! In the minds, hearts and souls of many, she is ever present, an example of dedication and self sacrifice to an ideal of solidarity and compassion.

For many, women particularly, she personifies a projection of the feminine need to place herself at the service of a cause of mercy to which she could hand herself over altogether. This hallowed need is however, rarely fulfilled, either because life has its way of drawing one into humdrum patterns, or because this need is only triggered when the call for help suddenly crosses one's way and shrieks of urgency.

Even then, the human need for comfort, security, and the instinct of self preservation outbalances the need of the soul to serve a great cause.

Thus the reason why Noor is so personally meaningful for so many women is because she represents what they would have liked to prove themselves to be by giving expression to an area of the soul where sacredness is realistic, that is, feasible in real life (a feminine characteristic which, in most cases, remains tentatively latent).

It is this dimension of feeling which is the stuff of which heroes are made. But the price is terrifying. The inevitable outcome of undaunted courage is the ordeal of torture and death in the most devastating circumstances as a victim of the cruelty and sadism of ruthless and merciless men and women, poisoned by hatred born of resentment. The humiliation, to which the captives delivered into the hands of their executioners are subjected, may prove even more excruciating than the bodily torture. Yet, here is an extreme case of the basic reconciliation of the irreconcilables behind all real-life situations, defined by Pir-o-Murshid Inayat Khan as "the Divine perfection suffering from the limitations of the existential condition." In this case, it is only the circumstances devised by the oppressors that are humiliating, but when one carries one's dedication to the service of the victims of tyranny to that point, one holds one's head high and unmasks the bad faith of the tyrants, instead of cringing. This is precisely what Noor did when she said, "The time will come when you will know the truth." It is a cruel paradox, that the one who ventured out to the rescue of the victims of torture in concentration camps should herself be subjected to the ordeal from which she wished to save them.

Actually, I recall reviewing with Noor the principles upon which we would establish our handling of the challenge of World War II as the cannon outbursts were groaning at the gates of Paris. Both of us agreed, as did our mother, that we had been spreading Pir-o-Murshid Inayat Khan's teaching and now the time had come to apply it. There can be no doubt; it is the teaching of kindness. Inayat means kindness. To be consequent, it implies sacrificing oneself for the sake of kindness to others. Of course this is the Message of Christ: unconditional love. Simple, yes, not metaphysics, just reality in all its painful realism, the axis around which the human drama revolves, and perhaps also, the drama of the universe in its breathtaking monumentality.

Here it was, right at our door, the call for mercy. People were being tortured; people were being contemptuously rejected like pariah dogs. There was a scent of war in the atmosphere; the folks were aghast, afraid, terrified, and cowardly. Of course, who would not be so except for the stalwart, knowing what it means to stick out one's head? In such situations, one can tell who is who; the silver coating is off. Everyone is in life according to the measure of the price one is prepared to pay from one's advantage or well-being or security for the sake of the other. For me, *this* is the criteria of spirituality, not *samadhi*.

How to Find Peace in the Cosmic Drama

This letter was written after the 1991 invasion of Iraq which was code named "Operation Desert Storm."

Whether more closely or more remotely involved in the present mess in which humanity has maneuvered itself, it would be insensitive on one's part not to feel distressed, disturbed, dismayed, and unsettled in our emotions. We may be angered and disgusted at the barbaric attrition which extremes of concupiscence in human nature have inflicted upon so many innocent victims, and yet on the other hand heartened by the courage and heroism of so many. Can one find equanimity, and is it helpful to seek serenity amidst the thoughts rushing through one's mind? Or would that be an escape? Alternatively we ask ourselves: what is it that we can do? Moreover, faced with the reality, we feel as though we are being challenged in our belief, in our faith.

If we could view things from the cosmic perspective, trying to reach beyond our personal perspective and middle range, we would see that, willy-nilly, we are plunged into the drama on Planet Earth that was impending all the time. We have failed to see, wrapped as we have been all the while in the false security of our complacency, oblivious of the drama and misery around us which we dismiss as "bad news" from the media. Seen in its wider context, the "Desert Storm" on Planet Earth is simply a pale reflection of the soul searchings, and the birth and continued re-birthing pangs, of the universe. Can we halt a moment and take stock of what it takes to make life at all possible, the issues behind the more immediate scenario on Planet Earth, in the hope that it might help us to understand better what is happening globally? Seeing what we are involved in unawares, we might better grasp what our role is or could be.

At the cosmic scale, can we have the slightest idea of what could be the intention behind the whole process of existence—the issues, and what is enacted in the process? Do we have any idea what the shift from thought to matter could mean at a cosmic scale? A good illustration of this would be a composer striving to give concrete expression to a powerful emotion that came upon him or her suddenly. What does it take for a motivation—any whatsoever, whether at the cosmic scale or human—to be followed up and vehicled by a whole organization programmed as its infrastructure? How does thought structure itself into what we call matter at a sidereal dimension? Just imagine our privilege as humans over animals and plants in being part of what is happening in this regard!

Now imagine what would be the cost of introducing freedom—that is personal incentive—in the system! This would require that the pattern on which the universe is built would need to shift continually from simpler models of harmonious orderliness to models exhibiting more and more complex orderliness that allow for the intervention of the free resolution of its constituents. In the interval between these there would inevitably be a transit situation where chaos sets in, in which the existing pattern is dismantled and the new one has not yet gelled. Thus this very "divine intention" would open up the risk of disruption, conceivably even the extreme hazard that the system runs amok and destroys itself. We are witnessing this in the decadence and corruption in the so-called advanced civilizations we pride ourselves in. Doubtless this is also the reason for our fear in the present crisis, that it should escalate ominously because the anger aroused by cruelty begets hatred, and the ensuing exasperation keeps unleashing yet greater violence.

Yet paradoxically, for a system to evolve rather than being bogged into its own pattern by vain repetitiveness or recycling, it needs to "fluctuate beyond equilibrium" (to use a word of Dr. Ilya Prigogine) until the previous order is sufficiently disrupted. Then the old order becomes obsolete and needs to be replaced by a new one. This is illustrated in nature or rather in the evolution of the chemistry of matter on Planet Earth, by the quantum leap from the inorganic to the organic. At the inorganic stage, atoms form a rather monotonous grid, rather like a repetitive wall paper. Suddenly in the evolutionary advance, some molecules shift into a more complex pattern whereby its atoms diversify. Each specializes in a different role in the overall architecture of the molecule. Thus they cooperate, and to cooperate, they become necessarily interdependent. An identical leap in the evolutionary advance takes place at the level of the chromosomes in the live cell which code for the variety of functions that make possible the advent of live organisms. Thus comes an ever more effective support system for the upsurge of intelligence in this corner of the universe.

At a higher level, we encounter an extraordinary complex and sophisticated infrastructure owing to the infinite diversity of functions in our civilized societies. There is the enhancement of the intelligence of the Planet with humanity at the prow. In fact the advent of the human on the Planet would not have been possible without this fluctuation beyond equilibrium from one order to another. But it must be understood that the gift of freedom needs to be supplemented by its imperative correlate: interdependence.

By dint of the application of the universal principle of economy, to avail itself of the fund of resourcefulness of the insights, incentives and initiatives of its constituents, the system would now need to concede some freedom to these in the determination of its program, decisionmaking, government, and hence destiny. However to avoid that the differences of opinion, of perspective, and the conflict of interest, should break loose in the inevitable surge of greed, ruthless exploitation of freedom to rob others of their free will, cruelty, atrocities, and all those appalling things that erupt already in peace and escalate in war conditions, freedom needs to be tempered by interdependence. The ideal would be where each and all of the participants find their respective place, cooperating in the interest of the whole, as we have witnessed in the organic molecules and in a healthy biological cell or cell formation where that cooperation makes the advent of more sophisticated forms of intelligence possible in the universe.

Here, more than ever, this evolutionary leap forward calls for a step in our realization of the imperative of introducing interdependence if we are to avail ourselves of the gift of freedom. This principle of cooperation is beginning to emerge in the consciousness of our more advanced human societies in what is now coined "the new world order." J. S. Bach pointed out that this requires, not the despotic dominance of one theme on others, but that each should contribute towards the whole, but restrict individual incentive in the interest of the whole.

Of course the marvel behind all of this is—far beyond the enhancing of intelligence—to be found in the advent of beauty. The splendor of the emotion behind the miracle of life manifests as beauty, first of all in natural structures, the perfect geometrical configuration of atomic, molecular and biological patterns, or the motions of the planets, stars, and galaxies. It also manifests in cosmic structures, filtered as it were through the human creative mind: the musical scales, harmony, the symphony, art, monuments. This is why, when chaos sets in and the forces of evil and corruption are let loose, one seeks refuge in beauty. In the very midst of ugliness, beauty confirms in us our shaken trust in the meaningfulness behind it all.

We need beauty! As a respite in stress and surrounded by defilement and violence and the attendant fear, our hearts resonate wherever there is beauty. But there is a yet subtler form of beauty where the splendor behind existence manifests, not in a special form, not in aesthetics, but in compassion, magnanimity, solidarity, dedication, and sacrifice for an ideal, unconditional love. Ultimately, the very pinnacle of this motivation which we can read into the programming of the universe is attained in prayer—I would say nonsectarian, or, alternately, in loyalty to one's spiritual heritage, yet with openness to religions other than one's own.

Unfortunately, as we have seen, the condition for the shift from one stage in the evolutionary advance to the next is a breakdown of a sclerosed order—this is the meaning of chaos; or shall we say this is its role in the cosmic programming. In the midst of this "destabilization," we are disoriented anxious, confused, and afraid. This is where we are tested in our understanding of what is happening and what are the issues enacted. We are being tested in our faith in the inherent meaningfulness and well-meaningness behind phenomena. From our commonplace perspective, we cannot possibly expect to grasp this; consequently our faith runs the risk of wearing thin. What is more, just as serenity and a sense of the sacredness is most needed, we find it more difficult to meditate or pray. It seems like opening one drawer after closing another, or burying one's head in the sand, fleeing reality.

If indeed the issue behind existence is the surge and preservation of the freedom of the individual, albeit tempered by interdependence, it follows that the "powers that be" have to constrain divine intervention. Yet does that mean abdication of any control whatsoever? Perhaps this would be best illustrated by a car-driving monitor, or pilot coach, handing over the steering wheel or stick to the pupil, restraining himself from stopping a false move until it becomes too hazardous, and then taking over. That power, which the Mazdeans ascribe to Ahura Mazda to maintain the ultimate control in the struggle between Spenta Mainu and Ahriman, Good and Evil, is called *kaza* by the Sufis. In tribulation, if we invoke God or the prophets, masters and saints who form the spiritual hierarchies of the Government of the World, it is in the desperate hope that they will be able to stem the tide of evil and avert disaster. But if indeed their overall commitment is to preserve the principle of the freedom of incentive and decision of the individual, then their intervention needs to be limited to simply avoid that the system should destroy itself. Would this means that the intervention of the *kaza* force is withheld until the eleventh hour, at the brink of disaster? No, not necessarily, *kaza* stands for inertia, in scientific terms homeostasis.

There is always a principle of stability, of balancing opposing forces written right into the programming of nature at all levels. This may be observed for example in politics or all human institutions where innovation is always countered and thereby balanced by a conservative force. In physics, it is called the "order out of disorder principle" for example in the Brownian movement within a liquid whereby the random movements of the individual molecules cancel each other out. Thus there is a safety mechanism programmed into nature that ensures that a system does not ultimately auto-destruct.

At the level of human affairs, this safety mechanism is embodied in the influence of the spiritual hierarchy, and more generally in the power of prayer and the propensity for peace inherent in people of good will throughout the world. The strength, range and reach of this power are enhanced by the number of its supporters, and the degree of their commitment. The bastion that we could build up by our prayers could, if backed by the uncountable billions of people of good will in the world, present a sizeable antidote to the forces of political dominance.

How does one maintain calm in tribulation? And more particularly, how does one maintain joy in suffering and despair? An apt illustration is given in the picture of Buddha sitting unperturbed in the middle of a storm. This must not be construed as failing to recognize the reality of the problem breaking loose as the storm. The problem needs to be dealt with. Peace needs to be availed of as the springboard for action—as a source of power, not as an escape. We know that the center of a hurricane is a vacuum: inertia balancing the turmoil and thereby staying it from running amok.

Where can we find this salutary principle of inertia in our psychological setup in life? Obviously if one withdraws one's attention from the environing drama, in splendid isolation, to meditate, oblivious of what is going on, which means unconcerned with human suffering, in a state of *samadhi* touching upon one's eternal being, one will doubtless find peace. But this seems rather like the despicable legendary ostrich act. However, there is a way of capturing the attunement encountered as we snatch a taste of our own eternity, but in the instant we call *now*—the present without change; and of the infinity vested in our human nature in the existential *here*.

In the ordinary course of experience, the instant is continually being flooded by the past that continues to live in our psyche, and by the future which we anticipate or apprehend. A good illustration of this would be a piece of music: while following the trend of the melodic or harmonic sequence, or rhythmic progression, one can often forestall the next step. The prior elements of the music flow into the oncoming ones, and the future ones are already anticipated, so that they overlap in the present. Thus the present is not limited to being a threshold, but is rather a moving transition that peters out in infinite regress on either side.

To understand what is meant by eternity, we could picture a pendulum. At one point, the point by which it is suspended, it remains stationary; at the other end, it moves in time-space. The *samadhi* state corresponds to the apex, the suspension point. However, there are two moments in the swing of the lower extremity of the pendulum where it also experiences a state of suspense: at the apogee of its orbit to the right and likewise to the left. One must be circumspect about imagining that time flows at a regular pace linearly; in fact it is landscaped. At those critical points (which could qualify as singularities) it is suspended; the process of becoming is arrested in a hiatus. Or could we posit that eternity is written right into the process of becoming, and what is more, we are endowed with the capacity of grasping it, not just in *samadhi*, but in the "here and now"? In fact this is what is meant by *awakening in life*.

How can we capture these moments in our lives, illustrated by the halt in the swing of the pendulum? We can learn from a Sufi technique of meditation which consists in evacuating the psyche of any memory of the past or any projects for the future in the instant where the arrow of time is arrested. We have for an instant emancipated ourselves from the constraint of the process of *becoming* in the here and now rather than escaping the here and now. This corroborates clearly with Dr. David Bohm's view regarding the "enfolding" of the totality of the bounty of the universe at any point of the universe in what he calls the implicate state, and of the encounter of the past and the future in what he calls the holo-movement. Rather than being bogged into the here and now, one sees how the "everywhere and always" converge into the "here and now."

It is in this instant, free of becoming, of homeostasis, illustrated by the Buddha, that we may find peace in the middle of the storm raging at present without escaping from it. The recipe is: wherever you can find an opportunity, put a screen upon your preoccupations with the past (remorse, recriminations, resentment) and stop worrying about the future (the desire for acquisition, greed, covetousness), but realize the privilege offered to you by the universe of experiencing the miracle of life in a breakthrough of realization!

Like Henri Bergson, the Sufis distinguish the instant from duration. Thanks to that sense of the timeless instant, one frees oneself from the way the future is conditioned by the past, so that one can determine it oneself as illustrated in Zen. In Herrigel's *Zen in the Art of Archery,* the teacher says: "The target determined the path of the arrow, not my hand."

Becoming represents our destiny, eternity our freedom.

Chapter 2
Science and Spirituality

Stalking the Light: Transmuting Fire into Light, Anger into Compassion

Light is a particularly important factor in our lives because it acts as a bridge between matter and the ineffable, beyond our perception. At the psychological level, we all know how it feels to be hot under the collar, burning with rage when abused, insulted, repressed, or when we are outraged with righteous indignation at witnessing an injustice or a blatant lie. It seems wise to contend that we condemn the ignominious act, not the person, but how real is it? Surely the action we condemn must reflect something of the person. We can intervene to counter evil like a noble knight, without hatred. A gesture of compassion can transform the fire of anger into the radiance of our countenance by the generous feeling of love—this is perhaps the greatest miracle of life. Pir-o-Murshid Inayat Khan told his students, "We are tested in our love." Being able to love a person who is obnoxious and unkind faces us with an almost unrealistic challenge. How strong is our love? I mean a wholesome, all-embracing, cosmic, unconditional love, not a sentimental love. One can be judgmental while protective. If we try to wean ourselves from our reactive ego, which is our defense system, we will suffer from psychological withdrawal symptoms, unless our love is very strong.

The phenomenon of light hands us a number of clues which convey realizations that open some escape from the enigma posed to our understanding. We discover that we cannot account for things on the strength of what we perceive. For one thing, light behaves—according to the test devised by scientists in laboratories—either as though it were constituted of particles (photons), or of waves. Particles collide but waves compose, forming a network as a wave-interference pattern. We imagine that particles occupy a definite location in space at a given moment, and collide if vying for the same space, whereas matter cannot be locatable as a wave.

Our human behavior follows the same principles. Our psyches can clash in conflict, or cooperate by completing each other. Waves can configure themselves in such a manner that they build up like a kind of knot, called a soliton; this is an instance of a standing wave. Such is also the case for us humans when, in the course of cooperating, somehow a conflicting situation arises.

If we consider our consciousness as a focal point located in space, light seems to radiate from a point located in space: the sun, the stars, a candle, an electric bulb. But when we turn within in our meditation, our consciousness, as it gets inverted, is diffused. Consequently our representation of light has shifted—it is diffused as "the all-pervading light."

Physicists never cease to be amazed by the paradoxical way light behaves when they try to track it down in laboratory experiments. They can only ascertain and measure what happens at the instant it interacts with their instruments, but light eschews giving any clues as to its behavior before, after or between the measurements. It might seem wrong to call light matter because, unlike any other form of matter, it does not have mass.

Light thus provides us with a useful model of the relationship between reality and actuality—the universe and the cosmos. Reality escapes any efforts on our part to track it down beyond the existential, perceptual world we commonly know. This familiar world looks like the cross section of a multiple, multidimensional, and many-tiered universe of which we only know what intersects it. This paradox becomes even more bewildering, because when we stalk it, reality appears as a virtuality that becomes an actuality in the existential condition.

We are baffled by the unknown, stymied, and ever wishing to decipher the secret of the mysterious unknown that affects us in such uncanny ways.

Reflecting upon the wavelike / particle-like antinomy, we ask ourselves whether our known world is not the crystallization of the reality beyond our understanding, just as we imagine waves to have crystallized as particles, or photons having crystallized as electrons to form a crystal.

Just stop to ponder the miracle whereby our thoughts or emotions configure the muscles of our face, and going further, how we may fashion the fabric of light of our aura into the countenance that transpires through our face.

To stalk reality beyond actuality, we would then have to reverse this process and transmute the electrons of our bodies into photons (as is the case with fireflies in the process of phosphorescence) or transmute the particle-like photons of our aura into wavelike, ineffable light. This would represent an intriguing prospect for life after life. Perhaps we could already start preparing for this right away, now. It would mean trying to stalk light as far as we can reach beyond its perceptual existential condition.

Should we attempt this—for example, trying to shift our consciousness into that of a master, saint, or prophet, or an angel, or a departed loved one—we would reach a point where the light that escapes our grasp, intangible yet luring us ever further, does not seem to be any different from the light of our intelligence.

What would it be like to live bereft of the body? Our advanced meditations "beyond existence," as Buddha phrases it, may offer us some clues. Imagine brainstorming creative ideas, while interfacing and interacting with the minds and attunements of other disincarnate beings, and fashioning these ideas into forms without substance (as an architect does), or tuning to a bountiful symphony of emotions without translating them into musical notes and rhythms (as a composer does). Imagine discovering new modes of meaningfulness without manipulating objects, working at the software of the universe, and knowing that your programming will, if viable and meaningful, be intuited by those on Earth who will carry them out concretely and practically.

Then imagine updating them by being receptive to the feedback from the Earth. The feedback of experience upgrades the feed forward of creativity acausally. The clues to soaring into worlds of celestial light are, first, in overcoming resentment and shifting our notion of light from its physical underpinning to its ineffable dimensions beyond the existential state, and then, rather than identifying ourselves with our aura, identifying ourselves with the light of our intelligence. Then we bring heavenly light to Earth through the glow of our eyes. This is the "Light upon a light" of the Qur'an.

"The light that can be seen" and "the light that sees," according to the Sufis, now seem like two poles of the same reality rather than being separated like the horns of a dilemma, as they appear to our commonplace thinking. Therefore to stalk the light of those we yearn to reach, beyond this limited world, and to be inspired, we need to transcend our commonplace thinking and allow our minds to be overwhelmed in what the Sufis calls "the consternation of intelligence." Our ordinary thinking sees "otherness," whereas our peripersonal thinking sees similarity and likeness, in a process of resonance. Pir-o-Murshid calls it the thinking of the soul, rather than of the mind. The state of bewonderment, and, more so, glorification, will spark our souls to ecstasy.

We do not have to condemn ourselves if we cannot forgive, but it is the clue to being luminous and radiant. It is our choice. Resentment traps us in our personal dimension, forgiveness will make us free to stalk light beyond its constraint at the existential level. In life after life, if one has not found freedom, one will be stuck in one's thoughts, regurgitating acrimony. One will fail to interface and interact creatively with wonderful beings in skyscapes of light and splendor. The message of Christ, "forgive those who offend us," is hard to follow, but it carries a great secret—perhaps the greatest secret—the sublimation of our human nature, like the way infrared light can be transmuted into ultraviolet (passing through the spectrum). Our incandescent aura becomes diaphanous: we have transmuted the fire of truth into the light of love.

Transformation, Mutation, Transmutation, Regeneration, Transfiguration, Resurrection

Achievement, however great, does not seem to grant most people a complete sense of satisfaction. Perhaps the greatest human need is transformation. No doubt this is because unconsciously we are tugged forward by the inexorable forward march of the evolutionary process of which we are participants.

Since time immemorial the best brains of our species have vied to unearth means of promoting and accelerating the process of human transformation at both the physical and psychic level. Alchemists searched their deep unconscious for clues, while believing that the coveted secret must be culled from a study of the processes that regulate the transmutation of materials. Metals, elixirs, chemicals, or crystals, were used. They posited that there must be a unified principle governing all transformation, whether at the level of the body or the psyche: "as above, so below." Their objective was "the spiritualization of the body and the materialization of the spirit."

Alchemists posited that if we could only wrest out the secrets using these principles, we could not only accelerate the processes of transformation in the laboratory, but similarly enhance the process of transformation in the psyche of humans. While working with the transmutation of metals, they were really discovering their own psyche and an infinite number of valuable clues. The simplest was *solve et coagule*: all transformation commences with a falling apart of the constituents, and then a new structuring. As applied to the psyche, this is called the royal art: *Ars Regia*.

Since the heyday of the alchemists, scientists, physicists, chemists, biologists, physiologists, psychologists and meditators have carried that early research a great deal further. Yet, the tenets of the mechanistic and positivistic theories neglected much of what the alchemists were conveying, albeit cryptically. The mutual interface of mind and body is now increasingly appearing on the scene. The holistic paradigm, and Heisenberg's Uncertainty Principle, and in general what one might define as a philosophy of science are emerging in our day. Dr. David Bohm intimated that "A change in our sense of meaning will affect the circuits of the brain." Such a far reaching declaration triggers in us a renewed vision of prospects. They might be actuated in many procedures devised to improve ourselves, and so fulfill our purpose in the universe.

Since the dawn of Indian thought, the Yogis have been working with mental and physical methods designed to promote the influence of the mind upon the body, and the impact of the body upon the mind. In the view of Buddhists the body provides us with a most resourceful vehicle in which to foster illumination. This is so providing its potentialities are exploited and its fabric transmuted.

We would like to know more about how precisely this works. What can we do to promote this transformation? Could it be promoted by the influence of our thinking and emoting upon the endocrine glands, and therefore on the enzymes that supervise the replication of the DNA? What can we do by exploring the way that our joy or sadness affects the light that we emit as an aura, or our electromagnetic field? The early Mazdeans, followed by the Sufis, highlighted the role played by thc subtle bodies in the transformation of the physical body.

Advances in science and technology have opened up new vistas as to how thoughts, images, and emotions affect the brain and particularly the endocrine functions. It may be said that the choreography of the molecules, atoms, and even electrons and photons of our bodies ensure the miracle by which the splendor of cosmic software endeavors to emerge through structures and functions of the existential realm. What is meant by subtle bodies or acupuncture meridians, or the "chi" force, still eludes the grasp of our middle-range thinking. We are only beginning to investigate how our resentment, guilt and violence, and our self image affect the immune system. Instead of thinking in terms of the psychosomatic, Dr. David Bohm considers the soma and the significance as the two constellated poles of a same reality which he calls the soma-significance. This way of looking at ourselves challenges us to explore new ways of fostering transformation.

Many techniques of meditation are devised to unmask the hoax of our commonplace thinking and emoting. Besides fostering transformation through insight (awakening), we are working with life energy (quickening).

Nature not only provides for the gestation of stars and atoms, but for an evolutionary drive in setting up more and more complex inorganic atomic structures. With the leap forward into the organic, the advent of the biological field, orderliness gets more and more intricate. Instead of structuring themselves in regular lattices, the molecules diversify to assume specific functions that are meaningfully coordinated. Thus there is increasing mental sophistication and inventiveness.

Doubtless, at the human scale, we need to account for the way the care and perfecting of body functions affects the personality. Conversely, we need to account for the impact of our grasp of significance upon this support system provided by nature as it evolves.

How this can be effected optimally is precisely the question before us. The cells of our bodies (with all their idiosyncrasies and volitions and dedication to the service of our understanding) need to be participants in the illumination of our minds. Our personalities need to live up to the challenge of our ultimate motivation.

Given that nature does provide for an evolutionary progression in its structuring of atoms, molecules, cells, organisms, etc., the early alchemists may be considered blacksmiths (the ancestors of the industrial revolution). They believed that metals were incubated in the womb of the earth. They posited that we humans could intervene in the operation of nature and accelerate the process in the athanor (the oven) or the alembic (the distiller). The secret was providing heat—which is, obviously, energy.

From the beginnings of time, the original state of randomness of atoms in the universe, called the primordial soup (the chaos), gets gradually ordered. It moves into clearly systematically programmed atomic structures, evidencing the impact of intelligence upon energy. The same applies to the way thoughts get structured by our sense of significance. According to the second law of thermodynamics, this costs energy. In the realm of the psyche it is our nostalgia and enthusiasm that represent energy.

This orderliness written into the programming of the universe falls apart if one does not inject energy into it: like a library in which the books are scattered randomly, it takes energy to put them back into their respective places. As in a computer, information is gained at the price of energy. This is called the law of entropy.

Note that the same applies to the psyche, as C. G. Jung showed. Its orderliness out of the chaotic unconscious was gained during the evolutionary process leading to the human condition throughout eons of time. It gets lost very easily unless one keeps putting ever renewed resolve into it. Besides, should we not also credit the influence of the sense of meaningfulness of which the atoms, molecules, cells and organs of our bodies are endowed?

Now supposing these beautifully structured molecules avail themselves of more energy. For example, as one heats them gently, gradually the molecules begin to free themselves from the constraint of a rigidly structured program. As Dr. Prigogine says, they self-organize, exploring new combinations or ways of being. The cosmic programming itself has now unfolded into infinite ramifications, thus enriching itself considerably.

There is a little-understood energy that is self-generated, illustrated at the physical level by chemical reactions that generate heat instead of absorbing heat. On the biological level it is illustrated by phosphorescence rather than fluorescence, for example in the firefly or deep sea fish. Regarding the psyche, one might say that enthusiasm is in some way related to the interfacing with the environment, whereas nostalgia is self-motivated.

Basically, we are faced with two steps in evolution: first the impact of the orderliness of the whole upon the parts; secondly the incentive of the parts that act upon the overall programming. The first stage incites one not to come in the way of the operation of the universe upon ourselves as a fraction thereof—called the divine operation by the Sufis—by interposing one's will or vagabonding into one's personal random musings. Evidence of the importance of this attitude is to be found in passive volition in biofeedback.

The will of the universe, called the Divine will in religious lore, seems to self-organize as it unfolds in one's psyche. Here long-range planning (the will of the universe) takes precedence over self determination (evidenced in our personal contribution to the programming of our being) and breaks through as creativity. At a threshold condition, which is difficult to determine, it is the personal will that shifts the system from equilibrium (as Dr. Prigogine shows) and opens the way for fluctuation, and hence new programs, and new ways of being.

As we observe them more deeply, the atoms, or cells, prove themselves to be not what we imagine matter to be. They display the mentation or consciousness or inventiveness that we have consistently denied them and attribute to ourselves. However, it is the availability of energy that actuates this meaningfulness into physical functions. This is much more marked at the organic or biological level.

At the level of the psyche, the clues we can infer from this intrusion into physical nature point to the role played by freedom from an imposed order in creativity; and therefore in the transformation of the personality. Conversely it demonstrates the role of incentive in freeing oneself from complacency in an imposed order.

Moreover, it is found that the impact of significance or purposefulness served by information economizes energy. This is called negentropy. The better organized one is, the more economically one runs one's business. Or in respect of one's personality, the clarity of one's understanding of the meaningfulness of one's life—called awakening—will spare much wasted energy. The secret resides in availing oneself of both the insight one gains in life, and the psychic energy of the human evolutionary thrust. In fact, it may well be that in a highly meaningfully-organized state one is generating fresh energy internally like a white hole instead of absorbing it from outside. This is one of our objectives in meditation.

The alchemists substitute the athanor (the oven) and sometimes the alembic (the distiller) for the womb of the earth in the incubation of metals, or crystals, or elixirs. The meditator envisions our body, magnetic field, aura etc., aspects of our total being in its holistic model, as constituting a temple—the psychic substitute for the athanor—and our subtle bodies form the altar of the temple.

The primary material the alchemists work with—called the *materia prima*—is our given nature before all the transformations it has undergone during existence. If indeed, "as above, so below," then it is just as in the blastema, the original cell in the embryo, in which all genes are present without yet having a determination. Which genes will be turned on and which turned off to diversify the cells of the unfolding embryo is undecided. Similarly, only a few of the infinite possibilities invested in what the Sufis, quoting Christ, call our divine inheritance, are turned on in our personalities. Most of them are recessive.

Just as the initial cell in the embryo is a hybrid in which the universe, having converged in multitudes of beings, cross-pollinates with that of numberless other beings, so the substrate of our subtle bodies carry the many-splendored bounty of untold denizens of the heavenly spheres.

This primeval material, of which we avail ourselves whether bodily or psychically, has both evolved and deteriorated during its involvement in the existential condition. Yet, just as the voice of Caruso is still buried in its pristine glory in the bad recording of the time, so the celestial counterpart of our being is unscathed even though defiled.

Human Understanding — Divine Meaningfulness

The pilot of our being is our mind-brain that extends throughout our body to our whole nervous system, right into the nuclei of each cell. It needs a wide scope of understanding and stimulation to reach a state of fulfillment.

Imagine that it took fifteen billion years of the cataclysmic convulsions in the birth pangs of uncounted cosmic galaxies to fashion the hundred million trillions of atomic particles constituting the fabric of our bodies. It took that amount of time to coordinate them to the point that they might, in their cooperation, offer a support system to the mind of the universe , which we call the mind of God, customized into what we call our thinking!

The very structure of our cells and organs, and the organization of our body functions, illustrate laws of harmonic resonance. It bears the stamp of the thinking of the universe which evolves as its material support systems become more elaborate. Reciprocally, the support system perfects itself as it evolves, just as our brain (and body for that matter) develops latent faculties as our thinking brightens, and as we exult in our grasp of meaningfulness. Our thinking perfects itself as our brain, and its extension as the nervous system, gets activated. Yes, the nuclei of our body cells are endowed with a degree of pragmatic understanding greatly enhanced by their cooperation.

In turn, by virtue of our tacit covenant with the universe of which we are a part, the cosmic mind, called the mind of God, is delegated to our minds. This opens vistas, albeit latent in the domain of responsibility assigned to us, to ensure the orderliness of that divine sovereignty. Thus we foster the mutation of the software of the universe, causing it to change by our personal incentive.

Since the divine mind (or mind of the universe) is the matrix of our mind, it can never be the object of our cognizance. Yet we can invite more of its bounty to percolate through as our thinking. To do this, we need to extirpate the mental restrictions we impose upon our thinking by our very notion of ourselves as a fraction of the totality, and by the same token as "other than God." That is the very principle of the Islamic Shahada: *La ilaha illa 'lla* ("All that exists is God").

Our limited way of thinking evidences our having failed in our commonplace thinking to make the step in the evolution of human thought marked by the holistic paradigm.

While the fraction of a hologram functions like the whole hologram, it functions less effectively, but acquires a uniqueness that makes for variety and cooperation in the interest of the whole which would not occur if everything were undifferentiated.

The functioning of our minds is illustrated most pertinently by the DNA. Each cell organizes the fabric of the environment absorbed in its tissue on the model of the blueprint of the universe, which ensures that the cells differentiate to cooperate in the interest of the whole body. Similarly every human psyche is formatted by the software of the cosmos, although each psyche customizes the principles governing that software in its own unique way and thus processes the environment differently from its neighbor. Thus the complex structure of our body serves as the support system for that very intelligence configured in the cosmic blueprint, by turning certain genes on and others off. It is even so with our minds. Although they carry potentially the mind of the universe, they are diversified, and thereby restricted by their vantage points and their specializations.

Karl Pribam showed that the brain functions jointly as a hologram, and as a network of circuits. May I add that doing so ensures both the transpersonal and the personal dimensions of our motivations. The more transpersonal, the more the holistic mode of our thinking prevails over our personal opinion. This is what is meant in mysticism by awakening to God consciousness. It is as though one were detaching one's personal constraints from one's understanding of meaningfulness, or, more precisely, one's personal interpretation of situations and problems—which is exactly what is meant by *maya*.

But the exhilarating aspect of the whole marvel of which we are a contributing part is that the springhead behind its superb alacrity is sheer excitement! The brain needs stimulation; the mind needs the joy of discovering ideas; and the psyche needs ecstasy.

Dr. Alfred Tomasis, a physiologist, found that our brain requires three thousand million stimuli a day to keep awake. These include, of course, light and sound, smell, taste and tactile impressions. These sensorial stimuli are translated by the brain as energy pulses stimulating the mitosis of nerve cells. We know that our body cells, particularly our nerve cells, absorb light from the environment. This catalyzes their powerhouse, freeing their electrons from their initial constraint for a split second of spree into a degree of freedom. We also know that they are picking up and communicating sound messages. Hence the importance of music as fuel for our brain.

Our communication with the physical environment is nothing less than a communion of light between the light fluoresced by the environmental objects, the sun, the stars; and the light thrust by our brain through the optic nerves and retinas into the environment.

But contemplate how the degree of excellence attained with the extraordinary variety of frequency resonances in the already complex atomic configuration of vocal cords, guts, wood and metals of musical instruments, already reflecting the orderliness of the blueprint of the universe, may be further configured by the mind of God when funneled by the human as in symphonies and choruses of our civilizations! Or when the latticework of the internal fabric of stones, glass and ceramic are assembled into a statue or cathedral. Or how the gossamer film of paints, which in many ways are of the nature of liquid crystals already, so splendid in themselves, are blended into a painting!

Paint, like sound, is a noble expression of the software of the universe, and does not need to copy perceived objects as the paintings of old did, or like Beethoven's description of a thunderstorm in the 6th Symphony, or Honneger's imitation of a train puffing along.

The form of a flower or the countenance of a human face figure at the prow of the evolution of divine thought configured as form, and the soul-searchings, the aspirations, the misgiving, the compassion and the wit, erupt in human emotions. These are described for example by Brahms, who dramatizes the mutations incurred by the divine being in the existential condition. The mutations represent a progress in comparison with the sounds of nature in mineral or plant life, sometimes depicted in the dehumanized austerity or exuberance of some of our modern music.

When these media are fashioned to express our creative thinking, they enrich the software of the universe. Our thinking customizes the divine thinking, and, having projected itself into matter that already carries the hallmark of thinking at the cosmic level, is recycled into the cosmic thinking. Our minds and emotions delight when carried beyond the trite commonplace by the inspiration of poets, rearranging the divine thinking in unexpected ways! We discover new horizons of meaningfulness evidencing the splendor seeking to transpire through the appearance of things. Our mind-brains feast at the banquet offered by the creative geniuses who have conceived our great civilizations. We are thereby enriched and transformed.

What of the light that we ourselves awaken (probably as phosphorescence) by our visualizations, as has been demonstrated by Dr. Motayama's experiments with meditators in lightproof cells equipped with photoelectric sensors? Can we imagine the delight of composers improvising musical themes emerging from inside, as it were projecting an inner mandala in a visible or audible structure? Like a toccata and fugue of Bach or a prelude of Chopin or a sonata of Brahms! Most all of us have that uncanny ability as we hum randomly, yet it gains incomparably in excellence when cultivated.

According to Pir-o-Murshid Inayat Khan, as we turn within in meditation, we discover our ability of awakening the sound of the universe, the audiosphere. This sound is written right into the fabric of our body cells. They carry not only the memory of the sonic outbursts accompanying the birth and demise of the nebulae, whose stardust has coagulated into the atomic fabric of our body cells, but the present resonance of the subatomic structures of our cells that are affected by our psychological attunements. What a miracle is the human skill which translates this ubiquitous symphony of the spheres into music meaningful to humans!

Further, Pir-o-Murshid Inayat Khan points out the way to arouse the light within that flares like a flame. The ebullient incandescence that burst out of the cataclysmic conflagration of the big bang is stored in the very fabric of our bodies. It is released as phosphorescence whereby we transform the atomic structure of our body cells into light—a capacity found in the glow worm and which we also possess, and which can be released by dint of the appropriate visualizations.

It is not just the energy of stimuli which charges the powerhouse of our brains, but the meaningfulness of the universal blueprint conveyed by these stimuli. There are configurations, of the atomic structure of the fabric of the environment and of our very flesh that our minds grasp because they are modeled on the mind of the universe. It is not that light or sound spells awakening, but the vistas that they trigger in our intelligence. Every "aha" moment triggers off a peak experience—a tidal wave of delight. The springhead of the whole phantasmagoria that we perceive as the universe, divine nostalgia, spills over into our psychological attunements as we discover the intention behind it all written right into our deep motivations. But this only happens when we reach beyond our limited thinking, limited vantage point, and limited self image. Imagine: our psyche is littered with our misassessments of the physical and psychological environment!

Consider the impact upon the brain cells (and similarly upon the whole body) of our mind's ability to reach beyond its middle range, and of our emotions reaching into the many-splendored shimmering gamuts of cosmic ecstasy! This is precisely what we achieve with our meditation skills, in *samadhi* practices, Vipassana, Kabbalah, the theology of Aquinas, the Sufi *dhikr*. A major aspect of meditation consists in learning how to think beyond the commonplace syllogism. P. D. Ouspensky announced in *Tertium Organum* the advent of a super-logic surpassing the simplistic syllogism (Men are mortal; Socrates is a man; ergo, Socrates is mortal).

> **Our ordinary logic helps us to gauge only the relations existing in the phenomena world. ... We must come to the conclusion that separateness and combination are not opposites in the real world, but exist together and at the same time without contradicting each other.**
>
> **Ouspensky**

The New Spirituality

In a large number of human activities the know-how must be continually updated. Meditation also needs to be updated. Armed with the information in the enormous pool of published material available in our day, we are now able to make a comprehensive study of the methods of meditation taught in the classical schools. By taking the opportunity to compare all these methods, we can gain a whole new grasp of the core issues facing our pioneering meditating predecessors. This in turn will help us to look ahead, and to brainstorm perspectives on the future of meditation at the scale of present day thinking.

Since the challenges of our times are in some ways more demanding than those faced by our predecessors, our free-wheeling into the future must integrate a greater complexity. For example, we will need to take into consideration futuristic views in physics (some of which have not yet gained acceptance in the party line of physics), or the latest developments in psychology. Meditation needs to give us the means to reduce stress, improve decisionmaking, to overcome resentment and poor self image. We need to honor our concerns about the environment, the population explosion, crime, and political oppression. We need to gain insight into the disenchantment about institutionalization, particularly in the field of spirituality, and join the nascent trend to explore new expressions of our need for the sacred, emancipated from hackneyed forms of sanctimoniousness, prescriptions, dogmatism, and superstitions.

Thanks to the momentous advances in communication (the media, technology, education, and the new paradigms), our way of considering the cosmos and the Planet Earth in particular, has taken a quantum leap. Looking at photos of the Earth from outer space is almost like having been out there personally. This has surreptitiously revolutionized our way of considering our Planet, which in turn revolutionizes our way of seeing ourselves.

We imagine outer space to be "out there," but has it ever occurred to you that actually planet Earth is in outer space? It all depends on how you look at it. This progressive vantage point is bound to open up new vistas in our meditation practices.

Consequently, for example, instead of sitting still in meditation, simply observing the body or mind (which is tantamount to observing a mere cross-section of reality), we can see the whole forward march of the evolution of bodiness from our ancestors to the present state and even anticipate the future of the evolution of bodiness. Our development from our animal ancestry has not finished; it keeps advancing. The human race keeps on improving, albeit at the cost of decadence at the jagged ends.

Instead of aiming at escaping the "here and now" to scan transcendental levels of reality (subliminal to the existential level) as did our ancestral meditators, we will endeavor to look at the "here and now" from an overview.

> **I ask for no less than the impossible possibility: infinity in a finite fact and eternity in a temporal act.**
> **Prentice Mulford**

Even this is too commonplace. It still evidences a static view of the existential state, whereas, as we have seen, existence is only a slice of reality in its dynamic state. Therefore, we will be learning how to see how the "everywhere and always" manifests in the forward march of becoming.

Furthermore, instead of modulating consciousness from one vantage point to another, we will need to learn to extrapolate between several vantage points. The consciousness of future humanity may well be called stereoscopic consciousness. This applies equally to the mind, which will learn to extrapolate between thinking in terms of categories and grasping the wholeness of a situation. In addition, as a corollary, we will learn to avoid accounting for things merely in terms of a causal chain in time, of which they are the effect, but we will also include causal chains moving from the transcendent dimension into the transient. We may even grasp the concatenation of many causal chains coming together in our time and space. As a consequence of this forward step, we will be able to meditate in movement, even dancing, which will reinforce the dynamic mode of meditation, rather than the static.

Quite understandably, the ancients, who had not yet acquired our knowledge of matter, witnessing the decay of the body after death, considered it to be like dust returning to the earth. Since we can now see our live cells in powerful microscopes, our whole perception of the fabric of our body has undergone a dramatic change. Instead of dismissing our bodies as other than ourselves, we are beginning to honor the involvement of our innate sense of meaningfulness with the very fabric of our bodiness. We are intrigued by the manner in which these two sides of the same coin interact and modify each other reciprocally. It is not just mind over body, but body over mind as well.

Consequently, we need to brainstorm a new method of meditation that incorporates the earlier methods and carries them into the future.

To extricate ourselves from the rut into which we may have inadvertently stranded ourselves by taking things for granted, or from the stalemate into which we may well have maneuvered ourselves owing to a faulty strategy in the game of life, we need to rethink our lives.

To achieve this, we need to hoist our vantage point from the commonplace narrow range of the immediate environment and look at things in a wider context. This is where some of the skills of meditation can prove helpful. It is somewhat like witnessing how different a familiar landscape looks when flying over it in a helicopter or suspended from a hang glider. Doing this, we realize that our assessments of our life situations change with the altitude, as it were. They are furthermore a function of our values which manifest the higher levels of our being and monitor our motivations. Moreover we realize that our sense of personal inadequacy or our pessimistic judgment in our assessment of a situation were due to our mind's having gotten entrapped in a way of thinking from which we failed to see a way out. Yes, one can get trapped in one's thinking and ascribe the prison to one's fate. The bind is in the mind.

To escape from this prison takes two things: a flash of insight and resolve. How do we trigger the flash of insight? We need to first ask ourselves: what if my assessment of my life situations (or of people around me), upon which I have relied all this time and which I have always taken for granted, is wrong? What is more, if this is true, any new assessment we might convince ourselves of at this point stand an equal chance of proving later to be erroneous. If we therefore forego not only previous assessments, but any attempt at a reassessment, then, faced with the collapse of our opinion, we find ourselves hopelessly groping our way in the dark night of understanding. Bereft of any crutches, a different mode of understanding dawns upon us. Imagine that, walking in pitch dark, suddenly you are able to see the auras of people and that the features of their real countenances are revealed to you in contrast with the features of their faces.

It takes courage to let go of all that one has built up over the years without any guarantee that a new light will dawn upon one's horizon. But we find ourselves sometimes confronted with the choice between situations which progress gradually like a bud unfurls, or where things remain at a standstill, or run the chance of reversing into decay, or where nature proceeds by leaps and bounds. There are situations which one cannot change in their outer circumstances, but will change by one's changing oneself or by a new way of handling them. In exceptional cases—perhaps the most meaningful—there is no slow transition from one perspective to the other, the transit is sudden. Here lies the difference between the moment of time where there is an overlap between past and future, and the instant where there is a sudden and irreversible break of continuity.

These rare conditions, called singularities in astrophysics, occur in our lives and in our thinking. They may be illustrated by a sunrise or sunset, a solar or lunar eclipse, or the equinoxes or solstices where there is an alignment in space between two luminaries at a given time. Let us bear in mind that the coincidence is only meaningful from our vantage point, as it relates the objective world to our subjective dimension.

A particularly rare coincidence between two numbers in mathematics illustrates our mind's ability suddenly to grasp coherence where two mental constructs seemed previously to be irreconcilable. More generally what we mean by our sense of meaningfulness is our mind's ability to click when it grasps a correspondence between two thoughts which had hitherto appeared unrelated. The grasp of congruence sparks our being with delight because it gives us a sense of thinking in sync with the thinking of the universe, and feeling in resonance with the emotion of the cosmos, and hence makes us aware of our holistic connectiveness with the totality which we call God, not just at the physical level but at all levels.

We are ourselves hybrids, born of the alchemical betrothal between heaven and earth.

We can rebirth ourselves by going through the steps that led us to our present state, altering them willfully and consciously. Here we witness in ourselves the very task we have investigated so far: conjugating in our very personality our celestial and ancestral inheritance so that they actually click.

C. G. Jung spent much ponderous enquiry upon this paradoxical conjunction between our psyche and the physical world. In paradoxical cases, rather than it being a perception or an event that impacts our psyche and gets processed by our psyche, it is our psyche that triggers the event. He called it *synchronicity*. Jung defines these rare and surprising cases that one would normally explain away as situations which cannot be causally determined as the simultaneous occurrence of two meaningful but not causally connected events.

Yet he still strived to grasp the mystery behind occurrences that could not be connected in a chronological sequence where one occurrence could have triggered the other. Rather they seemed to be causally connected in a network irrespective of the arrow of time. The connections of events may in certain circumstances be other than causal and may require another principle of explanation.

Then it occurred to him that rare events (like a syzygy or singularity) cannot be governed by the same laws that apply to statistics, for example. Indeed the conjunctions that take place in an instant of time are rare events as compared with the gradual transformations where at each moment, the past overlaps with the future.

Probability theory is able to predict with uncanny precision the overall outcome of processes made up out of a large number of individual happenings, each in itself is unpredictable.

Arthur Koestler

Of course, our minds can affect our body functions:

You see that deep changes of meaning is a change in the deep material structure of the brain; we already know that certain meanings can greatly disturb the brain, but other meanings may organize it in a new way.

David Bohm

But how does a grasp of meaning affect the outer physical world? (This is what is meant by psychokinesis.)

After years of painstaking research in psychokinesis, Dr. J. B. Rhine arrived at conclusions that throw some light on the problem. For Rhine, space and time are dependent upon psychic conditions.

A parallel with David Bohm is called for here:

But there is still a mental pole at every level of matter ... and eventually if you go to infinite depths of matter, we may reach something very close to what you reach in the depth of the mind.

David Bohm

We are touching upon a most important point: space-time is only meaningful regarding physical reality. Indeed, for the psyche space is only meaningful where one is recalling physical occurrences or the functions of the mind creatively in the act of imagination. Yoga distinguishes where the mind adopts, as it were, the form of that which is perceived or reminisced (*nirvetarka*), from the state where the mind absorbs the quintessence of the perceived irrespective of form (*nirvecara*), and at some point the mind loses notions of space altogether (*asmita*) and a further point at which the mind loses the sense of time (*asamprajnata samadhi*).

For Speiser, our psyche, at a certain level of our thinking, touches upon a level prior to causality.

> **It is an initial state which is not governed by mechanistic law, but is the pre-conditioning of law, the chance substrate upon which law is built.**
>
> **Andreas Speiser**

Compare with Bohm:

> **The mind has two-dimensional and three-dimensional modes of operation. It may be able to operate directly in the depths of the implicate order where this timeless state is the primary actuality. Then we could see the ordinary actuality as a secondary structure.**

Indeed, our commonplace understanding of causality is based upon our concept of time as being unidimensional: the event that we infer having been caused by another event followed it in a sequential order. In our ordinary thinking, we also assume that an event causes another if they are related in space. It could be by electromagnetic forces that extend in space or gravity that also extends in space or by the strong and weak forces between subatomic particles.

But modern physics questions the mechanistic theories of their predecessors, replacing them with acausal, nonlocal laws. If everything in the cosmos is connected with everything else as in the holistic paradigm, then location in space is irrelevant in the determination of events. It is simply easier for our minds to see the connection between the motion of a billiard ball and that of the one it has hit, than to see how the surge of a wave we think is in the Pacific could influence that of a wave which we think is in the English Channel. Yet, as Dr. David Bohm points out, a wave in the ocean is not caused by the previous one, but each wave is interjected back into the whole ocean and it is the whole ocean that projects itself in the next wave.

A form emerges or is creatively projected from the whole, and then it influences the whole, or is injected back into it. In the implicate order, it resonates with similar forms and then is projected back into the explicate order.

However, long before the holistic paradigm envisioned by General Smuts revolutionized science, the Sufis saw the insufficiency in reducing causality to the dimension of time which we call the process of becoming. One needs to account for at least another dimension of time moving from transcendence to transiency, and vice versa.

The Sufi Shahabuddin Suhrawardi felt that beyond the sidereal empyrean, other universes would be found in a hierarchical sequence of spheres of light of increasing subtlety. The higher ones precede the lower ones and enjoy a hierarchically higher value (precellence) and consequently sovereignty (prevalence); the lower ones proceed from the higher ones in a causal order in a different time order than the commonplace arrow of time—a kind of exponential order. This so-called vertical hierarchy which he refers to as the "world of mothers" then splits up in a lateral order where equality takes over from dominance. Here we find the prototypes of the species. It is at this level that our ordinary notions of the process of time take effect.

But it is in the conjunction between a physical phenomenon and a spontaneous thought that was not triggered by an actual occurrence that our delight reaches a degree of intensity such that it could spark our creative faculties—whether of a work of art or of our personality. One could define creativity as the act of exploring uncharted regions of the mind while grasping a correspondence between the mental constructs thus gleaned and a form or configurations or scenarios in the fabric of matter. Creativity is a congruent conjunction between the timeless and the transient, the heavenly and the earthly.

PRACTICES

What would be the kind of meditations embodying the progress in our thinking in our day and age and oriented towards the future? Having learnt how the mind works when it awakens beyond the existential realm, we need to learn to awaken in life—grasping our place, our role in the universe.

Let us follow retrospectively the trails of the two evolutionary networks that have intermeshed into the formation of our being as it is at present: (i) the legacy of our celestial origination, (ii) our genetic inheritance. To do this we need to reverse in our mind the forward thrust of the arrow of time and carry our memory right back in time—into prehistoric eons of time whose traces are stored (though recessively) in deep memory in the archives of the depths of the unconscious zones of our psyche.

1) Bear in mind that the fabric of your body originated in the big bang explosion at the onset of the present eon in the genesis of the universe (there were, however, previous universes!). Ponder upon the fact that your body is made out of the fabric of the stars.

2) Try to imagine what it would feel like to be a vibration—more precisely a high-frequency vibration of pure energy.

3) Imagine that this pristine state in which you were gels into a crystal.

4) Can you visualize the marvelous symmetry of latticework of the molecules and within them the atoms of your crystalline primeval body jiggling and sparkling?

5) Can you envision the glee of the electrons within the atoms as they avail themselves of the energy of ambient light to free themselves, even if for a split second, from the rigor of the constraint of the order of the universe maintaining them in their orbitals, and dance with abandon? Imagine the outburst of joy at participating with some measure of

freedom in the choreography of the cosmos!

6) Now imagine the sudden evolutionary leap of the molecules constituting your body from the mineral state to the plant—from the inorganic to the organic. Envision the intelligence of the universe self-organizing in an improved fashion through the awareness now emerging in the molecules, and finding a way of grouping gregariously with their neighbors to cooperate by specializing in their mutual contributions to the living cell. To illustrate this: instead of the repetitive series of frescoes on a wall paper, we have a flurry of proliferating forms and radiant colors.

7) Can you see the way the crystal connects with light after being entombed in the earth? Now experience the plant's ability to power its cyclic unfoldment, and more so its mutations by dint of light. Can you envision yourself as a flower at night fluttering in resonance with the trembling of a star? Can you feel the thrust of the evolutionary drive striving to free the plant of its roots that it may explore neighboring space as an animal whose instincts still conspire in us?

8) Or is it the impact of our heavenly legacy that seeks freedom from the strict conditioning in the more primitive developmental stages of our being, and makes for ever more variable structures in the material underpinning of our being? Notice that simply thinking of the celestial spheres conveys to you a sense of freedom. Now you may feel somehow the connection between your body, as it has evolved from its precursors, and your heavenly legacy.

9) At this stage, we are ready to understand the implications of the alchemical betrothal. Recollecting the two main genealogical streams generating your being, the celestial and the genetic, try and see how they have been intermeshing in both your body and your personality. If you recall some of the practices we did, envisioning our celestial bodies, fashioning them in accord with our thoughts and attunements and creative imagination, and observing how this

affected our countenance and even our demeanor, you will have established that connection. The same applies to our personality.

10) In meditative vein, envision yourself descending through the spheres. Now gauge the need you felt through your descent to understand how the intention governing the software of the universe gets actuated on earth. Realize that it was this need to understand that impelled the mutations in the very fabric of your body as it progressed though your precursors in the course of evolution, enabling your present body to be better able to serve the intelligence of which it is the support system.

11) Now consider that while you converge the universe and therefore incur a great measure of conditioning, you also act upon the universe. See how your incentive exercises an impact upon the legacy of the past in your body and personality which we have been recollecting.

12) Bearing in mind that the human condition is just a developmental stage in the evolutionary march, can you sense in yourself a longing to awaken beyond the human condition? Can you feel the evolutionary drive spurring you on? Can you see that if the initial springhead behind the whole evolutionary drive is the very freedom that resonates with your pristine celestial nature, then the Cosmos envisioned as one being (which is what is meant by God) tends to converge in each being. This is, incidentally, the holistic model. If this is so, then the more we converge of the bounty of the universe, the more self-sufficient we become. Think of yourself as aiming at becoming gradually a spinoff in which the universe rethinks and reconstructs itself.

13) Instead of visualizing the stars as they may appear from Planet Earth, now reach out there and imagine them as supporting civilizations different from ours and how our civilization might look from the vantage point of their intelligence.

14) If you ponder upon how the mind of the crystal evolved into the mind of a plant, then of an animal, then reached the human stage, realize that you can stretch your mind beyond its limits. The clue to spurring our mind to surpass itself is by jettisoning a lot of preconceived ideas—which is precisely what we have learned in this course. There could be no limits to this, but if indeed our minds are holistically sub-wholes of the mind of the cosmos, and if indeed the smaller the fraction of the holograph, the less well it reflects the original object, then the more we stretch out minds, the more truly our thinking will prove isomorphic with the thinking of the cosmos! Think: we are decoding the code of the universe!

15) However we should not limit our thinking to its cosmic dimension, its ability to extrapolate between more and more factors. We could highlight the transcendental dimension. As we shift our sense of identity from plane to plane we discover different levels of thinking. We normally ascribe the notions acquired by our thinking at higher levels to our sense of values. Values such as compassion, humor, or authenticity actuate themselves increasingly as evolution marches on.

16) Starting with your spontaneous thoughts, however random, prompted by inspiring emotions, try to grasp the archetypes of which these thoughts are the exemplars. You will find yourself exploring a whole different dimension—the world of metaphor. Now if you turn your mind downwards, as it were, you will find that these thoughts self-organize as forms, or landscapes, or scenarios, as in your dreams.

17) Now we arrive at a kind of pinnacle of cosmic cognition: See yourself in the universe, your origination, your purpose, your destiny, your past and future, your ability to shift your focus through the spheres by adjusting your attunement.

18) At this point we grasp the antinomy between thought and emotion as the two sides of the same coin, and shift between them. Consequently we can trace our origination to the emotion behind the universe beyond the software. The emotion moving the cosmos (the emotion behind the universe that manifested as the universe) passing though J. S. Bach's soul was crystallized into the notes of his music. In the same way you can feel the emotion spurring the universe at the cosmic scale configuring itself in the idiosyncrasies of your personality and the countenance of your face behind its external features.

19) You could willfully reinforce these emotions by indulging in the musings of your soul, by enjoying your sense of bewonderment at the marvel of yourself and the universe of which you are a part, and by giving vent to your need for glorification. Lo and behold, what at first seemed to be your personal emotion—rapture—culminates into impersonal, cosmic emotion—divine ecstasy

20) Now honor your intuition that behind all manifestation there is great splendor and that you are born of the divine nostalgia to manifest that splendor in every possible way in and through your being at all levels. Accept the divinity of your being. Awaken to the divinity of your being. Accept the beauty of your being if you can reconcile it with a sense of modesty. But do not confuse modesty with false humility. Priding oneself in one's self denigration avers itself to be a failure to recognize one's divine heritage, and proves self-defeating. The Sufis consider this to be an insult to the divine Artist.

21) We have been exploring methods of meditation whereby we may actuate the splendor of our divine investiture thanks to the ability of our intelligence to surpass its previous outreach, and by discovering in our high attunement, deeply rooted in the very springheads of our being, the divine nostalgia in search of beauty and love. Eventually we understand the enormous implications of a saying of

Pir-o-Murshid Inayat Khan, my father, embodying the very quintessence of the metaphysical traditions of the Sufis and representing the spiritual paradigm for the future. He said that awakening consists in seeing oneself as the fulfillment of the divine purpose and recognizing that purpose in the universe at large.

Chapter 3
Religious Faith and Experience

The 1984 Sinai Gathering

Some of us have just returned from a really exhilarating and fascinating meeting of religious leaders culminating on the top of Mount Sinai, a gesture of good will in a tough, violent world! That this historic meeting was not exposed to media publicity speaks, amongst other considerations, for the non-pretentious intention motivating it. Of course, everyone is aware that the Middle East ranks first among the most vulnerable areas, which, ignited beyond control, might be likely to trigger a nuclear holocaust. We also know that issues are so complex and intricate that governments, with all their expertise, fail to find a solution acceptable to all.

Consequently, although political feelings, claims, and grudges could not be overlooked or dismissed, there was a consensus that we were not habilitated or accredited or competent to meddle with purely political issues.

Why, then, did we meet? Could you believe that there are still a few idealists in the world who will leave their jobs and homes, cancel their busy schedules at their own expense, out of pure dedication, in the belief that since there is a religious factor in any war, let alone the Middle East conflict, it is incumbent upon the more progressive spiritual leaders of various religious denominations to demonstrate their solidarity in their dedication to a spiritual ideal while respecting their differences of outlook and ritual?

Obviously, numerically we represented a negligible fraction of the plethora of rabbis, priests, ministers, imams and bikkhus on the planet. Therefore, one might well question what impact our symbolic action might have upon the conflicting religious masses, especially since we were deprived of the powerful tool of mass media. "Small is beautiful..." and we believed that our gesture may loosen tensions a little bit in, let us say, the "software" of the programming of events materializing on the physical plane.

For the least, it may be said that we had a marvelous time sharing in the spectacle of the most diverse types of people and cultures and attires, and discovered the joy of communicating together with an open heart. For the Middle Easterners, the American New Age openheartedness, religious tolerance and optimism must have hit home as something totally surprising and very reassuring, and served as the "glue" that bonded us. It was a striking expression of the spirit of the message of unity to which we are dedicated.

We sang Hindu, Buddhist, Jewish, Christian, Muslim and Sufi songs at the top of the Mount where presumably Moses discovered the famous tablets. A Native American lit medicinal herbs at dawn. What a privilege to be ushered into the "holy of holies" at the St. Catherine's monastery, dating as early as the year 50 A.D.—a tribute to the fervor of the Hesychasts, the early monks of the desert whose caves are still to be seen where water flows generously betwixt the barren desert lands.

A remarkable feature of the event, which need not necessarily be put down to coincidence, was the fact that several Japanese religious groups had planned a similar event at the very same time. One more indication in favor of synchronicity in the planning of the "good force"! These groups added a lot to the sheerly picturesque—remarkable by their cool and noble discipline.

President Anwar Sadat's project for a peace center including three buildings, for Judaism, Christianity and Islam, seems to have been scrapped, but the spirit of Sadat hovers over the whole area. It was his favorite haunt. We felt that it was his spirit that had inspired us, and we were doing what we could to keep that ultimate hope for tolerance and good will alive, not only in the Middle East but in the world.

Towards a New Approach

Unless one is prepared to reconsider, restructure, and innovate, one is not part of the evolutionary process. In fact, the outdated religious beliefs and practices of those who have not made the contemporary leap in thinking are largely instrumental in fostering the intolerance which inevitably triggers the violence and wars that afflict our times.

We know that, having made the step required to be in sync with present thinking, there is no turning back; the paradigm shift is irreversible. But is it not foolhardy to devalidate or dismiss hackneyed attitudes and purport to start from scratch, when in fact our present is an organic sequence from the achievements of our predecessors? Each person stands on the shoulders of another so that one of them may see beyond. I consider it my duty to explore with you the features of the spirituality in keeping with our time.

What then would be the features of an updated spirituality? Purely off the cuff, I venture: a spirituality without a belief system, without a set of prescriptions, and without authority figures (that is, gurus or established ranks).

It is wise, however, to avoid throwing the baby out with the bath water. One overlooks easily the wisdom in time-consecrated procedures which one wishes to discard. On the one hand, the remarkable progress of science, technology, and social organization was only possible by questioning and updating previous thinking, methods, or procedures. On the other hand, we are beginning to discover the drawbacks: pollution, acid rain, the depletion of planetary resources, cancer, the population explosion, violence, and decadence.

Re: "belief." As one evolves, one questions belief founded upon authority and seeks direct experience. Yet one needs to take into account that experience is interpreted and our assessment is questionable. Moreover, we preclude and prefigure experience by our assumptions. Pir-o-Murshid Inayat Khan calls upon a totally different dimension which is faith rather than belief, based upon a kind of precognitive, proto-critical knowledge beyond the mind, something he calls the knowledge of the soul. Imagine—this basic human intuition gets blurred and devalidated by mind games that prove totally inadequate and misleading, so that people replace faith by belief or skepticism.

Yet, while opinions are relative, enlightened insight can reveal new vistas. Hence, people need guidelines, landmarks, bearings, and azimuths rather than goals.

Re: "do's" and "do nots." One will never like to take responsibility for one's actions if one bases them on the opinion of a person, however enlightened, or upon public opinion. Nonconformism to these prescriptions most often instills guilt complexes which obstruct genuine soul searching. When freed from this moral imposition, people are able to discover their conscience as their ultimate criterion.

Re: "counseling." Spiritual guides will have to make a policy of abstaining from advising, and at the same time, act as facilitators in order to help people untangle the incongruities in their own assessments and discover their real motivations. Undoubtedly, even as there are people who are more skilled than others in violin making or piano playing or cabinet making or physics, there will always be a need for teachers in every field including that of meditation or that most lofty of all skills, helping people to get in touch with the sublime dimension of their being.

Re: "gurus." Leadership, guidance, and pioneering are essential to human evolution, but our human expertise is not up to evaluating a person's degree of spirituality. Admittedly, there are certain norms. A person with a doctor's degree in medicine is allowed to practice medicine, but there are enormous differences in the skill of doctors. The world is graced with beautiful people without any pretense to spirituality, often more inspiring than those purporting to hold a spiritual rank.

While I recognize the need for organization, institutions, and schools, we will need to be wary in the future of claims to any established rank. Spiritual guides will have to prove themselves by the inspiration they communicate and by their radiance. This is the meaning of the Islamic formula: *khatum rasul il'llah* or The Seal of the Prophets. Claims to being "divinely special" may have had their place in credulous societies to establish credibility. Such claims are no longer acceptable in our time. Islam announced a landmark, which, in fact, defines democracy. The Prophet marked the transition by disclaiming any divinity, announcing himself as the servant of God. But the followers carried this teaching beyond its purpose, denying the divinity in all beings. But this is the very implication of *la ilaha illa 'lla* ("nothing exists but God"). If nothing exists but God, then the totality of existence may be thought of as God.

God as Archetype, the Human Being as Exemplar

To the question "how can one know God?" Ibn Arabi answers: "All that one knows of the archetype is what is exemplified in the exemplar." Roundness is only knowable through round tables, wheels, etc. This elicits a totally different relationship with what we think we mean by God. In our meditation practices, we shall learn to recognize in the idiosyncrasies of our personality the divine qualities that they exemplify. Rather than being like a cell of the body, we could see ourselves as exemplars carrying potentially the bounty present in the template or archetype which we exemplify. This elicits a totally different relationship with the totality we project as God.

However, there is a more profound way of looking at this: What in this view could the archetype of our personality be if we refuse to ascribe a personality to God?

> **It would be a great mistake to call God a personality, but it is a still greater mistake to deny God a personality. Each being is the flowering of the personality of God...the seed does not show the flower in it, yet it culminates in the flower: therefore the flower already existed in the seed.**
>
> **Pir-o-Murshid Inayat Khan.**

But the breakthrough is in awakening the God within:

Our notion of ourselves as the observer can be shunted backwards in infinite regress as one identifies more and more with that aspect of God which we represent as the Spectator.

To illustrate this, our consciousness is endowed with the ability to imagine how Planet Earth would look from outer space, or in some cases, how we are perceived by another person. Moreover, our minds are able to outreach any limits we may have assigned to their compass. As the French mathematician Henri Poincaré showed: "the concept of infinity evidences the mind's ability to always imagine a larger number than the one enunciated so far." In fact, our minds are coextensive with the mind of the universe. In the holistic paradigm, insofar as one can fraction the totality, every fraction of the totality does not simply act as a section (like a section of an orange, for example), yet the smaller the fragment, the less well it manifests the totality.

One needs to make a clear distinction between belief and faith. Belief is opinion based upon authority, or custom, routine, conditioning. Faith is reinforced by opinion based upon experience.

The mind gets easily caught in a bind. A bind is a situation in which thoughts follow one another in a circular fashion—popularly called a vicious circle. The pending catastrophe is rooted in the storms in human thinking. Thoughts thus caught as in a whirlwind become compulsory, and gain great emotional support by their addictive nature until they explode in violence. Imagine: it is this very flaw in the functioning of the mind that begets conflicts, disasters, ordeals of terrible human suffering and terror!

As seen from the serenity of a spiritual retreat, the disastrous effect of an ideology upon the destinies of masses of people stands out clearly. The excesses of cruelty that people will wreak upon others in the name of sheer opinion not based upon real life experience is appalling!

The mystics of the various religious denominations seek after real experience, whereas the thinking of the followers is governed by belief. The originating revelation gets gradually distorted by what Pir-o-Murshid Inayat Khan calls "the followers of the followers." Therefore the Sufis hold that one needs to base one's concept of God upon one's discovery of the traces (*ayat*) of God in real life. That is why the Prophet Mohammed said, "for each person, his religion." Because if that belief were to fail, if at some point doubts should arise as to why the mind finds difficulty in relating the belief to actual real life experience, then the mind becomes plunged in the dark night of understanding.

St. John of the Cross, who escaped his prison thanks to the darkness of the night, sees in this crisis in our thinking the way out of the bind. Now the mind revolts against its conditioning, against those who have held it trammeled. Once more there is revolution. When there is a paradigm shift in belief there is a revolution in values, in paradigms, and likewise when that shift is reversed. It is a great tour de force. But this requires some degree of consensus and marks a stage in people's evolutionary advance.

However, if the dark night serves to free one from the prison in the mind, it does not show the way. Therefore St. John cleaves to a tenuous spark of light in his understanding: the dawning of meaningfulness. Trust yourself to this fragile light as you advance towards it. It will grow as the effulgence of dawn. It represents a level of thinking beyond the kind of thinking that spins inexorably in a vicious circle. It dawns upon one's understanding as the horizon of one's understanding expands. Therefore the Sufis consider that it is revealed to one when one has found freedom from opinion.

From the moment that we realize to what extent our assessment of reality is distorted by referring everything to our notion of ourselves, we appreciate our ability to look at things in reverse. For example, "I am seen" rather than "I see," or "I am thought of" instead of "I think," or "I am the convergence of an infinite and eternal reality" instead of "I experience reality."

What is the criterion distinguishing this intuitive mode of cognizance and opinion based upon belief? One would need to investigate the levels of thinking of the human mind.

At the bottom line: experience of the physical environment imputed through the senses and hearsay, opinion, and psychological data are interpreted from the limited vantage point of our commonplace consciousness. At a higher level, our minds project their grasp of reality, which our consciousness cannot encompass, into metaphors. This is why mystics express their conviction in the splendor behind real life in terms of poetry. To value what comes through in the experience of the world, one needs to tap one's inborn sense of beauty and meaningfulness.

This virtual sense is "revealed" if one does not limit one's opinion to the way things look from the vantage point of consciousness focalized by our commonplace notion of "I-ness," nor to opinions borrowed from others. According to the Sufi Niffari, one is suspended on the threshold until one is ready for that revelation which he calls the divine revelation. For how could the mind transcend by striving to carry experience to the edge of the unknowable, while still confined to its sense of I-ness? Rather it can only be revealed thanks to the *significatio passiva* (being passive to the divine operation). By trying to define God, one confines God to the narrowness of one's mind, however expanded. Therefore let us not limit God by seeing in this a proof of God's reality.

This is revelation: the meaningfulness of the universe as a total being erupts in each fraction of that being when that fraction reaches out beyond its horizon and plugs into the thinking of the universe. Here lies the next phase in human evolution. Evolution advances by dint of the revolution in our minds and a harmonious resolution.

Psychological and Transformational Stages of the Mass

Some of the more traditional religious ceremonies are preceded by a procession exhibiting festive pageantry. Participating in a procession fulfills our need to discover whatever is holding us back from our quest and release ourselves from it.

But it is in the custom of performing ablutions that our sense of guilt is sparked. It brings home to us the importance of confronting our conscience as we recollect having offended or abused or harmed a fellow being. By the same token it draws our attention to the immaculate nature of that deep core in our being in which we discover the sacred.

Just as in the Catholic Mass, we first need to go through the *Kyrie* and *Christe Eleison* before participating in the *Gloria.* We cannot approach the immaculate center of our being without coming to terms with our guilt. To be honest with ourselves (otherwise it would be a masquerade), we resort to ponderous soul-searchings. Memories of forgotten incidents besiege our minds and pummel our emotions. Our reason will come to our rescue, furnishing us with the most unconvincing arguments intended to justify ourselves. We may fall for these unaware, yet our conscience may not feel totally assuaged.

Our assessment of our guilt avers itself not to be too reliable. It easily overlaps with our resentment. We may feel guilty for having allowed ourselves to be abused, or co-dependent. Anger serves as our defense system. But we need to clearly distinguish between rage and outrage. Consider rage as the personal dimension of outrage and outrage as the impersonal dimension of rage. Rage can degenerate as hatred; outrage can erupt into heroism.

Toying with the impelling emotions generated in the drama of our lives, religion avers itself to be our saving grace. By grasping the splendor in the heavens behind the iniquity in the earthly drama we are lured out of our self pity, which helps us to heal. Is it worth missing out on the *Gloria* by being waylaid by our hurts in our storms in our teacups, when life in all its glory beckons us to participate in the cosmic celebration?

Is it the act of glorification, rising aloft from the fervor of the congregation into the high vaults amidst the rafters adorning the colossal masonry of the nave, as incense echoes the celebration in the heavens—or is it our incantations that enchant those celestial beings by an eerie sortilege into an upsurge of jubilation? It is as though a skylight had been suddenly opened between earth and heaven.

The *Gloria* of the Mass serves as a reminder that it is only out of an act of glorification that we can raise ourselves above our commonplace self image in which we are encapsulated by our trite emotions, our greed, our lack of mercy and compassion. It brings home to us that it is our ability to honor our intuition about a splendor that is continually trying to break through the painful circumstances constraining us in the existential condition that fosters our transformations.

Of course those realms that we ascribe to the heavens are not located elsewhere; they are not confined to us either.

But we accede to these by confecting that very temple built in the fabric of our own person—our body, magnetic field, aura, and psyche. This secures a psychological area offering us protection against the sacrilege rampant in the world and also within ourselves.

It is indeed our faith in our intuition—a kind of inborn sense of meaningfulness not based upon the judgments of our limited minds—that gives us access to the higher dimensions of our being, and by the same token, of the universe. Incidentally, let us not confuse faith with belief that is based on authority.

This is where the *Credo* comes in, bolstered by the power of our personal convictions. It is a mode of cognizance, not based upon our assessment of situations but upon the fact that our thinking is of an identical nature to the thinking of the universe when not limited by our personal focal center. This perspective emerges only when we are able to grasp the cosmic and transcendental outreach of our being.

It is prayer, the act of glorification that shifts our thinking from the commonplace mode to this cosmic and transcendent mode. The effect of prayer challenges our minds by revealing hidden causes behind events that do not make sense in our lives or those of others. In our ignorance of that which is enacted behind situations, sometimes dramatically, we tend to make serious mistakes in our handling of our affairs, with dire consequences for ourselves and others. It is difficult for our minds, functioning in their limited fashion, to grasp the interaction between destiny and free will. It is difficult to gauge the cosmic laws whereby the interplay between our covetousness and our dedication to service affects our destiny—or how this affects our personality, our attunement and our fulfillment of our life's purpose. That the act of giving, sacrifice, and relinquishing, even to the point of surrender, should be the ultimate issue in our lives defies rational common sense. Why this moral injunction about sacrifice, epitomized in the rituals of all religions, and illustrated in the oblation of the Agnus Dei, the Lamb of God, or in the immolation of Isaac, and culminating in the *Crucifixus* of the Mass?

> **Those who are crucified on earth will be free in the heavens and those who are free on earth will be crucified in the heavens.**
>
> **Pir-o-Murshid Inayat Khan**

It is not much use trying to argue with whatever we ascribe to destiny—that is, the enigmatic intentions of the programming of the universe. It is clear that we cannot appraise this intention from our limited perspective.

The only sense renunciation could possibly make is in resurrection—*Resurrexit.* That the quintessence of whatever has been achieved in the process of becoming is fed back into the pool of resourcefulness of the cosmos makes metaphysical sense. What has been achieved by existentiation is that the virtual Totality should be diversified in each of us. This points to the original contribution of our personal dimension—that the quintessence of our personality and know-how must be resurrected.

It becomes obvious to one's soul-searching that one cannot expect one's being to be resurrected unless purified of its blemishes. To extract the quintessence, alchemists need to drain away the dross. This is where one finds that asking for forgiveness is not good enough; one needs to repent, which means renewing ones pledge never to repeat the offense: the *Confiteor.*

This pledge to service illustrated by Isaiah's "send me" is a commitment to accept whatever the office asks of one in terms of sacrifice to the point of persecution, torture, and martyrdom. There is a feeling that those called to cosmic service are being eulogized by heavenly beings—the *Sanctus.* Moreover something in the human spirit surges forth to honor, venerate, and sanctify our heroes who have lived up to this higher calling—the *Hosanna.* They figure in our sacred treasure house as living examples of the value we treasure most. Only after this may the celebrant approach in the *Introit*, the altar, the holy of holies to participate of the *Eucharist*.

> **Hic est enim Corpus Meum; Hic est enim Calix Sanguinis Mea.**
>
> **This is my body, this is the chalice of my blood.**

According to Pierre Teilhard de Chardin:

> **The body of Christ represents the matter of the universe that is continually being transmuted into spirit (energy), and the blood is the suffering implied by the incarnate condition, being transfigured into joy.**

The ritual serves as a reminder that we do carry within us the inheritance of the whole universe which may be looked upon as the body of God. But if we are not aware of our divine inheritance, it remains recessive in us—we cannot actuate it in our personal idiosyncrasies.*

> **Be ye perfect as your Father.**

The celebrants now return to their seats replenished by the many-splendored bounty lying in wait in their own being. Conversely by following the psychological stages celebrated in the Mass the contemplative may in personal orison experience this Holy Communion with the whole universe at all its levels.

---

*Reference could be made here to the Greek myth of Zagreus, the son of Zeus. When Zeus vacated his throne, his son Zagreus sat upon it. While stupefied at the discovery of his resemblance to his father as he looked into the mirror presented to him by the Titans, they precipitated him into the abyss and devoured him. Zeus shattered the Titans with his thunderbolt and men were born out of the ashes of the Titans who had ingested the body of the son of God.

The altar is amongst the stars.

Teilhard de Chardin

The kind of peace that passeth all understanding in the *Dona Nobis Pacem* could not possibly be reached unless one has gone through the cosmic drama, enjoying the privilege of the gift of life and suffering defeat, humiliation and despair. There is no peace equal to that at the aftermath of a storm—when one has confronted the challenge and come to terms with it. Hence the last words of Christ: *It has been fulfilled.*

Ita Missa Est—the Mass is completed.

Chapter 4

Meditation

The Other Side of Life

When one realizes to what extent one has allowed oneself to be conditioned by the way things look and how one has let oneself be confined by one's self image, and when one nurtures a hunch that there must be dimensions of the universe that one fails to countenance, one is moved by an impelling need to know something about the other side of life.

One imagines that perhaps it is in dreams that one might snatch an ephemeral peep beyond the curtain into other spheres concealed behind the phantasmagoria of confused impressions in the sorting-house of the mind.

Curiously enough, the more one tries to do this in one's day-consciousness, the less one achieves even the slightest haul. At those moments when one awaits it least, a fleeting landscape of the soul transpires—just as one may catch a furtive overview of the land from a plane or a hang glider in the instant of break in the clouds. "It has passed before one has noticed it," says the Upanishad.

Why is our most cherished nostalgia so difficult to attain? It is because, as the Sufi Al Hallaj said,

> **"It is our wish of God that stands in the way of the experience of God."**

Perhaps we might understand this better by calling upon a double metaphor. Suppose that we converge the physical world like a whirlpool converges a lake. It follows that we are coextensive with it and, by the same token, with the fabric of the higher spheres and, what is more, with the consciousness and will of the universe that is the knowing subject.

The paradox is really that behind the commonplace subject-object relationship we entertain with the physical aspect of the universe. There is a deeper form of cognizance whereby one realizes that what one experiences is actually one's self.

"That which is experienced is that which experiences," says St. Francis. In this mode, experience is self discovery.

The key to grasping this paradox is to realize that because we think of ourselves as a fraction of the universe, we fail to experience the higher dimensions of the physical universe that we ourselves are. If we are indeed the convergence of the universe at all levels, we are those spheres which we think are out of our reach. It is in ourselves that they are to be found. This would explain the words of the Sufi Abdullah Ansari, who said,

> **"I searched for God and only found myself and then I searched for myself and found God."**

This is where the second metaphor comes in. Suppose the vortex were three-dimensional. As we get closer to the apex, the bounty present in the base would be badly squeezed and impoverished, just as the details of a landscape are reduced on a photograph to fit it all into a small confined space. This is why, deceptively, the splendor we ascribe to these planes or spheres gets so badly limited, distorted, despoiled and desecrated in what we think is ourselves. We have "converged" all that wonder that is behind our trite beings so much that it is most times difficult to detect whatever splendor has been pressed within.

To see what beauty lurks behind a wounded and disenchanted face, or what modicum of intuition still looms behind a conditioned mind, one has to have the eyes of

Majnun the lover, say the Sufis. Consider (as Prentice Mulford has said) "...infinity in finite act and eternity in a transient act." I would add that behind the beauty of snow-covered landscapes is hidden a still greater beauty; the snow crystals.

If one could see the flickering and sparkling of light, or hear the incredible melodies produced in the molecules and cells of even the hair that we shed as they reproduce in mitosis or, more so, the shrewdness of the enzymes that unlock the transcription of the DNA by the RNA, one's spirit would be sparkled with ecstasy. And what of the light display of the galaxies and the symphony of the spheres! It beats even the most ravishing sunrise. And what do we know of the splendor of the heavenly spheres, since whatever transpires in us, even in the eyes of some children, can only be a dull replica thereof! "In comparison with the beauty of God, the beauty of the creature is *nada*," says St. John of the Cross. From our limited personal vantage points, we cannot countenance it. One would have to discover and identify with the heavenly counterpart in oneself.

Yet see what richness our civilized life offers us in amenities and sheer beauty of art and music and architecture and theater and dance and poetry and technology through the incentives of so many Pleiades of creative beings since the early stirrings of life on the Planet. The beauty that comes through the inspired mind aroused by ecstasy is inestimable, monumental and unending.

Thus, the other side of life avers itself not to be like the opposite side of a coin, but the all-encompassing reality of the apex of a cone, within which, in our ignorance, we confine our notion of ourselves.

On Retreat

Yes, it has really happened. Years of dreaming, of yearning for the cave. Alone at last in the wilderness: the rocks, the gurgling water echoing the wind, the sun pouring its magnanimity upon this body near seventy, exulting in the merging with its ground, Mother Earth at her most ravishing.

Why the impelling, ever recurring dream of the cave? I ask myself this as I exult in the night chill in the welcome warmth of the wood fire in the cave I have so longed for. It occurs to me that the glow of the sun I had enjoyed a few hours ago, the initial outburst of the big bang, is vouchsafed to me in the depths and darkness of my rocky reclusion by the bodies of the trees that have stored that mighty effulgence better than I can, kindling yet more light in my aura.

So what am I escaping from? Is it an escape from the very thing these logs are doing for me, from the goodies of life, making life beautiful in the nitty gritty? To pursue practical well being, one would need to involve oneself in life. But one needs to balance the giving out of energy in one's worldly pursuits by rekindling, replenishing oneself at the source.

For a short spell, it is not an escape, but a very necessary rededication. This is therapy. Life communicates life, especially in the silence, the aloneness, the solitude. And what of the internal energy emerging to resonate with the energy accruing from nature? Meditation's dialogues with space itself have lost its meaningfulness.

I mused upon Buddha on retreat and imagined how he would have loved to have a computer in the wilderness (pure conjecture).

While sitting in rapture amongst the glistening cascades and pools, the rocks incandescent in the sun, the cacti, I reached beyond the physical scene and it occurred to me that the more breathtakingly beautiful nature is, the more splendid can one imagine the fullness of reality behind it. Remembering how it looked, I could now offset my consciousness from the physical perspective. To do this, I had to let myself go and lose myself in the rocks and water, wind and sun, to step beyond. The consequence was that my sense of identity got totally shifted. At those rare moments, one occupies a vast space, and identifies with the universe. One can watch one's body and mind as one identifies with a reality of a different nature. I tried not to attach a label to the new reality by calling it intelligence, because I did not want to slip back into a mind trip. As soon as one calls off the activity of consciousness and meditation, one can see oneself clearly as not being either body or mind. However much some thoughts struck me as being relevant, I kept grasping the intelligence behind it all. Actually, there are several layers of the mind. If one lets go of the common-place layer, an archetypal layer takes over.

Remembering how the mind thinks ordinarily, I dismissed my mind and proceeded without objective or motivation, identifying myself with my higher self. By imagining the splendor behind the rocks, the flowers and the stars, one discovers that very splendor in one's own being. Gradually, every aspect of one's being that has become jaded becomes dispelled, until one literally *becomes* that splendor. I asked myself, "Is splendor what we experience of the heavens, magnified up there, or are we creating it out of the latencies within ourselves by the act of glorification?"

It became clear to me that one cannot dismiss one's ego personality in order to reach into the transcendental areas of one's being; one needs to sanctify it, then it is easier to tow it along in one's high quest. Idiosyncrasies get set in and become nearly indelible. Only spiritual power will transform beyond recognition. At a certain stage in the process, spiritual power comes through, surprisingly. Spiritual power arises out of developing the magnetism of the soul, which in time, arises out of the emotion of the soul. The emotion of the heart, lovely as it is, links one to the world.

The magnetism of the soul is other worldly. It represents a value beyond life that moves all things, overriding the emotion of the heart, great and beautiful as the heart's emotion certainly is. To develop the magnetism of the soul is for the few, because it means giving up attachments and their accompanying concerns, which is most challenging to our humanness. This signifies renunciation which is undoubtedly the way of the ascetic. I know.... and yet we are preaching fulfillment, accomplishment, and unfoldment, which means involvement. Can one ever reconcile these two irreconcilables? I wish I had the answer. To honor one's personal loves, one covets worldly power as the protector, the patron, the provider. To develop spiritual power, one needs to give up thoughts stirred by human emotions. Then one asks oneself, "Who am I?" And one watches one's involvement objectively. Now one can discriminate between acting when motivated by attachment, or by a sense of responsibility and dedication.

In this perspective, one understands so well what Pir-o-Murshid and the Sufi dervishes said in moments of cosmic consciousness: One has the soul of a king, but one's self image that has accrued to one, owing to one's ancestral inheritance, is the source of all weakness. Here lies the secret. One is cosmic, but one thinks that one is inadequate because one is impressed by the evidence of the body and the mind. Should one dismiss this identity, the change that occurs proves quite unbelievable.

Of course, I am, you are, the being of God, however constricted, despoiled, degraded at the jagged ends. But one needs to distinguish between that aspect of one which is the Knower and the Creator, who knows Himself through that focalization of divine consciousness that is one's own consciousness, and who manifests the divine nature transpiring through one's personality, and that aspect of oneself that is the means to fulfill this. Both are God, but the second one is a deterioration of the being of God. That is why Ibn Arabi says, "He is both the Seer and that through which He sees, but know whereby thou art God and whereby thou art not God."

Awakening and Enlightenment

> **To carry the self forward and realize the ten thousand dharmas is delusion; that the ten thousand dharmas advance and realize the self, is enlightenment.**
>
> **Zen Master Eihei Dogen's Genjo koan**

Attaining this way in one's daily life is the realization of ultimate reality. Attaining this place in daily life is the realization of the ultimate reality.

What does one mean by awakening? What does one mean by illumination? Are they the same? How does one attain these? The paradox is that when one tries to define these, one cannot but confuse their meaning, like explaining non-Euclidian geometry to a person locked into the thinking of Euclidian geometry, or again, the way one distorts an electron by trying to observe it. Therefore, Zen masters ponder koans—riddles one needs to decipher or unhoax.

Do not think that realization must become the object of one's knowledge and vision and be practiced conceptually. When Buddhas are truly Buddhas, one need not be aware of being Buddha. Realization is, therefore, something one needs to experience before one can know what it is, while one would normally expect that one would need to have an idea as to what we are talking about in order to try to practice it.

Awakening is a term used by Vedanta and Sufism which stands for a sudden switch from one's commonplace perspective of things as they appear to our senses and the interpretation that we make from our personal vantage point, to an impersonal overview. This shifts the notion of self from an individual to identifying oneself with the totality, not just of the universe, but of the thinking and feeling of which the universe is a projection or manifestation.

Enlightenment, the term used by Buddhists, signifies precisely the same, except that the clarity that ensues is so reminiscent of one's physical experience of luminosity that one feels like a being of light, and everything seems translucent and radiant. Hence the term, "the clear light of bliss" coined by the Tibetans. Note the inclusion of the emotional overtone that is unleashed by that sudden quantum leap of perspective: bliss beyond joy.

The Sufis draw one's attention so that one has not only shifted one's sense of identity to an impersonal cosmic dimension of one's being, but has also shifted one's sense of identity transcendentally, thinking of oneself now as pure, luminous intelligence. The body and psyche are looked upon as the support system. The important issue is that when one is observing and experiencing, one should envision oneself as a consciousness, the same as the reality behind the appearance of the universe. Then there is no more duality, and therefore there is no observation, no experience. Consciousness has withdrawn into its ground, which is pure transcending consciousness, reaching beyond the ego transcendentally (one thinks upwards). This is only the first step and actually proves misleading because it revolves around the personal vantage point which is very limited.

The Astronaut of the Mind

Reflections of a nomad in a past life, having become a skipper in this life and dreaming of becoming an astronaut (of the mind) in a future life.

> **One has seen his life's purpose as light seen in port from the sea.**
>
> **Pir-o-Murshid Inayat Khan**

On watch by night, it becomes clear to me that the safety of my fellow passengers depends upon my being awake.

As from deep under water, one may scan the shore, even so from the abysmal depths of my slumber I espied, as if beyond a threshold, evanescent flashes of what the awakened state was and could be like. A powerful thought impinged upon my dimmed consciousness enjoining upon me to awaken to capture it. Yet what a struggle to keep my mind alert amid the jumble of thoughts that beset slumber! How impelling the temptation of surrender to sleep! How comforting an escape!

Sinking, I watch the desperate struggle of the mind for coherence against the entropy of blurred thoughts. I vaguely discern apparently unrelated words, even gibberish sentences surfacing at the edge of my mind and then meshing in a somewhat meaningful way, only to vanish beyond range. Sleep seemed to befuddle the mind in waves of nebulous inanity and lay a snare upon my faltering resolve to rise from my torpor. But safety is at stake! The safety of all of us, including myself, depends upon both my sight and my insight subtended by that dwindling resolve that keeps evading my grip.

Yes it is the sense of urgency that comes to the rescue, fortifying my determination to steer our way with foresight, determine where I am heading and why. I am in a desperate bid to eschew catastrophes while off guard. I must admit an insatiable curiosity to make sense of life and to understand what is enacted in the drama of life all around. And to guess why I am doing what I am doing is also essential to my orientation.

Navigating by the planets soon proves misleading to a nomad who places more reliance on the "fixed stars." Besides they would look very different as seen from Mt. Palomar or Capetown. Moreover the expectation of dawn is for those who are at the time on the dark side of the planet. For the astronaut there is no dawn because there is no sunset, with the exception of the rare case of an eclipse. And the stars would look very different if I were hurtling through space at the speed of light.

But if I were to space-walk, can I really say that I am flying above San Francisco rather than London? My sense of location in space has shifted and so my sense of meaningfulness. Incidentally what does it mean to be located in space? Pushed beyond its customary range, the mind reels. Planet Earth is in outer space; ergo, am I not in outer space when my body is on the Planet? Yet paradoxically my aura which is also my body extends in the starry sky.

My intuition tells me that the guidelines for our joint safe faring rest upon a sense of meaningfulness rather than aimless rambling, and that such meaningfulness can only lie beyond my personal horizon of meaningfulness. I ponder upon the meaning of my life and life in general. Brainstorming my mind for explanations within the purview of my understanding would inevitably stand in the way of the understanding they seek to support.

Explanations are the steps to understanding; yet lingering upon them will obstruct the very understanding that they led to. Are we not limiting our grasp of the meaningfulness of the universe by our rudimentary assumptions that the universe should be logical? Are not contradictions part of its meaningfulness? Is it not our aversion to accepting the contradictions of our thinking that has so far debarred us from accessing the thinking of the universe? And is it not a feature of the freedom of the mind to refuse to demur to the constraint of logical consistency?

Under pressure, I come to realize that it is my insight that alerts my sight, spurring it to espy beyond its range, sniffing out clues which surreptitiously spring into sight as dawn adorns the shadow world with flashes of uncanny effulgence. By what jugglery of mind am I able to muster these clues into guidelines, giving me a sense of orientation beyond the range of my horizon?

But what do I mean by a horizon? It only exists in my mind, not in reality. A horizon is the function of a vantage point which spells a limitation. Consequently it has the virtue of making me aware that it hangs precariously on the measure of my ignorance—one more evidence of my failure of having availed myself so far of the many dimensions of my mind.

Indeed I had not realized that my mind is not just a fraction of the mind of the universe, but coextensive with the mind of the universe. Is that what one means by the mind of God? What does one mean by God? The being of which the physical universe is the body? Or is one not limiting what one ascribes to God by one's anthropomorphical projection upon infinity of the finitude of what one assumes is one's own mind? That is why theologians insist upon the "transcendence" of God.

Incidentally, could it not be that it is my reliance upon the impact of the mind of God upon my mind that keeps me within that illusory horizon? Such a horizon does not really exist except from my perspective. That is: it is because I assume that my mind is limited that I call upon "other than myself," when in fact these are further dimensions of me.

Yet one still needs to account for transcendence—"beyond the beyond."

The way I think of myself changes with my perspective, and so also my understanding. But if the safety of my fellow passengers depends upon my sense of meaningfulness, and this depends upon how I think of myself in the universe, imagine the challenge I am facing!

How could I not feel unequal to the challenge to my mind? It is in a spirit of modesty (in which I clandestinely pride myself) that I say that my mind is limited, comparing it with the mind of the universe. Do I realize that it is my assumption of being what I think I am that spells my ignorance? Imagine it is my self image that screens my own self knowledge that keeps striving to make itself known to me? Is it not this very assumption that obstructs my accessing the boundless reaches of my mind?

By positing that my mind circumscribes a limited range within an unlimited compass, by assuming that the universe or God is "other than myself," I fail to apply the holistic paradigm: namely that my mind like a wave in the ocean expresses the mind of the whole universe albeit less well than the mind of the universe. Yet I must ever remind myself to leave room for the majesty of the divine thinking: divine transcendence way beyond the holistic level that I share. The two areas of my thinking, the circumscribed and the boundless, work against each other!

Yet I can see why many mystics await the grace of divine revelation, thinking of God as "other." Maybe this is a worthy means of accessing further reaches of understanding by bypassing the limiting effect of the personal self image. Maybe applying passive volition unleashes further dimensions of being. Some Sufis, however, change the terms of this antinomy by imagining what the converse perspective would be like.

I follow the clue: I flip my sense of identity to the other side of that fictitious horizon. Suddenly I watch those emerging thoughts that now aver themselves clearly to be contrivances of a hologram, projected from my real being, not the thoughts of my real being! I observe that they obey certain rather rudimentary laws of the middle range mentation programmed into humans within a bearable measure, like radio sets for domestic use, not for high-tech users. How on earth did I allow myself to be fooled all this time!

Now I realize that the limitation I ascribed to my mind was due to my using it as a buffer, to protect me against the power of boundless thought lest it annihilate my viewpoint. It is like emerging from Plato's cave into the glaring sun, overwhelmed but shattered by the magnificence. It would take the released prisoner time to cope with the bounty of meaningfulness, hypothesized the philosopher, but what a wonder! Yes life does make the most ultimate sense, but it takes this altitude to encompass it! I can see why when entrapped in the middle range thinking, it could not possibly make sense.

As I watch by night while my fellow passengers are sunken in the slumber of blissful oblivion, while our safety depends upon the prospect of exploring the uncharted reaches of the mind—of the universe? Of me? My understanding struggles to shake off its support system. There is a moment of illumination—a flash of meaningfulness at a cosmic scale. Is this illumination? Then the gravity pull of the nonexistent yet fictitious ego takes over—back to mediocrity.

Oh, to roam in the outer space of intelligence at a cosmic scale as an astronaut of the mind, to contemplate the sun of sheer perspicaciousness forever, but for the short spell of an eclipse, rather than being immersed in the arctic winter when the sun emerges but a few minutes above the horizon to plunge one back into the dismal night! But why the eclipse? How could one know of light if not for the contrast of darkness?

By the way, I have been absentmindedly referring to "me," speaking about reaching beyond "my understanding" throughout; but if my understanding is co-extensive with that of God or that of the universe (except less efficient), is this right? Or is this further transcended by divine omniscience? Then what do I mean by *me*? By me in the universe?

As I watch in the night of understanding, while my fellow companions trust themselves to my looking beyond my self-styled horizon, flashes of lucidity strike my soul as I leave my mind behind; it is not the light I see, though, it is the light that I am in reality, if only I knew that I know!

Our Solar Initiation

You know, we exist on several levels—there is the level of the mind and the level of emotion. You have to work with the intermediary levels. That means that you have to purify your emotions from any dark emotions: covetousness, resentment, hatred, jealousy, intolerance, judgmentalism, and then, dishonesty, dire manipulation, intrigues, so that the emotions become glorious, luminous, diaphanous, golden, very beautiful emotions. That will have an immediate effect on your aura. Thoughts become crystal clear, no more ambiguity, because there is some relationship between the emotions and thoughts. If your emotions are murky, thoughts get confused, ambiguous. When the emotions have become clear, like when a cloud is moved and the sun shines upon the landscape, then the thoughts become crystal clear, crisp and clearly defined. You are carrying your thinking into further dimensions, further frontiers of thought in the evolutionary process.

In this condition consider the starry sky. Just imagine that your body is in some way anchored upon Planet Earth; it is part of the proliferation of the Planet, yet somehow your consciousness is able to reach out into the stars. Isn't that extraordinary? What does a flower know of the stars? We are able, just with our thoughts, to reach out into the stars. What an extraordinary feat of evolution! The flower has become the human being in the course of evolution and is able to have a more encompassing grasp over the whole meaningfulness of the universe.

In the past, you've practiced getting into the consciousness of beings by experiencing what it would be like to be your friend, for example, someone you are very close to. Consider the sun as it rises above the horizon of Planet Earth. Then consider that you could take off and the sun would not be rising above the horizon of the Earth because the Earth would be far away somewhere, and the sun would be seen now continually.

Now, instead of looking at the sun as an object of your vision, enter into the consciousness of the sun. You realize that your body was originally the sun because the planets emerged out of the sun, or at least the companion to the sun. It's not quite certain which theory is correct, but in any case, your body is of the nature of the fabric of the sun, the galaxy and the Big Bang. Not only your body, but can you earmark those qualities in your personality that you have inherited from that being of which the sun, which we observe with our eyes, is only the body. Don't think of the sun as being a glob of burning fire suspended in the sky but think of it as a being whose body we experience as a burning spark of fire.

Giving life by burning, that is the sun. The Sufis call the sun an Archangel. They call it Prince Huraksh. Shams Tabriz had lost himself totally in the consciousness of Prince Huraksh. That's why he shattered the being of Jelaluddin Rumi by the radiance of his being. That's the secret. So if you can identify with your solar inheritance, realize that you are not only your body, but you have inherited some aspect of your being from the archangel of the sun, Prince Huraksh. The being is covered by 22,000 veils, but all you have to do is peel off those veils, which represent layers of your personality, to find, deep down in your being, the idiosyncrasies of the archangel of the sun. Then you will understand the words of Jelaluddin Rumi, "I want burning." By burning on the sacrificial altar of holocausts you give out light and illuminate all creatures with your light.

Shahabuddin Suhrawardi called this a solar initiation. You have to recognize in yourself the quality that is the nature of the archangel of the sun. That quality is *Haqq*—Truth. Dissipate the clouds of ambiguity; bring everything to light. When you do that you are operating as a sun. Unmask the hoax. One of the aspects of the hoax is self deception. The dervish becomes like the sun, truthful. Now you proceed into the starry sky. You leave the orbit of the planetary system and you have to broaden your horizons. Remember, the Earth bathes in the sun. The sun does not have a boundary, so we are in the sun. The Earth is in the sun, not outside the sun. The sun itself is bathing in the galaxy so you are not reaching out from the planetary system. If you did reach out in a spacecraft beyond the planetary system, it would be easier to grasp the immensity of the galaxy. Once more you would realize that it is a most incredibly powerful archangel, enormous, even more glorious than Prince Huraksh.

Can you imagine a being whose body is ten million stars—the intelligence, the emotion, the scope, the attunement of such a being? Remember, if you are just in a spacecraft, you would still be in your physical self image, self identity, but suppose that you jumped out of the spacecraft and started to float in outer space and while you were doing that, instead of identifying with your body, you would think of yourself as an aura. Your aura is spread out throughout the starry sky. Now the stars are not the object of your cognizance anymore because your aura is made of the light of the stars. It is contiguous—coextensive—with the light of the stars. In fact, the stars are not those little dots in the sky but reach out into immensity. There's no space anymore. You forget space; you reach beyond the idea of space.

You are part of it all. So the physical world is no more the object of your cognizance. What is more, in that condition, you realize that your thinking is of the nature of the thinking of the universe, otherwise you would never understand the universe unless you thought the same way as the universe thinks. In fact, at some level of your being, you are of the nature of the Archangel of the galaxy. That's what is meant by the splendor of the universe—the splendor of the being whose body may be beautiful as the galaxy is beautiful—but splendor is beyond its manifestation in the Now. You are carried beyond any emotion that you could ever possibly have experienced—into cosmic ecstasy. It is so incredible! You are ashamed of yourself for having paid so much attention or attributed so much importance to your puny problems on Planet Earth. It's like picking up the crumbs when you're invited to the banquet of the stars. It is participation in the cosmic celebration of the heavens. You realize that the power of the archangel of Dominion is the wondrousness of sheer majesty participating in the glorification of the cosmic celebration. You see the whole universe born out of the cosmic celebration.

The whole physical universe is simply a derived reality that is trying to express the splendor and the meaningfulness behind it. Now you see that you are a pilgrim on the Planet Earth, and you forgot who you were. Instead of climbing down the mountain, you are climbing up the mountain and beyond it into lofty realms. You see how inadequate our lives are when we've lost contact with our real Self. No wonder we get confused, disenchanted, and embittered. We've lost the battle of life. Identifying with your solar inheritance is your saving grace.

The Dance of the Cells

The Dervish says, "I am dancing with the galaxies by the power of love reaching beyond my body." We're going to make a little visit to the galaxies.

First of all, start realizing the marvel of being able to participate in the galaxies in your very body. Perhaps you could look upon your body with a kind of overview and think, yes, I have the privilege of somehow being able to connect up with this chunk of the living matter of the universe. It is, of course, the same matter as the as the Planet but it's been so fantastically improved, so marvelously processed. The cells of my body are like the molecules of crystals. Just imagine, they are doing a lot of extraordinary things; for example, they are burning. They are in a state of combustion just like the sun. That is why I have a certain degree of temperature. In the process called phosphorescence, the cells are radiating light by burning. This radiant dance of light is the burning of which Jelaluddin Rumi speaks.

The cells also act like crystals in that they have the faculty of absorbing light, not only from the sun, but also from the stars and from cosmic rays. The whole of the universe is not just studded with lights as we imagine them to be, but the whole space is an ocean of light and we are participating in that ocean of light. I want you to feel the absorbing fact that the cells of your body absorb the light of the stars of the universe, and energized and dynamized by this light, they begin literally to dance. The electrons within the atoms within the molecules within the cells start using that energy of light to free themselves from their routine sort of orbitals and begin to reach beyond the constraint of the normal orbital and dance. The freedom that they enjoy because they are feeding on light is something that one has to experience. The dance of the atoms! As matter of fact, they exult in joy. If we become conscious of what's happening in our body, then our souls exult in joy, and that is the reason for the whirling of the dervishes. They give expression in that joy by somehow participating in the choreography of the heavens.

Now when the electrons have used up all the light energy that they are able to absorb, then any light remaining gets radiated as fluorescence, so that our body is fluorescing, like fluorescent light. That is what we call the aura. I want you also to experience the fact that gifted with this energy, the cells divide. They are using that energy, plus many other forms of energy, to kind of explode, to proliferate. As they divide in the process of mitosis, there is an explosion of light, so they are flashing light. If you could just imagine the cells of your body flashing light all the time, and the overall light of your aura radiating into the universe, then you would realize that body is not that heavy sort of matter that you think it is. It is alive with light, sparking! The consequence is that you will start becoming radiant. If you keep on being aware of this you will enhance the light of your aura. More important still, your eyes will shine with a lot of light, and whenever you enter a room you will communicate light to people by the effulgence of your glance.

Your aura, your glance, the crown of light above your head (the corona) and the colors of the aura corresponding to the spectrum—red at the base, light blue and violet at the top, all different colors of the rainbow in between, saffron, orange and gold, green and blue, and then the whole array of rainbows around your aura—intermesh as rainbows, changing their color according to your attunement, shimmering at the top of the head with all of the colors emerging. The aura is very bright around the body and the more you concentrate on it the brighter it will become—so much so, that if you have eyes to see and come across a great being, you'll find that you can start seeing the aura.

The way to see this is to cast your eyes—your glance—at infinity. Remember that the light accumulates around and inside the body, permeating the body. There is a continual exchange between protons and electrons, but the important thing to know is that the light of your aura is hurtling through space at the speed of 186,000 miles a second! Since light is produced from the matter of your body, your body is extending into the galaxies. So it is purely illusory to think that we are bounded by our skin. Our light is intermeshed with the light of all other beings and the light of the stars, forming a huge wave interference pattern of light. This also means that you are not just here but you are everywhere, spread out in the universe. You are without boundary; at least as far as your aura is concerned there is no boundary. As a matter of fact, your aura is pulsing, just like some of the stars. There is ebb and flow; it is absorbing or converging light; it is radiating light as you breathe in and breathe out, so try to feel that. That is a centripetal/centrifugal cosmic dimension.

Now you can revert to the other way of breathing, moving up from the bottom of the spine, holding your breath, exhaling downwards, so passing in review the different colors as you inhale and all the rainbows radiating out of each chakra. Pay particular attention to the golden color in your heart towards the middle of your inhaling. The heart is looked upon as a miniature sun. As you inhale you keep moving upwards from the heart to the pituitary gland chakra—called *bindu*—which is like a diamond, a colorless light which gives you the impression of being white like snow. The whole array of colors radiating from that diamond at the crown center is visualized toward the end of your inhaling. Then, as you hold your breath, you make a real quantum leap from identifying yourself with your body and aura, to identifying yourself with what you have been prior to your incarnation, right in the beginning, before your descent into the spheres. You were a being of luminous intelligence. That's not light in the physical sense. Your aura, your body and your magnetic field are the scaffolding, the underpinning support system for the essential reality of your being, which is luminous intelligence.

Can you just experience the intensity of intelligence in you? That's what you really are—luminous intelligence—awareness beyond ego consciousness. That is called illumination. When you are able to see, when something clicks in you, you awaken from your body identity and you suddenly realize. "This is what I am! I am the spectator; I am pure intelligence." Consciousness results from intelligence when confronted with an object, so you are even beyond consciousness.

It's not light in the physical sense, and that's why the early Catholic Church fathers used to call it "the uncreated light." But it's just like light; it makes everything clear. The Sufis say, "It is the light that sees, instead of the light that is seen." Now, as you exhale, you become aware of the impact of the intensity of your luminous intelligence upon your aura. You know how, when suddenly you see a point which you hadn't grasped, all of a sudden your face illuminates with a smile—Oh yes, I see that! Your whole aura flashes with light at the moment when you realize that you are luminous intelligence. That is what is meant in The Qur'an by "a light upon a light." As a matter of fact, your cells begin to flash light more intensely than ever before and start proliferating; electrons start dancing; your whole being is alive with light!

Meditation After-effect

At a certain point in our search for meaningfulness, it may suddenly dawn upon us that our quest of trance-like meditations or retreats may arise from a perhaps unconscious wish to escape from a life situation (for example, parental authority or the ruthless, merciless civilization we are living in: its violence, its greed, its manipulation). Moreover, it has become evident in recent years that meditation practices can and do lead people to drop out of life in general and eschew taking responsibility in their lives for loved ones or fellow beings.

Further, we just may be trying to validate our own personality in our own view or that of others by being special or different! Actually, we may be missing out on the inestimable value of that which has been acquired by humans throughout the ages in terms of beauty, material convenience, and orderliness: the marvel, the excitement, the courage, the vulnerability and the enriching effect of sharing joy and pain, relationship, friendship, loyalty, and service in which God is to be found as a living reality. It is tragic to cloister oneself in an anesthetized psyche that shields one from confronting the challenges of the drama of life, which both actuates the celebration in the heavens in a concrete way, and tests our mettle.

There is a way of being high without being spaced out!

When meditating (or prescribing meditation), it is important to be clear about the after-effect that the shift of focus of consciousness may be expected to have upon our personality, attunement, and worldview, and to know which practices trigger which effect.

1) Since our notion of ourselves needs to be expanded when extending consciousness, we contemplate vaster and

vaster reaches of space, and we identify with zones of our being beyond our notion of a skin-bound material body. We may become aware of and identify with our magnetic field and/or aura. As these do not have a boundary, we then envision ourselves as being like a vortex (boundless). What is more, we tend to assume that we lose ourselves by merging with the totality of the universe.

It is important here to keep in mind that one is both a vortex and, at the same time, something like a cell, bounded by a membrane, albeit porous. We need to work with both in combination, not just one or the other. Our minds in their commonplace thinking mode find it difficult to reconcile these two paradigms. This problem is similar to the one that physicists encountered in accepting that, since photons of light behave either as waves or as particles according to the way the experiment is conducted, they may be considered as displaying both of these properties. So it is with our notion of ourselves.

Our bodies (including the subtle bodies, the psyche, personality, and consciousness, etc.) are indeed holistically related to the totality of the fabric of the universe. This means that they carry potentially in them the bounty of the totality of the fabric of the universe, just as every drop of water has the same properties as the water of the ocean. In fact, every cell of the body has the same genes as every other, but in one some will be activated and in others different ones, so that by diversifying they create the change to cooperate. Thus they differ while being potentially identical, and in that sense may be considered as "discrete entities." It is in this diversity that our freedom is rooted. A vortex is open to its environment, and in fact incorporates its environment indiscriminately, whereas a cell, thanks to its membrane, may select the elements it takes in from the environment, or secretes to the environment, while still being open to some measure of osmosis.

If we identify just with the vortex model, we are overlooking the containment which ensures our protection against undesirable impressions, honors our idiosyncrasies, and confers upon us our incentive. If we neglect our boundaries, we run the psychological risk of finding ourselves disoriented, spaced out, and unable to confront circumstances as real. One may even invoke the concept of *maya* to justify this attitude. What is more, just as we generally fail to realize that an eddy does not lose its identity by joining with other eddies in a wave-interference pattern (whirlpool), and can even be retrieved, we tend to believe that we lose ourselves as we merge blissfully with the totality of the universe or the being of God. However, the objective of the universe is that the bounty of the totality should be customized in each of its sub-wholes in a unique way! Annihilation in God does not mean that one loses oneself, but only one's commonplace notion of oneself.

2) In meditation we learn to "turn within," which can easily be misconstrued as encapsulating ourselves in our psyche while blocking any impressions, physical or psychological, from the environment. Here it is the opposite: by setting up a boundary segregating ourselves from the environment, we tend to merge with the totality in an inverted space. A person might find it difficult to know what one might mean by "inverted space." It may therefore be preferable to envision that our magnetic field or aura intersperses with that of other such fields, like the eddies on the surface of a lake as they compose to form a wave-interference pattern. It is difficult for us to realize that this does not imply that they spread out or diffract in space. A good analogy would be the difference between a short musical theme, each note following the other, and the notes forming a chord without being stretched out as a melody. This happens in our dreams, where impressions are jumbled; in order to retrieve them in our memory, we sort them out in a space-time framework.

If, however, as we turn within in meditation, instead of setting up a boundary encapsulating ourselves in our thoughts, we envision that we are protected by a porous membrane that filters impressions from the environment (at all levels of reality) and that we are consequently able to radiate into the environment, then we will enjoy an incomparably richer experience. Now, envision that you are not just filtering these impressions, but transmuting them, just as we digest our food in order to use it, since we can only deal with chains of amino acids that match our own. Just as in digestion, we need to break down the ingested elements and rebuild them on the model of our own idiosyncrasies and reject those elements which, being too alien to our own beings, would prove to be difficult to incorporate, or might even be harmful. Here our sense of having boundaries will help us reject unwanted impressions, on the one hand, or filter and transmute those impressions that can be put to good use if adjusted to our particular attunement, on the other hand.

3) Transcendence: there can be no doubt that our involvement with life at its lowest common denominator fosters greed, limitations in the field of consciousness, and conflict, while our quest for freedom from conditioning opens the doors to the wonder and meaningfulness behind what seems to be happening at the existential level.

Another way of putting this is to say that we must instill something of the way of the hermit into the way of the knight. Our need for freedom is as compelling as our need for involvement. Are they necessarily mutually exclusive? There is a way of reconciling the irreconcilables. One example is to love without being dependent upon being loved. In meditation, detachment frees one from the conditioning of one's thinking and the constraint of one's self image. Freedom from the usual setting of consciousness will enable us to shift consciousness into an inner space or, alternatively, into a mode of self transcendence.

Chapter 5

In Life

Spirituality in Real Life

What do we mean by spirituality in real life? There is no doubt that in using the word spirituality, we are referring to a whole other dimension than the usual commonplace dimension. But are we really talking about something other than a way of thinking? If so, it must be substantiated by a level of experience beyond the ordinary, and be verifiable and repeatable, according to the scientist. Certainly the verifiability is in whether it makes a person luminous, joyous, alert and noble. If something is real, it must have tangible effects. Its repeatability is observed in the fact that most of the authentic mystics known in our human heritage refer to identical experiences. If real, spirituality must have its implications in our way of handling problems. It must govern our whole value system, determine our priorities: what we strive for, what we shun.

Those caught up in the "here and now" get easily burnt out, disenchanted, even sardonic, or alternatively, if under a lucky star, selfish, arrogant, bumptious. Those hankering after the "everywhere and always beyond the beyond" tend to get out of touch with the nitty gritty, shun responsibility, and alienate themselves through fantasy.

We are in search of a healthy and invigorating spirituality at the level of the dimension of realization that humanity as a whole has attained in our day and age. This spirituality is at the leading edge that pioneering thinkers are feeling out.

A number of those who were deeply immersed in spirituality have been put off by the abuses of some gurus. Others find that they have less leisure or interest for such flights of fantasy owing to their family and job commitments, and feel that any connection with spirituality alienates them from their co-workers, even puts their credibility in jeopardy. Yet if spirituality has far-reaching implications in our understanding, and in the determination of our objectives and achievements, then by neglecting spirituality, one would be missing out on dealing with prevailing concerns that eventually affect the personality, the family, and the job.

Suppose that a being only capable of interpolating two dimensions should occasionally have uncanny hunches of being part of a three dimensional world. He or she would strive awkwardly to infer what a three dimensional world would be like from the way the two dimensional world looks. This example shows why our inferences about the higher spheres or the nature of the soul are full of conjectures so disconcerting for the practical man or woman. On the other hand, if our two dimensional being followed up hunches about other dimensions of being, one would hoist oneself into an incommensurably different level of realization and achievement.

How would this simile apply to the mundane need of dealing with human problems? It would mean dealing with the implications of the problem rather than the symptoms. Here we are not talking about a further dimension of space/time, but of understanding. Grasping the factors that caused the events is a first further dimension of understanding that is not limited by a linear time sequence, admittedly more difficult to cull. What are the qualities in me or in the persons involved in the problem that are at stake? How does my decision or way of handling things affect the higher counterparts of my being which must, by resonance, affect the higher counterparts of those in contact with me? These higher counterparts must eventually sprout through in my personality and of necessity, affect others by osmosis. What does our reciprocal interaction involve in the larger scheme of things?

The challenge may prove insuperable. For example: reconciling strength with kindness, the need for personal fulfillment and that of service; reconciling freedom with involvement, joy with solidarity with suffering, the divine with the human; giving to Caesar what belongs to Caesar, not paying with your soul for the goodies of the world. What is your real motivation? The more all-encompassing one's perspective, the more socially altruistic and less personal will be the objective, a reconciliation of the way of the master with the way of the saint. The new perspective is a matter of bringing the divine desire into the human will, the "everywhere and always" into the here and now.

This is where spirituality, awakening to the higher dimensions of one's being, does affect the nitty gritty of our lives. Failing to give it the attention it deserves spells a failure to become "what we could be if we would be what we might be."

The Human Drama

Before we realize it, we are involved in the human drama willy-nilly, irretrievably. Life may prove exhilarating, disenchanting, awesome, disturbing, depressing, or just humdrum.

Our co-actors on the scene may prove to be friendly, supportive, or inimical, compassionate or vindictive, loyal or manipulative, harmonious or treacherous, insolent or gracious, inspiring or repugnant, or just indifferent and incompatible… or some or all of these contradictory traits paradoxically lumped together.

At every move our intentions are tested—shall we say by life itself? We are ourselves mostly little aware of these motivations, except that life itself unmasks us. Our motivations emerge to the eye of the aware even if we ourselves fail to espy the proof in the proved. Even when our covetousness or grudge, or axe to grind, or cantankerousness, or conceit, or power trip, or failure to take responsibility had devastating consequences, perhaps decades later, we may deplore our poor judgment or our folly or our inane decision, but still belie our intention, perhaps because it masks something deeper: our need for self validation, for self esteem, for attention, for security, for achievement, for love. We may also uncover the precious motivations: idealism, dedication, a spirit of service or self sacrifice, altruism, compassion, mercy, an unscrupulous concern for truthfulness, purity, innocence, beauty, glorification, holiness, and a need to partake of the intoxication of divine ecstasy. These may aver themselves to be the moving drives behind our handling of situations.

Our involvement with people, with situations, with the apparently-uncalled-for problems that arise can pummel our heart into agonies of excruciating pain, or more rarely spur it to outbursts of joy, or just pleasure or a sense of well-being at the venture of life.

The interplay of destiny and incentive baffles our understanding. Are we the victims or the doers? As in the game of chess, sometimes we assume that it is our move, but how far are we reacting to the move of our partner, looking back into his or her mind, witnessing in the move the signature of the intention? Or how far are we projecting into the future; that is forecasting what another's move could be if we decide to move this way or that way? Yet even when reacting to our partner's intentional move our move is still motivated unmistakably by our own intentions.

Moreover, what do we know of the role played by a cosmic motivation behind our moves? Let us not think of it as other than our motivation, but as the cosmic dimension of our motivation—something like the harmony of the stars and galaxies, the Pythagorean harmonic relationship that governs the intricate mechanism of which we are a part. The more we become conscious of this dimension of our own being, the greater our achievements. Here lies the real meaning of spirituality.

Of course the intricacies of our motivations in life's drama are incomparably more complex and paradoxical then in the game of chess; and consequently the influence of this cosmic factor is more readily detectable. Here in real life our motivations give away where we are at. Here lies the criterion of our mettle at this point in time—which hopefully may improve. Here the real person is revealed in all nudity and authenticity, eluding any pretence. But also here "the hand of God" which we often ascribe to fate or destiny is made noticeable to the intuition of the seer.

Since unmasking our intention proves to be a criterion as to what we are in our person, it constitutes an incalculable feedback system right there at our disposal. And doubtless our ability to avail ourselves of it depends upon our readiness to confront ourselves, and call our own bluff. But it becomes difficult to earmark the way the universe fulfills purposefulness through or rather *as* us, which the Sufis call the divine intention behind our intention; or to discover the conflict between this and our personal intention—which is really tantamount to a conflict of allegiance to different values within ourselves.

It is as difficult as assessing whether the trace that a physicist detects on a screen is the same electron that reappears, or whether this trace betrays the "probability" of another one substituting itself for the first one. Or is it another one? Or is it just the whole process appearing and disappearing in its parts? Thus the problem is that we may read the other's intention as our intention. This problem is far greater than we may have judged it to be in our introspection. Therefore beware of misassessing yourself in your self confrontation.

Behind the thrust of our motivations lie deeper roots: our innate qualities, or foibles, or rather those that have been so far actuated in us, and which are precisely those which we believe we possess. Unfortunately our self assessment is often mistakenly based upon our success or failure in our performance in the challenge of life, which cannot by any means, be the ultimate criterion. A victory may aver itself to be a defeat and defeat a victory.

The push that it takes to move out of a rut or to go out on a limb into an undertaking whose success remains questionable may be sparked by the values we believe in, but is powered by our belief in our potentials. Our real value is stored in our potential which is ultimately infinite. It is the activated fragment of this potential that has real life effectiveness—the measure of our potentials that is turned on, in contrast with those infinite bounties that lie in wait, unknown to us because unexplored. For example we only discover our power when we are called upon to overcome obstacles, or our compassion when faced with someone suffering, or our perspicacity when unmasking a fraud.

Our motivations spur these potentials or their shadows on into existence in the human drama. For example if one's motivation is service to people, one's potentiality for compassion will emerge more markedly; and one's dedication to service will have the effect of allaying one's resentment, so that one will prove more magnanimous towards the person who has offended one. If one's motivation is personal gain and dominance, one's personality will no doubt manifest more power, but this kind of ego trip may be looked upon as the shadow of genuine power. It distinguishes itself from real power by its ruthlessness. Here the potentialities of one's being have been constricted, defiled, and deviated from.

It is as though life offers us the most incredible array of bountiful values that corroborate the values that we ourselves cherish and uphold. Just consider what our civilizations have bequeathed us as works of art and architecture, of music and poetic lore, of ingeniousness, of know-how of organization, of skill, of discipline, of inventiveness! Consider the wealth of emotion that has filtered through the human being and been customized by our inventiveness! The acts of dedication and mercy and heroism! The whole universe is enacted in the human drama including that little patch that seems to belong to us: our problems and life situations, our achievements, our fates and destinies! Our lives are traversed, in fact fermented and suffused by the fruits of the inspirations of creative beings in the past and all around us. The bottom line in our lives is what our contribution is to all this bounty. We are not only the products of these civilizations and of the genius of their outstanding pioneers, but we are also their successors and nominees.

Moreover we need to extend our grasp beyond our terrestrial civilizations, and include all that lies behind the moving scene of the human drama on Planet Earth. Do we know what spawns the stars? What emotions or aspirations convulse the galaxies? What beings lie beyond our ken? Do we espy traces of the symphony of the spheres or the cosmic celebration in those emotions that make our heart beat faster, or shatter and delight our soul, or spark our spirit? It is these springheads of cosmic moment that lie behind our motivations and potentials, sometimes dormant, sometimes hopefully active.

A formidable power lies at our doorstep. The Sufis call it the divine power, which actually is the potentiality of our divine inheritance. While at the transcendental pole of our being (let us say in the seed of our personality), the bounty of the qualities that flower in the existential universe lay potentially dormant. These qualities contrast with their actualization in the existential pole of our being (let us call it the plant) in excelling everything one might imagine by their awesome perfection. In becoming conscious of our divine inheritance, we start integrating the opposites while paradoxically bypassing them: for example being powerful and radiant at the same time—that is manifesting power without being stern; or being both loving and at the same time free inside; or wise without being smart.

To avail ourselves of these features of the divine perfection invested in our being, we need to extend our thinking beyond the middle range. Evolution advances by burning the hurdles on the way and continually making the leap to the next step, which always takes off from a springboard that integrates all the previous steps, thus carrying them further.

The clue lies in espying the motivation of the universe behind our motivations, and the qualities the Sufis call the divine qualities behind the qualities that we have actuated so far, and in assessing the values that are being enacted in our own fragment of the human drama, while realizing that in fact it is not a fragment. Everything involves everything else, so that we are irrevocably involved in the cosmic drama, and this is the measure of our grasp of what it is all about.

To track down this infinite dimension of ourselves, albeit remotely, the first step is conceptualizing God. In so doing, one is nurturing one's creative imagination which is the self-same power that projects the software of the universe as its hardware. The act of conceptualizing needs a support system which actually recognizes first the values that one cherishes in nature, and then the qualities that are being enacted behind the drama of our lives. We then recognize these qualities in our own nature, and finally embody them—thus making God a reality.

Bringing Spirituality Into Everyday Life

The ancients used to divide the world between the sacred and the profane. The temple represented an area considered sacred. The *sanctum sanctorum* (the holy of holies) within the temple was out of bounds for anyone except the priests, who were organized in a way that was conducive to the strictest dedication to a spiritual way of life. In our day and age, we are doing away with the barriers. Under the guise of bringing spirituality into everyday life, we run the risk of profaning the *sanctum sanctorum* with the gross and rather uncouth attunement of those who are vying for personal gain.

The link between you and me is chiefly in our quest for our spiritual home. The real *sanctum sanctorum* is in the very depth of our beings.

The mystical tendency in people seeks for the personal experience of that which is formalized and organized in any religious institutionalization. We are the real temple. Truly, a person who has become deeply attuned to the atmosphere of the divine presence becomes sacred. Entering into his or her presence is an experience of communication with the pristine condition of God.

It might be helpful to grasp the subtle difference between saying that "all is God" and "all is divinity," a distinction illustrated by the difference between the drop and the sea, or, better still, the seed and the plant.

Hazrat Inayat Khan says: "Divinity is like the seed that grows in the plant and it comes again in the heart of the flower. In a similar way, the God who was manifested as the seed of the plant of this creation rises again towards fulfillment, and in that fulfillment He produces a seed in the heart of that flower, which is divinity. The seed comes last after the life of trunk, branch, fruit and flower. And as the seed is sufficient in itself and capable of producing another plant, so man is the product of all the planes, spiritual and material, and yet in him alone shines forth that primal intelligence that caused the whole—the seed of existence—God."

Though the plant is the unfoldment of the seed, the plant still never expresses all the many splendored bounty potentially present in its seed. Besides, just as the plant may get tarnished and eventually will disintegrate, even so, disintegration sets into the body of God, into the universe, since it is the condition for rebuilding and evolving. Just as in the body, the hair and nails are less important than the cells of the brain, even so, one might grasp that there are degrees of Godness. At the jagged ends, the universe and creatures get tarnished.

Getting in tune with this immaculate nascent sacredness in its pristine state prior to its becoming tarnished does make one rather out of sync with any grossness, or just worldliness or selfishness. This is why the hermits build up barriers like the precincts of the temple and the out-of-bounds regions to protect their attunement from the profanity of the world. Meanwhile, hopefully, the faithful may be observing ablution rituals with the effect of washing away some of the inevitable psychological pollution. Since one feels the need to adapt oneself to the common denominator, maybe one does not observe this tarnishing in the midst of life. When one is programmed into the personal vantage point, one fails to see that which transpires behind that which appears. One gets alienated from one's spiritual home, the holy of holies, and one feels sullied and profaned.

Therefore, after freeing oneself from the conditioning of the environment, the next step consists in consciously building a temple out of the very fabric of one's being and establishing thresholds to protect the *sanctum sanctorum* so that the outer world cannot invade it and pollute it.

That temple, made of the fabric of our being, ranges from gross matter to the most subtle gossamer. All living structures in the universe, including our bodies, are based on the same formative process as the galaxies, more elaborate than a vortex. In fact, the formation of galaxies is a double helix on the principle of the caduceus of Aesculapius: two crisscrossing spirals generated by an axis that is considered to be a vacuum but which represents the threshold into an inverted space. It can only maintain its continuity in the process of becoming by continually dissolving and reforming itself, and it edges off into the stars. It is pulsing, sparkling, radiating and whirling in many dimensions. The inlets and outlets are what the yogis call the chakras. One may discern an altar corresponding to the heart (*anahata*) chakra, mounted upon the tabernacle, which is the solar plexus (*manipura*) chakra opening into the inverted space where one has access into the treasure house of the many splendored bounty of the universe. For the Sufis, it is the "hidden treasure that desired to be known." At the vortex, in the middle of the resplendent radiance, flashing out like a fountain, is a channel wherein one may experience the descent of pure spirit, which again is a dimension of our being.

By the sheer act of envisioning this temple, one will dynamize it and form its structure. Reciprocally, the energy so generated catapults one's consciousness into the higher spheres. At a further step, one envisions the temple as made of light, the aura. As soon as one realizes that the light of the aura is hurtling through space at the pace of 186,000 miles a second, one cannot look upon the temple as made of a membrane any more but as an expanding vortex reaching into the universe, intermeshed with the light of the whole universe while still maintaining some paradoxical mode of identity. If one observes the axis of one's aura, one will notice that it is like a flame, red at the bottom and violet at the top, surrounded with a corolla likened to a rainbow. In addition, one may consider one's akashic body as a further sheath of that temple, a body of vibrations which also diffuses, in this case, in the symphony of the spheres, while still retaining its own specific signature tunes or frequency patterns.

In considering the inner temple, moral codes represent the provisions taken by society to ensure a basic order and protect its members from exploitation and abuse. Its buttresses are built of the taboos we have come to observe to avoid being humiliated in our spirit. This is brought home to us particularly forcefully when we become aware of the divine nostalgia within us, bursting in the pursuit of excellence of the divine creator which is our innermost being, as a challenge and eventually, victory over any defilement in us. It is climbing the hill of divine orderliness, overcoming the entropy of slackness, disenchantment and destructiveness. It is a pilgrimage to the sources of life, much as the throngs of pilgrims trek to the source of the Ganges in the high Himalayas.

The world is a treasure house of splendor manifesting as beauty wherever it can overcome the resistance of those who obstruct it. By what grim twist do people choose ugliness when there is so much beauty about! It is very sad. There is no accounting for taste. Beauty is an expression of that sacred source of inspiration. The beauty of one's being flows through when one plugs into the splendor of the divine being where it is to be found, in its pristine state in the holy of holies, within the depths of our own being. Such is the mystery of the sacred heart.

High Key versus Low Key

There is a story which Hazrat Inayat Khan tells of a spiritual teacher and someone who was placed before his door who told awful, untrue stories about the teacher. Only those seekers who had eyes to see the truth piercing through the falsehood recognized the teacher and came inside the door.

Many initiates who were living dedicated lives have now found their way into the active life. In fact, such seems to be the overall trend at this juncture. I believe this is the logical next step, in line with the *leitmotif* of the Sufi teaching. Many spiritual groups are criticized for encouraging a dropout from real life and making people unadapted to deal with their problems, and therefore a burden on society. So we are gratified to evidence that we have had the opposite effect.

Jobs can be challenging and prove to be very time consuming and exacting, sometimes discouraging and depleting. The family scene with its joys and cares has its fascination and solace. For women, it may turn out to be a twenty-four-hour chore, with its bright spots, but very demanding.

Those who went back to school know how competitive and tedious it can be. Some of the less compatible couples may have their problems, leading in the more dire cases to painful soul-searchings. Beautiful friendships, when genuine, prove often to be the saving grace of a lifetime. Otherwise, the commonplace humdrum middle class existence just falls short of inspiring the more sensitive or idealistic people to find fulfillment. At worst, people get burned out, and an insidious sense of frustration may surreptitiously creep into the unconscious, making people feel that they have failed to fulfill their highest aspirations and that life is slipping by.

For those who have previously involved themselves in the "spiritual process," two options present themselves. For some, since they have become so entangled in day-to-day commitments and have lost touch with their erstwhile spiritual attunement, the only solution seems to be a brief but radical break from the active life to the contemplative life, and taking leave of the consuming responsibilities, at least for a few days. This of course, accounts for the increasing demand for retreats, by people who, in the ordinary rhythm of their lives, do not find any way of attending classes or doing their practices. It is then easier to immerse oneself into the spiritual life in the appropriate setting and with guided instructions. Some initiates find, however, that having now adapted to the ordinary run of life; they have lost the ability to re-attune themselves to the spiritual pitch. Spiritual guides particularly, being deeply enmeshed and committed in life, feel it is an incredible strain to hoist themselves up sufficiently to meet the demands of guiding others. This often proves to be at the cost of effectiveness in one's job, which may require all one's energy.

In the more extreme cases, some people are harassed by a burning, quizzical, and unsettling thought: could it be that I was caught up in a kind of spiritual mirage and now I am where things really are (although admittedly, it is devastatingly sobering and low key, and even rather disenchanting)?

The clue to this enigma is obvious: when immersed in the commonplace middle range thinking in which most people have been programmed, one sees things from one's individual, focalized vantage point. You know, the way things look from a vantage point is not the way things are, but just the way they look from that vantage point. Consequently, one's outlook is one-sided, short-sighted, and unimaginative. It is living in a slice of the multi-tiered universe, and failing to participate in all the bounty that is offered.

Friends, we desperately need something to hoist us beyond ourselves: a strong experience that liberates us from the constraint of our trite self image and our inadequate assessment of life's events and situations. Rather, more than an experience: we need a breathtaking awakening into an overview, grasping the meaningfulness of ourselves in the universe, and fulfilling our own purpose in relation to the purpose of the whole. Is it not an exciting feature of our gift as humans that we not only partake in our flesh of the physical nature of the fabric of the universe, but in our psyche of that very being that is the universe, and more so that we have access into the thinking, the programming, the software of the universe? This is the only thing that makes sense in life.

Imagine that you are a cell within a body, and as you evolve, you can see your function within the network of functions of the whole body, and can enter into the mind that programs the body. Thus, you would fulfill your purpose as a cell by overreaching yourself. Since it is so difficult to maintain this attunement in life, one can well understand why people have sought to drop out from the workday existence either in the Indian tradition of the *sannyasin* or by the dangerous drug trip where the experience so dearly sought is distorted by a chemical stress on the brain. But neither of these alternatives is satisfactory, since one is missing out on life with all its challenge, excitement, fulfillment and attainment. Admittedly, at least in the case of the *sannyasin* or dervish, one would at least be high, sovereign, luminous, peaceful, and free. The inescapable answer of our day and age is obviously the "reconciliation of the irreconcilable," not the middle way which is tepid, undaring, and holds back both ways. It is to bring more life and punch and joy, laughter, intent and insight into life, reinforcing this by an occasional retreat—so long as the retreat is an occasion for an overview on life, insight into one's problems, recharging the battery of one's psychic energy and fostering creativity in one's personality.

After a retreat, one is more able to keep up with one's everyday meditation practices. One has been rededicated. Then, back to life with more zest than ever!

Be vibrant, alive, aware, and life giving. There is a French motto: *Reculer pour mieux sauter*—Back up an instant in order to spring forward more effectively.

Of course, it means growing up. It means being intensely alert and aware and luminous—not just aware of the "here and now," but of the "everywhere and always" (which, incidentally, must not be confused with the "nowhere and never"—often the outcome of spacing out, easily taken to be *samadhi*). Being aware does not just mean being acutely observant of what is happening around and about one, with particular regard to its relevance to one's objective, but it means to be aware of all that lies behind the apparent situation and the implications of this objective, and what is more, of what are the issues behind one's objective.

To be precise—it encompasses several scores. First, setting a goal as definite as possible. This is admittedly difficult because our human representations of our objectives are based upon our own scale of values, which we are continually reassessing and which fluctuate according to our attunement. Murshid says, "Shatter your ideals upon the rock of truth." Second, as we mature we become more realistic as to how to implement these imponderable values into tangible objectives. If we are really progressing, whatever we conceived of as our purpose is continually superseded by a further one. "The purpose of life is like the horizon: the further one advances, the further it recedes" (Pir-o-Murshid Inayat Khan). Not only is this true, but if one is truly creative in life, one constructs the path upon which one treads not unlike an aircraft (in contrast to a car that has to follow a prepared road).

Here, our own incentive will determine an azimuth upon the horizon which itself may vary, should one choose to reschedule the itinerary on the way. Furthermore, one would prove foolhardy to pursue one's proposed objective glibly without the slightest regard for what is going on around one. In fact, one is continually reprogramming one's objective on the strength of the wisdom that one gains by learning from the experience of one's fellow humans, and from the feedback to one's ideas and actions gleaned from the life situations around one.

Having then some sense of one's purpose, it is advisable to foresee possible obstacles, although most are unpredictable. Obviously, one will have to be prepared to deal with these as they arise. However definite one is about one's purpose, one may be advised to be versatile enough to totally reprogram one's course in view of the lay of the territory encountered.

The challenge of life requires one to be highly astute. First, one may be able to observe how people, perhaps unwittingly, tend to draw one into their problems. If one is inclined towards tender-heartedness, one inevitably does get oneself inextricably entangled, which, incidentally, is not necessarily salutary for the person one is accommodating. In this case, the second modulation of consciousness advocated in meditation is extremely revealing: shift one's consciousness into the consciousness of another person. What a different perspective from one's own! One soon discovers how people both suffer and rejoice for having made themselves dependent upon one by, in fact, making one dependent upon them. Their fear of being unable to cope without one may be so desperate that one prefers just putting up with the pain oneself. One likes to boast to oneself of being stronger than the persons concerned, not realizing what it does to one's morale and personal unfoldment.

When one gets inveigled into worldly affairs and dallies in small talk, not only does one lose one's contact with the heavenly dimension, but one starts disliking oneself, and consequently develops hardness and bitterness. What is more, one may nurture resentment against the people who were dragging one down, overlooking the fact that maybe they were looking to one to inspire them and give them an uplift!

As one matures, one learns how to help without being burdened, how to function like a *sannyasin*, an initiate, in life. It is true that one needs to be alone to do a lot of repair work upon one's psyche and to see things in perspective. One may well understand Buddha. Yet in our day and age, it is more challenging and wiser to awaken, to become very alert and aware right in the middle of "all of this," standing steadfastly while lending a helpful hand by thrusting the light of one's insight upon people's problems. This means earmarking the deeper issues behind their problems, to avoid letting oneself be trapped by or embroiled in the commonplace thinking, judgmentalism, and personal likes and dislikes of so many people, while keeping one's spirit in good tune. All of this, on the assumption, of course, that one is not being judgmental of them oneself. One is really more aware than they are of the way their interpretation of events and their dealing with events has tarnished them, and how this happens surreptitiously. One sees clearly where each person is "at" and what they would do to one's attunement, to one's thinking and values, how they would affect the pursuit of one's objective if one permitted.

Such clarity will undoubtedly bring one to handle life situations and all relationships wisely, harmoniously and beautifully in future dealings. Obviously, the emergence of a new awareness will carry as a consequence a difficulty in continuing to adjust to situations previously taken for granted and even coveted. Of course, as people grow, they inevitably need to readjust their relationships accordingly. They are no longer the persons they used to be. Relationships have to be re-wooed, updated, and never taken for granted. Redressing current situations and relationships after reassessing them requires even more insight, assiduity and courage than dealing with new situations, because one has to safeguard people's pride while weaning them. One discovers that the wisest way of doing this is by strengthening them in their trust in their own resourcefulness. This can only happen by giving them a chance of having to rely, themselves, upon that untapped store of resources which they can only discover by actuating them.

This requires one to watch the process very carefully and monitor it painstakingly, rather than go about crushing people's feelings recklessly like an elephant in a glass castle. However, sometimes a sharp change of tack is less painful than a lingering severing, leaving a person in a feeling of uncertainty as to one's true intentions. One needs to awaken people to the views that one cherishes rather than nurture resentment for the fact that they are constraining or restricting one. For this, it is best simply to communicate one's point of view, one's insight. People love clarity, and are excited by new points of view, and will value these, providing one does not criticize their narrowness, of which they are themselves not aware, even as we have a blind spot in our own eyes. On the other hand, people tend to feel threatened by a point of view that takes away the walls of the false security of their commonplace values.

On the Champs-Elysees

Sitting on the Champs-Elysees doubtlessly has its very special Parisian charm. People do this for various reasons:

if nothing else, to get out of the confining offices, shops or factories. More pondering minds find this a perfect opportunity to watch the moving scene of life. For me, here is a prompt to reflect upon what is going on in the souls and hearts and minds of so many different types of people. What is the relevance to spirituality here? Musing on my rather more metaphysical grasp of what spirituality really means in my high tech, modern aluminum cave in the Pyrenees helps me to x-ray what strikes the eye, as the ceaseless crowds crisscross right in front of me—a living film on the moving scene of life.

Remember, I say to myself, the real cave is not carved in the stone, but is an attunement (that paradoxical psychological chemistry of the objectivity of detachment with the subjectivity of involvement). How can I understand these beings if I do not recognize their idiosyncrasies in me? Of what value are my subjective impressions of them unless I were to involve myself with them, at least talk to them? *La vie est un noeud de relations.* Life is a network of relationships, said St. Exupéry. Life is interaction; we are intermeshed with each other. If we think of "that person" as "other" in what Martin Buber called the "I-it relationship," we become judgmental. We are lacking in love. So this is where spirituality comes in.

But now comes the test. That man with sunken cheeks right in front of me has so obviously been beaten by life, is so disappointed, so forlorn, so bereft of hope. How can all my preaching about glorification have even the slightest meaning for him? When fate has proven to be so unfair, how can one enjoin its victim to believe in God?

In my seminars and retreats, I show how, by transcending the personal vantage point, one realizes that there is splendor behind "all this," but how can one not be locked into the personal perspective when fighting a losing battle for survival? What would be the use of presenting him this sublime teaching? Even if I had the opportunity of talking to him, it would fall upon his psyche like water on a duck's back. It took a leap into the sublime to overcome the floundering of my soul as I gazed upon the abyss in his soul. I smiled upon him. He couldn't believe anybody could smile upon him. He did not have the strength to smile back. But after a double take, I could see that something stirred in the unsounded depths of his being. Here it was easy to love; facing suffering, it is easy to love. This was his only cure, love, not glorification—the emotion of the heart rather than the emotion of the soul. But I could only have found that love by getting in touch with the emotion of my soul.

But what about that thug (please excuse the obviously judgmental term) slouching down the Champs-Elysees, yelling swear words, molesting the girls, throwing his beer can on the pavement and snatching the purse of a fashionable old lady right in front of my eyes in broad daylight to the dismay and sheer incredulity of the passers-by, and then taking flight? Love comes less easily here; in fact, is it at all realistic?

It would be a platitude to say that it is just because he has so alienated himself from the sacredness of the very act of life that this could ever occur. This is where only our sense of paradox helps us face such aberration. "All faces are My Face," says God, according to the Qur'an. Could the Face of God have become spoliate? Fruit putrefies; the seed remains unscathed. Yes, all is God, providing we grasp what lies behind the immanent God who, according to Meister Eckhart, "becomes and unbecomes." We grasp the transcendent dimension of God in God's perfection. Perfection, all inclusive, must include freedom, with the consequence that things can get out of hand.

Do we recognize ourselves in that thug? The propensities are inherent. Do we not nurture resentment? This is what has brought him to this point. He may well have been humiliated and abused as a child and disenchanted by the hypocrisy of the very people who profess spirituality. In this case, a smile would not help. What help does spirituality have to offer here? One would have to start from scratch; it would involve a whole educative process. It means overcoming heavily embedded sardonic disenchantment, indelible resentment and bitter irony. The people in Plato's cave with their backs to the light could not understand what people meant when they said the grass was green and the sky blue, nor do fish know the sea they are floating in. Some might ascribe the condition to a lack of spirituality from the start. I would say, perhaps the lacuna is in the way spirituality is ordinarily meted out to the young, totally out of phase with the thinking of our time.

The young are living in a tougher world than ever before, suspended upon an atmosphere of hopelessness which all the permissiveness in the world cannot allay. Youths need to have something to look forward to: outrun their father's records, unmask their blunders, free-wheel creatively, build a brave new world. Take this away and young persons become disgruntled, apathetic, sardonic, sometimes violent or degenerate. Spirituality, that totally incommensurate dimension that crowns our human values and spins one's mind and emotions beyond their middle range, has inspired civilizations to produce great cultures. It still remains the live force spurring us to outreach ourselves, but spirituality needs to be updated. Space age spirituality, further dimensions of reality—that is the pointer.

This realization came across overwhelmingly when a nun was passing by. Here at least, I had expected that spiritual dimension missing in the thug (in my estimation). But I missed the joy, the radiance, and the sparkle of St. Teresa of Lisieux or the compassion of Mother Teresa of Calcutta. I sensed humility misconstrued into self denigration, reinforced by a guilt complex. I sensed a cult of suffering bordering upon masochism. I do not wish to generalize, but Christ could not have wished for this. I see him earnest because conscious of the suffering of the world but full of joy. “Be ye of good cheer,” he says to the forlorn poor in spirit.

Updated spirituality, is that to be found in the new age flower people? Here was a typical hippie conforming to non-conformism, unleashed, shipwrecked in the ocean of his psyche and taking it to be spirituality. Is it spirituality to so damage the delicately programmed brain we are invested with?

There was the colorful ramble of the good, steady mainstream loners. And now, standing out in the crowd, a one with sunlight in the eyes, nobility in the gait, strength blended with gentleness in the demeanor, restraint and wisdom in the voice. Our glances crossed, just as my glance did when I passed that rishi at an earlier Kumbha Mela or communed with that dervish at Shams Tabriz’s tomb. But here, no robes, no role playing, no pretense at spirituality. Just a mutual attunement, unspoken mutual realization, and mutual recognition. Such is spirituality in real life.

Finding A Wider Perspective

If we look at Notre Dame in Paris from only one angle, we haven’t seen Notre Dame. Likewise, if we look at a problem from our personal vantage point—what we think we are—then we can’t have a real sense of what the problem is. Just to say, “It is not what I think it is” is a negative statement. The positive way to do it is to start looking at the problem from alternative points of view to our own point of view. What I suggest is to think of a problem, but as seen from the point of view of another person who’s involved with us in that problem. That doesn’t mean that another person’s point of view is more valid than our own, but at least we now see the situation from two angles instead of one.

Generally we think of another person as the object of our awareness, but in meditating, we discover we are literally able to transpose our consciousness into that of another person. That person's way of looking at things may be as limited as ours, or may be better than ours, or more limited, but it does alter our perspective. For example, if that person were attuned to a very high state, then what we grasp of that person is going to be different from the way that person would be if dealing with the nitty-gritty of human problems. We can imagine how we appear to that person, and we realize the image that person has of us is not what we think we are and neither necessarily better nor worse, but then, I am not saying this is the real thing. No, I'm saying that we then have the ability to see something about ourselves that maybe we didn't see when we were in our personal perspective. Our eyes can't see themselves.

The next step is to expand our consciousness to more people—three people, four people, and many more people—and eventually, we can just feel the joy of our consciousness expanding. It's like we have been sitting in the office or in the house the whole day, and then we have the opportunity to make a trip to the mountains and sit on the mountaintop and watch a fantastic dawn. What a joy to be out of that prison! Marcel Marceau does a famous mime routine. He's walled in, and he keeps on pushing the walls, and they get further and further away, and the further away they go, the better he is able to dance, and eventually he dances the dance of freedom. Now that is essential to our work, pushing out our limitations.

There is another way of doing it. We imagine the starry sky, and clusters of galaxies, and realize that the very fabric of our body is the fabric of those galaxies. The fabric of our body originated in the Big Bang as a pure outbreak of light, of pure radiance, and this light crystallized itself into what we call matter—although for a physicist, light is already matter. Imagine light that has gelled into a crystal. Our bodies are much more elaborate than crystals. They are not frozen as a crystal, so from the moment we reach out in our thoughts to the vastness of space, and we realize that we ourselves, our body itself, is part of this starry universe—they can't be separated—that has a dramatic effect on our way of thinking of ourselves. We no longer see ourselves as a discrete entity with a boundary, the skin. We are not just expanding our consciousness. We are altering our sense of identity, or rather gleaning awareness of the vastness of our identity.

It is true that as we extend our consciousness, we lose the sense of our individuality, so it's good to balance that with the opposite. When we exhale, we experience this wonderful expansion of our consciousness reaching out further and further, losing the sense of our individual center. We then do the opposite as we inhale; we see how the totality of the universe converges as us. It converges just like a three-dimensional panorama converging into a two-dimensional photograph. The consciousness of the cosmos has become focalized, like light is focalized through a lens. We are focalized as our consciousness. Our consciousness is not different, not other. It is the consciousness of the totality.

We have the ability to toggle between an all-encompassing setting of consciousness and a personal one. For example, when we read the pages of a book, our eyesight is highly focalized, but when we look at a panorama, our eyesight is all-encompassing. We could toggle between the two. We could read a book while sitting in beautiful mountain scenery, and then look at the panorama, and look at the book again, toggling between the two. We can do the same thing with our consciousness. When our consciousness is expanded, we can see our problems in context. That means we can see the implications of our problems instead of just seeing them from our limited, personal bias. Then we realize that what we thought was our problem, is simply our participation in the drama of the universe.

That is a way of liberating ourselves from the constraint of our commonplace assessment of situations, and our self image which we carry in our psyche throughout our lives.

We are carrying in our psyche a false assessment of our situations, of ourselves, of our relationship with the universe, convinced that that's the way it is. We suffer because of it. We are confused because of it. The expanding of our consciousness does have an effect upon our identity. We can expand our consciousness like our eyesight. We then have a wider sense of our identity. It doesn't seem logical to think that we are a fraction of the totality. We think, "How can you say that? I am a totality." Some mystics say that, but we wonder if they're crazy. We can't understand how they could say anything like that. It's something we have to gradually train ourselves to in meditation.

In our commonplace assessment, we would never, for example, be able to make sense of radio waves. The radio processes those waves by impoverishing them, by limiting them, so that we can make sense of them. The same thing is true of our lives. We have difficulty in integrating different situations. Remember Cinerama, where there were three screens in the cinema, and the idea was to grasp this wide panorama, and we found that in fact we were scanning anyway. We didn't have the faculty of being able to encompass all this richness. If we trained ourselves, we would be able to integrate those different images and make sense of the whole. That's what we do with our eyes. The vision of each eye is different, but we are able to integrate those two visions. This is what we are learning to do in meditation, to be able to make sense of our lives in the context of the whole humanity, instead of being caught in our personal trip. That makes for maturity. We become a mature being. We become more and more cosmic, and less personal. That's the reason we use the word *Tatagatha* for Buddha instead of *Siddartha* or *Gautama*, because *Tatagatha* means "Thus." We become Thus. Impersonal.

What we are doing now is to try and reach beyond our narrow self image, which not only distorts our understanding of our lives, but also affects our self esteem. Our self esteem is important, helping us to find fulfillment in our lives. We are proceeding in a counterproductive manner in our lives by standing in the way of the fulfillment of our lives—by limiting ourselves to our self image. We need to notice that we are always relating our self image to the totality, and totality to the self. We are always connecting the two. That is why the Sufis speak about the Divine Consciousness. It seems at first, in our minds, because we think in categories, that the Divine Consciousness is out there somewhere, and this is my consciousness. In our meditation, we start working with expanding our consciousness over a period of time. It might take months and months, even years. We might reach that point which St. Francis talked about when he said, "I thought I was looking at the universe, but the universe is looking at me." That's a breakthrough in meditation. The Sufis would say, "I thought I wanted to know God, but it is God who is discovering Him/Herself through me." Or "I can only know myself by trying to have a sense of the knowledge that God has by discovering Him/Herself as me." That's Sufism.

Maybe it's difficult. In theory, in poetry, it sounds beautiful, wonderful, and paradoxical. We have the faculty of transporting our consciousness into that of another person, then the capacity of transporting it in the consciousness of more and more people, then in infinite regress, we are able to transport our consciousness into the consciousness of the universe. In order to do that, we have to downplay our personal consciousness, or the purpose of our personal consciousness, and highlight the consciousness of the universe. That's what happens in a very advanced state of meditation.

There is a difference between the cosmos and the universe. The cosmos is the body of the universe. Think of the universe as a being, composed of lots of cells—just like the cells of our body—which are endowed with a certain amount of consciousness, will, and awareness. Our consciousness is the focalization of this total consciousness, this global consciousness. That means it is part of that global consciousness. That means our knowledge of the cosmos makes a contribution to the knowledge the cosmos has of itself. When we are looking at the stars, the stars are discovering themselves through our glance. Now perhaps we can better understand the words of Ibn Arabi, who says "God discovers Him/Herself as you," meaning the way the totality is actuated in a unique way in each fragment of itself. It's not God static, it's God dynamic.

Discovering God awakening by becoming existential—activating God as us—is a very different way of thinking. We no longer think of God up there and us down here as miserable worms. It's a completely different way of looking at it. This way of thinking is going to open the door to having a sense of the sacred, because we respect each being as an expression of the Divine Being. This is what is called God-consciousness. "Is it possible that the being of God, whom I imagined to be up there somewhere remote, is present within my own being?" We realize it is only our concept of ourselves, self image we call it, our refusal to accept the Divine gift of our being, that stands in the way of our ecstasy and makes us low key. In the breakthrough of ecstasy we realize the totality of Being at all levels—not just the physical world, but all levels. Being is coming through us, or is us, or is being aroused as us—this is an incredible thought.

Imagine Einstein pushing a pram in streets of New York. A lot of people pushed prams in the streets of New York, but while he was doing it, he was thinking of space and time and galaxies. Most people think that they're pushing their pram, right there in the streets of New York. They cannot see that that is only a very small piece of the totality. It is so easy to be caught in a perspective.

The first American astronaut who landed on the moon gave a seminar at the Zenith Institute. He said, "You can't imagine the thrill of hurtling back home through space at tremendous speed and thinking, "My family is down there, down there on that planet. Over there it is very far away."

And thinking, "Well, yes, I am looking forward to meeting my wife and children and all the circumstances, but I just hope that I won't lose that sense that I have gained of the vastness of reality." In fact, he never lost it.

We don't have to take a space ship to gain a sense of the vastness of reality. This is what we are doing in meditation now. It's a matter of our realization. That is the way out of the prison, and it makes for the maturation of our being. We can't come back through the door through which we came to this state. We can only come back through another door.

What is Spirituality?

As I try to explore new horizons in what has been called "spirituality," I am led to determine as clearly as possible what "awakening in life" would really mean in practice. One might question the validity of practicing away from the scene where things actually happen: the value of learning to pilot a plane on a simulator, the effectiveness of meditating on divine qualities in a meditation cell, isolated from the real life situations in which one is being challenged in affirming these qualities in one's actual handling of problems.

Granted, in a first step, one may autosuggest a built-in programming, bearing in mind that one is just earmarking in oneself a quality that is already latent in oneself and actually effective in the entire universe. The neo-Platonic philosopher, Plotinus, once said: that which one fails to intuit in contemplation, one seeks to experience in the environment. In one's ivory tower, in splendid isolation, one may well glean something of the universe within oneself. Being conscious of the bounty, splendor, and grandeur of the qualities inherited, converged, confluent, from the entire universe at all levels, one's divine inheritance, one would walk the streets with the majesty of a king or queen.

But I would advocate as a second step, while meditating, when one is still protected from the actual stress of impinging situations, to clearly envision those circumstances in one's daily life calling for the particular quality one is meditating upon. Clearly imagine yourself as you would be if you were faced with this very situation and were able then to manifest this quality more intensely than before, thanks to the emphasis given by concentrating upon it.

But it is in the third step that one actually gets down to doing it. This is where things are really at. Presently, one finds oneself launched into real life. In a battle of wills, people are trying to blackmail one into submitting to their will. One did not quite realize it except that one felt frustrated. One resented the people for being bullies. Yet maybe one thought they knew more and had more experience. One is hoodwinked by their self confidence. Anyway, one feels one does not have what it takes to bend their wills.

Besides, it is all too much of a hassle, and so tiring to keep on fighting. So one yields, resenting them, resenting oneself for copping out, resenting fate for having placed one in this insidious situation. Half the battle consists in realizing the situation, in clearly seeing what people are doing to one.

What is the second half? Discovering in oneself the selfsame power that moves the stars and the planets, the atoms, the sea, and propels the sap in the trees and breaks through as the power of a kingly personality. One has it, too, in oneself. Maybe it is difficult to believe. Abraham believed in it; that is why he became a patriarch. If one were Abraham, these people would not be trying to undermine one's will. People have a sure sense of how far they can try it on a person. But one has the same latencies within as Abraham. Why is it they are doing this to one? Because one does not believe one has the same power as Abraham.

While meditating, maybe one could actually see it theoretically. "Pir Vilayat keeps on referring to the DNA in each cell that carries the same programming as the whole body." Each fraction of the totality carries the bounty of the whole potentially, albeit less effectively the smaller the fraction.

But when on the battlefield of life, the theory seems far-fetched, star-flung, just a mind trip when faced with the stark reality. This is where awakening in life proves more effective than awakening beyond life, and the knowledge gained by experience more effective than our intuitive pre-knowledge.

Yet involvement in life tends to draw one into one's personal vantage point and self image. The chances are that in like manner, one has allowed oneself to sink into that lowest common denominator. Awakening in life does not mean being caught in the constraint of the personal perspective. It means being aware of it while reconciling it to a cosmic and transcendental perspective. Both together. Now you pull yourself together and awaken! Immediately, one is aware of an overwhelming cosmic force in one—this is in the nature of one's real being. Presumably one did not have the trust or courage to call upon one's real being faced with the aggressive ego impacting one. Now one has clinched it, thanks to having learned to avoid slipping into one's personal vantage point.

The question now arises whether this of itself will enable one to surmount the challenge. The answer is no. First, one's inborn courtesy and politeness, and also compassion and generosity of heart, will certainly stay one's hand in bringing to bear all the power on tap. Secondly, how does one allay megalomania? Remember: pride in the divine inheritance, together with humility for how one limits this bounty by one's own concept of oneself—both together—the reconciliation of the irreconcilables.

One tends to sidestep the problem by thinking, "I wish to be the instrument of the divine will," evidencing once more one's built-in conditioning of thinking in terms of categories. No! One's will *is* the divine will, funneled down, limited, distorted, but still the divine will.

But will that do it? Or was there a hitch? Was it really power that one needed? Or was it mastery? Why is it that, having inherited divine power, one cannot muster enough of it in real life? Is one's self standing in the way of manifesting one's innate power? Could it be that one is unwillingly giving in to impulses leading to a sense of failure or inadequacy or helplessness? Undoubtedly, a sense of self denigration would pull one further in one's self image and stand in the way of one's confidence in one's divine inheritance. "If one cannot control one's horse, the reason may be because one is not master of oneself, of one's own fingers," says Murshid.

Shall we take up courage and be even more drastic with ourselves? Could it be that one is ashamed about something one is doing, that one has a guilty conscience about being dishonest, deceiving people? This would make it difficult to have self confidence, except by putting on a show of force that could crack up if the truth should explode. Maybe here is the crux of the cause. Of what use is trying to draw power from one's hidden resources if one is blocking it oneself? You do not expect people to respect you unless you respect yourself!

The clue to the whole hang-up has now been unmasked. The answer now is in making a decision to change an action in life. Immediately—but immediately!—one is able to walk down the street conscious of one's divine inheritance, with the majesty of a king or queen, while being aware of one's personality identity. Both together, this time in perfect sync. And furthermore, one is aware of filtering one's real being into one's personality to extend its boundaries and become more and more cosmic. There was no point in repeating the *wazifa* (name of a divine quality) unless it were consistent with one's action.

The above would be a practical way of enacting one's practices in real life situations. We have built a bridge between what we imagine the divine nature to be and our personality, because we cannot know these archetypes except by exemplifying them in our own personality. The new knowledge is built on a preknowledge, but substantiated and "customized" by personal experience. "By discovering God in my being, I confer upon God a mode of reality," says Ibn Arabi. Yet to actuate latencies is not enough; the divine archetypes are enriched when we mutate them in our personalities. Therefore, Ibn Arabi adds, "By actuating God in my being, I confer upon God a mode of knowledge."

New perspectives in spirituality! Exploring the new spirituality. More realistic. More honest!

The Test of Authenticity

It is significant that it is mainly amongst contemplatives that we find people who are in a high state of attunement. We ourselves may also spark a spell of ecstasy in our meditations. Also, the prayers of glorification of the devout may lift their souls to a state of exaltation.

People, particularly initiates, lament that they fail to maintain that "high" in everyday life. The social environment, particularly the trauma of pain, exercises a compelling impact upon the setting of our consciousness, coercing it into our ego, which devises strategies for our self defense. Projections, denials, pretensions are strategies which parade a useful though deceptive image of our real self to safeguard our self image, which is not by any means what we really are. By the same token our concern about adapting ourselves to the challenge of the environment has the effect of constraining us in our self image, which is not what we are but what we think we are.

Accomplished contemplatives are able to maintain their "high" by observing a combination of two complementary outlooks:

(1) the doubt that their assessment of situations, including their self image, is reliable (this is applying the theory of *maya*—unmasking the personal bias) and

(2) continually (with unrelenting diligence and observation) maintaining the alternate perspectives (the wide

embrace, looking out from inside, and the overview) which need to be examined here in more detail.

Contemplatives or devouts are able to escape from the commonplace conditioning, and thereby maintain or recapture their high, because of an enhanced sensitivity to the grossness, greed, and guile that they ascribe to "the ways of the world." And there is a passion for the "sacred" to which they give priority beyond their "earthly" needs. These must be met in the appropriate proportion. All depends on how either figures in our list of values.

The trouble is that to attune to the sacred, it is helpful or easier if we find ourselves in an environment, both physical and social, which favors that attunement. Our fragile attunement seeks to lean upon a support system. Inevitably, owing to the flaws in our human nature, this support system may prove manipulative, may be administered in the form of a *display* of spirituality whereby the adherent ascribes sacredness to the device rather than what it represents, hence the destruction of idols in Islam. The same may apply to ascribing sacredness to the personal dimension of role models, instead of their cosmic or transcendent dimension. This is idolatry. The Sufis replace *tassawuri Murshid*, the image of the Murshid, with *tawwajeh*—to resonate to the pitch to which the teacher is attuned at the crest of conscious reach, rather than envision the teacher's face.

Since the Sufis were conversant with the nomadic life, they could not rely upon having a temple or church, mosque or synagogue as a support system, although the prayer carpet introduced an extraterritorial space in the profane environment. Consequently Sufis had to construct the temple out of their own body, and a temple of light out of their own aura, finally discovering that what they thought was a temple averred itself to be the priest or priestess in themselves and in others.

If the altar which embodies our projections as a sacred object, a totem, avers itself to be made of gilded cardboard boxes (as in Bernstein's Mass) and the guru a phantasmagoria of make-believe (as has often proven on further inspection to be the case amongst self-styled role models), then our faith which is vested in them collapses in dismay, outrage, offense, and indignation.

When the hoax is unveiled, the feeling of having allowed ourselves to be fooled reeks of betrayal, and proves demeaning to our very self esteem which was riding high on the spell sparked by the display.

It is our concern for authenticity, together with our realization, that triggers doubt, which in turn unmasks the hoax of our belief in wishful thinking, and eschews reliance upon a support system for our "high." This has the effect of opening the door to genuine experience and the ensuing realization. It was the wise man, not the heckler, in the Bernstein Mass who pointed out that the wonderful scenario was in fact a piece of sorcery, an enchanting display. How judicious is it to trash people's simple faith—when their only way to uphold it is through belief?

It is only safe to let go of the support system if one can replace it by genuine spiritual experience, as is the problem in withdrawal symptoms after addiction. Otherwise one falls in a hole which is the dark night. One cannot exit from that dark night by the same door through which one entered. That can only occur if the fictitious display, and the role model parading sanctimoniously to exercise dominance over the believers, is replaced in real life by a clear sense of the immaculate and germane sacredness inherent within its distortion. That transition is personified in the Bernstein Mass by the transfer of leadership (or rather the metamorphosis) from the high priest to the redeeming child with the candle, chanting, followed by the crowd who had been stymied in the dark night. The art of so doing consists of being able to keep riding the tide of doubt in an ongoing way while promoting the progressive transformation, without allowing ourselves to be caught by it.

This is precisely the process that any spiritual group needs to go through to respond to its own need for authenticity. This is why Pir-o-Murshid Inayat Khan beckons us to self-generate the sacred in ourselves by "awakening (arousing) the God within." All genuine spiritual groups embody a transmission equipped with a support system that needs to be updated to meet the process that their adherents go through. The risk, however, is that unless we are sharply perspicacious, when we are bereft of the sacred support system, our doubt may induce us to slip back into our trite personal self image, our middle range vantage point, and our commonplace thinking.

The soul manifests in the world in order that it may experience the different phases of manifestation, and yet not lose its way, and that it may regain its original freedom in addition to the experience and knowledge it has gained in the world.

The doubts of pupils prove troubling to their teachers. The teachers themselves need to honor the truthfulness of their own doubts rather than denying them or circumventing them. It is by making that journey, passing though the dark night of doubt while clearly seeing the way out—by themselves negotiating that transit from the apparent to the real—that those leading may give a helping hand to those floundering.

When the teacher wants to offer a hand, the teacher must know that she or he is in the water at the same time. The one who is sinking is sinking, but the teacher also is in the water. The sinking people might drag the teacher down with them and make him or her sink. The teacher must be moving both legs and hands to stay afloat while at the same time holding the mureed from sinking down.

For this the teacher needs to spot where the incongruity in his or her own thinking, and that of others, is causing the problem.

There comes a time when a mureed gets an idea which does not fit in with the teacher's idea. It does not mean that it actually does not fit in with the teacher's idea, but the mureed does not allow the teachers idea to fit in.

The clue resides in the fact that, unless we are clearly self aware, we tend to confuse our real being with our self image, which is only the notion that we make of who we are. Indeed the personal dimension of our total being carries within it the potentialities of our total being in the holistic paradigm, and therefore opens a door to the extensive being somnolent within us (the Creator buried in His creation) and of which our personal being is a relative and temporary sub-whole. If we can envision this fragment of our being in relation to our total being, as carrying within it the potential of our whole being, then through its door we can arouse its bountiful potential, but not if we identify with our misleading self image. This is the criterion of discernment. The awakening that we seek hangs upon this discernment—our ability and acuity in spotting this disparity.

If someone asks us how we feel, unless we are very perspicacious, we tend to fall unawares upon the "I" with whom we identify, not the "I" that we are. Here lies the conundrum.

This requires us to have explored in meditation the wider areas of our being, beyond the personal nexus of our psyche and body, and consequently to see for ourselves how constraining and deceptive our self image is in our assessment of our problems and our validation of ourselves.

> **We occupy as much horizon as is within our consciousness, or as much as we are conscious of. We are as great as our spirit, we are as wide as our spirit, we are as low as our spirit, we are as small as our spirit.**
>
> **Pir-o-Murshid Inayat Khan**

Having seen this, we are now able to see the personal dimension of our being in its context—in its relation with the whole. This will save us from confusing our self image with the personal dimension of our total self.

Then we reverse our perspective.

> **When I open my eyes to the outer world I feel myself as a drop in the sea; but when I close my eyes and look within, I see the whole universe as a bubble raised in the ocean of my heart. The one who tunes himself not only to the external but to the inner being and to the essence of all things gets an insight into the essence of the whole being; and therefore he can, to the same extent, find and enjoy even in the seed the fragrance and beauty that delights him in a rose. He, so to speak, touches the soul of the thought.**
>
> **Pir-o-Murshid Inayat Khan**

Now we can see how our personal bias in our representation of occurrences perceived as "outside" load our psyche with misrepresentations which undermine our self esteem. Consequently we seem to reach what we thought to be "outside" from "inside," and moreover we capture the budding of our recurrently renewed being as it surfaces from inside.

In the person who participates actively in his or her own creativity, God can gain a greater degree of perfection.

Then we need to reconnoiter the psychological gravity pull exercised upon our psyche by our concupiscence—which enlists "the way of the world," with its trail of unkindness, manipulation, and suffering—and give vent to our bewonderment at the splendor and meaningfulness, which we ascribe at first to God as "other" in an awakening "beyond life." In an overview we see it coming through real life—awakening in life.

There is a stage where, by touching a particular phase of existence, one feels raised above the limitations of life and given that power and peace and freedom, that light and life which belongs to the source of all beings. In that moment of supreme exaltation, one is not only united with the source of all beings, but dissolved in it, for the source is one's self.

Now only can we zero in on the personal dimension of our being, envisioning it in its relation, in its context, with the totality in the cosmic outreach and transcendent mystery crowning our being without slipping back into our trite self image.

The key to spiritual attainment is to be conscious of the perfect One who is formed in the heart.

Pir-o-Murshid Inayat Khan

Awakening Beyond Life; Awakening in Life

WHAT DOES IT MEAN?

The usual inadequacy in our understanding of what is being enacted in our lives presents a resistance to further unfurling of our personality potentials. The resultant vulnerable self image and dissatisfaction in our accomplishments is owing to our being entrapped in our personal perspective; thus we fail to avail ourselves of all the resourcefulness of our being. This is the crux which may determine ultimately "who we are."

How can we free ourselves from such constraint of personal perspective, or complete ourselves with additional wider perspectives?

If you look at a cube drawn on a blackboard, you can toggle your glance and alternate between seeing it "this way" or "that way" in what may be considered complementary perspectives. How does the setup of our nervous circuits operate that fluctuation? The unconscious automated programming of our neurological sensory pathways is sensitively balanced in a state of near-equilibrium so that it may shift easily from one pattern to its complementary function. That precarious balance (*kemal* in Sufi terms) avoids the disadvantage of a system getting bogged into a sclerosed impasse which resists change, and therefore favors the advance of the evolutionary thrust.

In our psyche, this delicate balance is ensured by the antinomy between interest and indifference.

From interest, the chance of freeing ourselves from the rut into which we may easily slip lies in the degree of our enthusiasm for, dedication to, and motivation for what we value. This is sometimes accessed by our intuition in what at first seems a hunch regarding an alternate perspective to the commonplace one, a perspective heartening in its excellence and splendor. To this alternative one may toggle the setting of ones consciousness from the commonplace perspective in which one gets so easily entrapped.

Secondly, in indifference the chance lies in giving vent to our nostalgia for freedom, our ability to extract, redeem ourselves from our dependence, addiction, selfishness. This provides the power to shift the perspective of our consciousness in meditation as in real life situations. This nostalgia is the quest for the unattainable which has the power of shifting our perspective from the compulsiveness of *maya*. The choice of that word "unattainable" indicates that it always lies further—we can never claim to have "got it."

However, the paradox lies in the fact that it is the power of love which involves us in the existential condition (the way of the householder, according to the Sufis), while it is the power of freedom (the way of the ascetic) that frees us from being entrapped in a constrained and deluding perspective. Toggle between joy and pain and ecstasy, between awakening in life or beyond life. Now try to integrate these two poles of your being which are of necessity interrelated and interdependent, rather than toggle. To reach beyond the middle range, we need not just to shift our sense of bodiness and self image into discovering ourselves as subtle bodies, or better still as auras of light, but also activate the process of transmutation of matter into spirit in our very constitution—an alchemical process.

Our quest for the unattainable actuates our curiosity to peer beyond the veil: to espy not only the "programming" of our lives and life in general, but what is the originating intention set up in the "software," and more so to appraise the way that our incentives affect and update the programming of our lives and of life in general. Let us bear in mind that, much as the knowledge of the programming exhilarates us by stirring our understanding beyond its limits, it is for the sake of the house that the blueprint is designed. The blueprint only enlists a small sampling of all the creative potentialities that it customizes. This could be illustrated by the fact that the radio simplifies the bounty of the wave-interference network, from which the sounds that we hear are derived, by limiting the frequencies in a manner that our ears can handle.

The paradox is upon us in our life as soon as we seek to make sense of it. We are shattered by joy flawed with pain, and overwhelmed by pain illuminated by flashes of joy, and ecstasy beyond. The precious gift, which is it? Hope and despair interwoven? Like a kaleidoscope, the scene or rather the scenario of life passes on unaccountably.

The encounters of beings are tokens of our involvement in life. Sometimes ephemerally like ships in the night, sometimes compellingly involving, they may bid rapture or wreak constraint upon our freedom; their impact may prove intrusive or enriching and healing. One may be lucky to come across such encounters that trigger illumination, realization, a breakthrough of alacrity, apparently providentially—or those that spark a sense of déja vu that shatters and enchants our soul. What a miracle—life!

Heaven and Earth Interspersed— Part I

We are at a stage where the need for illumination has become imperative. One can say that ultimately illumination is the only thing that makes sense of life and for many there is an almost desperate need to obtain it.

Illumination is associated with awakening and awakening may be described in terms of experience such as suddenly seeing things from a different perspective. An example would be walking in the woods and having a sense of being in a transfigured world, one that is absolutely magical. Or being convinced that your assessment of a problem is the way you thought it was, and all of a sudden something switches in you and you see it in another way. Or walking in a street and instead of seeing a lot of people, you see that it's all One Being, ourselves being the fractions, although ultimately the total Being can never be fractionated. So we see that our usual representation of the world is the result of the commonplace focus of our consciousness which is rather limited. One's vantage point can change, and the consequence is that one's perspective on what one means by reality switches over, clicks into a totally different perspective.

We say that we are in pursuit of spirituality but there is no way in which we can define it or have a clear idea of what we mean by spirituality. We would like to make it a little more real, however, otherwise it becomes like lip service to a belief system. One way of doing this would be to think that what one is trying to do is to introduce another dimension into our commonplace lives which brings in an element that has a transforming effect. And this idea is substantiated by the thought "bring heaven to earth." But when we say bring heaven to earth we are thinking in terms of duality; we are thinking heaven up there is to be brought down to earth. There is some contradiction in this. The reason for this is that our picture of ourselves is usually limited and so the heaven would be other than what we think is ourselves, maybe like angelic beings. We need to realize that there are no boundaries to our being, and the heavenly realms are part of ourselves just like, for example, the people you love become part of you and are continually present in you. So if we think of the heavens as other than ourselves, then we will not discover the features of the heavens within us. To know the heaven in us we have to unfurl the potentialities of the celestial features of ourselves, so it's a knowing that results from doing instead of just knowing. Of course we would like to simply try to define those features which we could ascribe to the celestial dimension of our being, as compared to those we call human. But then again we're thinking in terms of duality because in fact they are interspersed.

So if our thinking stands in the way of our experience, then we have to invest our thinking with greater wisdom. Then we are able to overcome the limitation of our mind that is standing in the way of not only our experience but of our unfoldment. An example of the limitation could be illustrated by a loaf of bread which you could slice and then you could select any slice. Or if think of yourself as being made of different components, you could call on a certain component to try to unfurl it.

The usual way of thinking is that we have all kinds of qualities like compassion and truth and joy and peace and so on, but the holistic paradigm in our time presents us with a much richer understanding. This could be illustrated by a hologram incorporating several images which are superimposed and interspersed, unlike a slice of bread that you can separate. So you can toggle between the focus that brings out the perspective on one image, from the focus of consciousness which brings out another image.

As with a hologram, somehow our brain has the capacity to integrate those two images and the consequence is that we see three-dimensionally, otherwise we would not recognize three dimensions. And the same thing is true in what we call spirituality. Instead of thinking of the heavens up there and the earth down here, or even thinking that there are features in us down here that are of the nature of the heavens, we need to see that in fact the heavens are interspersed with our humanness. For example in India it was believed that the *sannyasin* was different from the householder but now we're trying to see in which way they relate.

We could of course highlight certain features in us that would typify the angelic in us as a guideline. This is in accordance with the teaching of Christ to be in the world but not of the world. What Christ is saying is precisely what I'm trying to clarify in our minds. We see people who are typically of the world in their ways of thinking and doing, and we are surrounded by them, suffocated by them. If we follow the prescriptions of Christ, which are crucial to our objective, we need to see what it is in us that is not typically of the world, but which we could actualize in our behavior so that we are not pulled between two different objectives or motivations. Any such attempt at definition is bound to be perfunctory, but still one needs to start doing this.

The thing that strikes me particularly about the angelic in us is innocence. There is a kind of cleanliness about innocence, as opposed to the kind of psychological pollution which we see around us which I think is sacrilege. The dividing line is very difficult to find. So it is our natural innate sense of the sacred which gives us the ability to ascertain what is inappropriate for us because it violates this sense of the sacred. The consequence is that one becomes very sensitive to any manipulative tendencies in one, any guile, or lack of truthfulness. So the beauty of the child is that the child will come out with the way he or she thinks without any concern for what it does to another. But the consequence is that the child is extremely vulnerable and fragile, and can so easily be hurt.

Of course the celestial dimension of our being is very vulnerable. In order to defend itself, it creates a defense system which unfortunately takes over, covering the most essential celestial aspect of our being in order to protect oneself. The consequence is that we are drawn into guile, manipulation, being divisive, being ruthless, and availing ourselves of the kind of support system that gives us a sense of security against our vulnerability. The whole Western civilization is clearly a support system with all kinds of amenities which aim at being comfortable. It protects us from the storms of life and the precarious nature of our lives. The one thing that it can't really do is to protect us against pain, so our vulnerability is still there. Therefore the support system tends to take over so that one has little time to care for one's soul.

One's spirit is very vulnerable and just a little disappointment or dishonor or anger will harm it. Caring for the soul is something that the support system just cannot do. In fact we must be careful that the support system does not harm the soul. As Christ said, "*what point is there in gaining the whole world if you lose your soul*?" That is our concern in life. If we protect ourselves, then we can't experience life in all its fullness, so it means taking the good with the bad and accepting one's vulnerability, trying to make a dream come true and being prepared to find that one's ideal can never totally gel the nitty-gritty of the situation, because that's not what life is about. Life is an opportunity so that we may become better people—wiser, more loving and illumined—as we progress in evolution.

Heaven and Earth Interspersed—Part II

The question in the mind of Buddha, and also of sages in the Hindu tradition, was whether pain is due to our giving in to our humanness, and whether we can find protection against pain by withdrawing our need to fulfill our desires. I believe that is similar to anesthetizing oneself. Cancer patients who have the choice of doping themselves with painkillers have to decide to what extent they feel comfortable about doing so, or to what extent they feel that it is separating them from the reality of life.

Maybe there is another way of looking at this. The consequence of trying to highlight and also unfurl the celestial aspects of our being is that we encounter pain when our celestial ideal is being violated. So the pain is in the way of translating our celestial ideal into earthly conditions. The curious thing is that, in fact, if we look at it we will realize that it is love that typifies the celestial aspect of our being as opposed to desire. Desire can lead one to slip into wanting things that are comfortable or even wanting people in our relationships to give satisfaction to our ego, and that's not love.

Of course in love there is the greatest of all vulnerabilities, as is illustrated in the songs of the Sufis, where one is on tenterhooks as to whether one's love is reciprocated. We can illustrate it as the heavenly beings being rejected by the egos of the denizens of the earth, with the consequence of being bereft of their ability to nourish the earth with that special dimension which they represent. It's a kind of refusal of beauty. It's a very strange thing but it's something that one wouldn't believe unless one saw it happening today—replacing love by desire.

By love I mean unconditional love, which you could see as a yeast which has a transforming effect, but which also makes one extremely vulnerable. Paradoxically this vulnerability avers itself to be a great power: it's the power of truth. As we know, youthfulness has a resilience that is lost when the personality becomes jaded. This innocence bespeaks reliance upon the parents and has a lesson to teach us as adults, however important our incentive, that there are times when we need to trust ourselves to the self-organizing faculty within us and beware of interfering with it by our personal volition. This is precisely what the Sufis call reliance upon God.

So if we introduce this into our way of doing and thinking, then we have an immediate measuring rod which gives a sense of what we are doing in our lives that goes counter to bringing heaven on earth. We have a feedback system there. Then it becomes very clear that what we are doing to Mother Earth is the result of greed, of desire having snowballed and reached the point of gross exploitation. Ruthless cruelty is the opposite of love. This has been the message throughout the ages but somehow it has been downplayed, even in the name of religion as in the terrible persecutions in Spain at the time of the Reformation.

So far I've highlighted innocence as being one of the features of the heavenly states, and then love. I think we also have to feature beauty, or we could think of it as splendor rather than beauty. Beauty is just the way that splendor assumes a form. It could be the beauty of our thoughts, or it could be the beauty of our way of handling things, or it could be the beauty of our aspirations, the beauty of our willingness to be of service, or of making personal sacrifices. There are many ways in which the kind of beauty which we ascribe to the heavens becomes a reality on earth. Of course it is on earth that beauty is to be found. That is why we need to change that tendency of thinking that the heavens are up there, and that's where we want to reach. Perhaps we will reach it when we die.

If you seek beauty it will elude you. If you unfurl the beauty latent in your being, it will attract beauty. This is the reason why seeking for the angel in the heavens is misleading. Instead, find the heavenly dimensions of your being and the environment will be transformed.

The state of the heavens is embryonic, which means that it is a virtuality. It means that the reality is down here, because this is where the celestial virtualities of our being are unfurled in our personality like an egg that has unfurled into a blastema, an embryo, and then a baby, and so on. So think of the heavens as being in a seminal state, but then it doesn't have to be up there, it's in us. It's not contained in us, but if you think of the hologram again, this is a virtuality that can be highlighted, and by being highlighted it can be really called into existence.

At the very thought of the divine splendor there is a kind of ecstasy that Sufis have often called an inebriation. Now one projects it as a reality up there, but the great breakthrough is when one discovers the splendor in oneself. One doesn't dare to do this because one thinks that it is too grandiose. But that is why Abu Yazid Bastami said, "how great is my glory." So he did make that step which we have difficulty in making, at least I do. One can only do this by accepting that we have in us both the aristocracy of the soul and the democracy of the ego. Otherwise if one were to claim that one is the splendor, then one would be guilty of megalomania. So it's much easier to project and think that one is enamored or enthused or inebriated by the splendor of the heavens.

It seems rather presumptuous to be enthused by the splendor that one discovers in oneself. It seems very self assertive, and yet ultimately it's the same as discovering divine splendor; but one needs to see that it is the same thing by overcoming one's sense of otherness. By highlighting one's problems one tends to slip into a very commonplace picture of life which does not honor the needs of one's soul, even though one is in theory trying to actualize spirituality into real life. A criterion that might prove helpful is the difference between one's needs and one's wants, and moreover the needs of the soul, in contrast to the needs of the psyche, although these are both interspersed and reciprocally relevant.

Our pain is the wounded child, so it is the celestial in us that feels rejected by the human. On the other hand the child has an extraordinary capacity of laughing and crying at the same time. If we dwell in our pain, then we are allowing the angelic in us to be bogged down in the human condition. Therefore the joy that we ascribe to the heavens is an emotion liberating us from the constraint of our humanness. If we do not avail ourselves of this resort, we get bogged down by our human condition. Those who are trying to actuate spirituality in daily life continually encounter the tendency to get caught in the perspective of human problems, to the extent that one has lost sight of the spiritual values behind them even while one is trying to actuate those values. It's like the perspective in the hologram. If you highlight one, then of course the other tends to fade away, and it's very, very difficult to integrate both at the same time. So our attentions are right in line with the need in our time, which is to make God a reality. But the soul in its search for fulfillment on earth tends to lose its way. That's the reason one needs to refer back to the original motivation of one's soul, and to realize that our minds tend to sclerose the dynamic intention into concepts. When this happens we get caught in our concepts of spirituality—and that's not spirituality, it's our concepts.

Therefore shatter your concepts of your ideal for the sake of being realistic. Then you will find that your ideal will find further outreach, further perspectives that will free it from its limitation in your mind. But never give up your ideal because then you are lost.

The Human Drama and the Cosmic Celebration

When the mind idles ponderingly, reflecting upon the meaningfulness of life, the human drama comes into relief with all its emotional charge and paradox. The being of the Planet Earth as it proliferates and mutates, evidences the incredible achievement of humans in the wonder of works of art, the skill of inventors, and social organization. We see everywhere the human emotional drama of joy, triumph, defeat, the thrills and pangs of love, fulfillment, resentment, the miracle of birth, the terror of death, friendship, aversion, loyalty, treason, the jubilations of acts of worship, the agony of those forlorn in the battle of life, the desperate struggle for self esteem, the venture to unlock the unknown, the heroism of some, the depravation of others, cruelty, sadism, violence, vulgarity, self denigration, self defeatism. How powerful are the forces at play, how sublime, how violent, how paradoxical! What is the meaning of it all? To what extent is it programmed? Could there be randomness? Could it all fly off the handle in a disaster?

As one begins to unmask the mind games and debunk the ego trips, all the ephemeral illusions we have built into precarious constructs evaporate in the clear light of bliss. It is the moment of moments: the breakthrough of awakening.

"Every atom, every being awaits its moment of awakening," says Pir-o-Murshid Inayat Khan. Doubtless, some languorous nostalgia for the lost innocence subsists wistfully, like the afterglow of a raging fire as the shimmer of dawn enfolds the landscape in its clarity. But how much more fulfilling is that clarity!

It becomes clear that all those people in the human drama that we admire or resent or try to emulate or criticize, are expressions of the yet-unmanifested expressions of idiosyncrasies in ourselves that we assess favorably or unfavorably. These idiosyncrasies may have been repressed because we have condemned them, or have tried and possibly failed to unfold them. We are both the actor and the enacted in the human drama. We are potentially the hero and the coward, the magnanimous and the mean ones, the uncouth and the subtle, the jubilant and the melancholic, the agitated and the peaceful, the arrogant and the shy, the truthful and the divisive, the ingénue and the manipulative, the inventive and the conditioned, the witty and the boring ones. We are both enchanted and alarmed at what we unwittingly recognize of ourselves as a reflection in the "other."

Relentlessly, the drama forges ahead. As confusion dwindles in the clarity of awareness, one's participation becomes more purpose-oriented, better motivated, designed by the maturity thus gained. What is being enacted in the human drama? What are the issues? What are the dimensions involved? What are the springheads spurring people to act as they do? What are the issues they or we fail to see whose relevance would unmask the hoax in which we are entrapped? We need to recognize, in our minds' thinking or realizing, all the dimensions of the human drama.

If we acknowledge that our brain cells know precious little about our thought, are we to be surprised at the extent of our ignorance of our spiritual dimensions? Could we be oblivious of our invisible partners in our human drama? Yet do we not espy the features of the angel filtered through those of a child or hear echoes of other worlds in inspired music? Moreover, what superhuman impulse could drive a person to brave death exacerbated by torture for the sake of a cause one believes in?

What do our brain cells know of our thinking, though they participate in that thinking? What do our minds know of the thinking of the universe? If indeed our minds grasp something of the thinking of the universe, it is because they are isomorphic and coextensive with it in the holistic mode. This holds true for the cosmic dimension of our minds, and by analogy, as far as the transcendental dimension is concerned, we need to recognize, in our minds' levels of thinking, realizing, and even emoting, a hierarchically ordered infinite regress that must hold true for the mind of the universe. "You are to God, as the corporeal body is to you, and God is to you as the spirit that governs your body," says Ibn Arabi.

What do we know of the many splendored transpersonal dimensions of our being, of our participation in the sphere of metaphor, of our body of pure splendor, or the spheres of the beings of pure splendor? There is a great difference between listening to a piece of music and entering into the mind of the composer as it is composed, or watching a flower as opposed to grasping the way the cosmic celebration is contriving to express its splendor in the form and color and perfume of a flower, or judging the personality of a person and grasping the splendor, the marvel that is striving to come through together with the person's resistance in accepting the glory of their divine inheritance.

It becomes clear that if we were to include all the dimensions of the human drama, that is to give heed to the role of the cosmic celebration plotting and crowning the human drama, we would make a quantum leap in our understanding. This is where meditation avers itself to be the key to getting in touch with one's subtle counterparts and the corresponding celestial spheres. However, we must bear in mind that the divine motivation is both mitigated and enhanced by our very free will. Because, for the software of the universe to mutate, it needs to fluctuate from a point or stable equilibrium (Prigogine)—variations on a theme! Both randomness and motivation vie in this evolutionary change, and this is precisely what we see in the human drama: randomness where there has been a loss of the sense of one's cosmic dimensions, and on the other hand stifling conformism where one is not aware of one's personal incentive. Watch the drama in this light.

You will earmark people stepping out on a limb and fashioning the treasures that give us a sense of release from the narrowness of the flattened out human framework, within which we tend to assess the bounty of the universe. The ballerina, surreptitiously perhaps, filters through in her movements something of the emotion and thinking of the choreography of the stars or the atoms inherent in her genes. Who knows what monumental glory the choreography of the stars filters through what we call the divine harmony—pure splendor beyond any mode of expression whatsoever, and yet whose material expression must inevitably limit it while manifesting it? The playwright highlights typical human features at grips with the human drama, sometimes so unaccountable as to be ascribed to a blind destiny. But the contemplative is trying to grasp the divine archetypes that get distorted as human idiosyncrasies.

And as the mind ponders upon meaningfulness, are any clues to be traced of the cryptic devolution of a fulfillment gained by the universe as a whole in the human drama, where transcendent values are actuated in the melting pot of human strivings, jubilations and ordeals? Can a cosmic celebration really be sensed filtering through the human drama? It is when humans try to find a means of expression of their inveterate need for glorification, that divine features inborn in our humanness begin to emerge. Admittedly our fumblings with religion aver themselves to be most inadequate and often have given vent to undesirable emotions: sanctimoniousness, self righteousness, intolerance, sadism, persecution, hatred, violence, or simply superstition, conformism, conventionalism, fundamentalism, and institutionalism and the complacency of the flock mentality.

As the mind ponders upon meaningfulness, it cannot suffice itself with dissecting the past. It projects ahead. A breath of fresh air sparkles the spirit with hope, as one brainstorms and pioneers for a liberated spirituality at the scale of our time. In this light, one detects in the inane imbroglio of the human drama, a promising ingredient: the catalyst. Enzymes are an example of this on a bodily level. It is not good enough to go out on a limb and act creatively, overcoming the inertia of all existential things, and the conformism that sets into life situations. It is more creative to trigger creativity in others.

This is the age of collective action, with each being triggering the potentialities of every other being, reciprocally quantifying each other in a bold bid to build a beautiful world of beautiful people. This I see as the next step in spiritual organizations, rather than telling people what to do.

Chapter 6

Psychology

The Leading Edge

Yes, we are somewhere about an emergent leading edge—if—we take the next step.

The ancients were more interested in discovering first principles or experiencing wonder. People in our day and age are concerned with the nitty-gritty: the unfoldment of the human person. I see here, a clue to Murshid's teaching and a confirmation of its relevance to our time. While most traditional schools were or are striving to reach beyond the middle range (for example, expanding consciousness), we are trying to identify with our planetary, solar, galactic, and even angelic inheritance as the boundaries of our consciousness dissolve. See the difference? By the very fact of endeavoring to reach beyond, one is evidencing the assumption that the universe lies beyond some invisible boundary, delineating oneself, whereas in reality, one incorporates the universe (not only the physical) albeit by limiting it, even as a focal point converges a broad array of light, for example.

The more progressive schools in psychology such as transpersonal psychology are now recognizing factors in the human psyche that lie beyond the boundaries of the zone that their predecessors defined as the human psyche, carrying Jung's collective conscious a step further. Yet most psychotherapists are still reinforcing people's confinement within their self image by emphasizing the need to heal the trauma of earlier trials, rather than luring them out of that confinement by helping them to identify with the more vast dimensions of their being, thus revealing to them how they "could be if they would be as they might be." Admittedly, it seems logical that one needs to first remove the obstacles to growth before fostering that growth. But one must realize that trauma reinforces people in the exploitation by their unconscious, allowing an excuse for having failed to become what they would have liked to be.

Causality is one of two parameters, the other being purposefulness. If you throw an arrow at a target, it is the bull's eye that determines the nervous impulse that triggers the launch. The pull of the future is more important than the push of the past. If a person had the slightest inkling as to what one could be if one would be what one might be, that person would have an incentive to remove whatever relic of the past was obstructing his or her objective.

Many handicapped persons excel in alternate or closely related fields to those in which they are incapacitated, by dint of nature's mechanism called overcompensation. Many piano tuners are blind; the violinist, Perlman, is paralyzed in his legs but shows incredible dexterity in his fingers; one of the most outstanding brains of our time, the British physicist, Dr. Hawking, is paralyzed to the extent of not being able to talk distinctly or write at all, Demosthenes and Churchill had a stutter; Beethoven composed while deaf. However psychologically damaged a person might be there are creative areas in which that person may excel. One becomes so convinced that one is the image that one makes of oneself, not realizing that it is just a "notion," that is, a construct of one's imagination. What appears at the surface of one's being is only like the tip of the iceberg in comparison with the iceberg. From the moment one grasps that the notion is an imaginary construct, one realizes by the same token, that one can change it, since change is within the power of one's imagination. What is more, within certain limits, one can make one's image into what one wishes.

In fact, the leading edge in psychology today is signposted by the magical words "creative imagination" as pioneered by Dr. Rollo May et al. and this is precisely the gist of our work in the Sufi Order. We are onto something of great moment if we do make the next step, which in this case, is to make ideas materialize, because progressive psychologists are trying to make use of the know-how gained in classical schools of meditation. We are amongst the few esoteric schools who are trying to interface our meditative practices with the latest developments in psychology, in order to apply whatever insight we gain in meditation to helping people in their urge to grow through undergoing a process of transformation.

You may ask, "Why especially the Sufis?" Well, the answer springs to evidence. Sufis traditionally, and most particularly, Pir-o-Murshid Inayat Khan, place the accent on finding God in and as ourselves, rather than seeking God "up there" as other than ourselves. The DNA illustrates this reality by pointing out that the whole body is present in totality in each cell of the body.

The Sufis say we not only inherit the divine nature but *are* that inheritance, albeit limited and tarnished. We could interpret this in the holistic paradigm of our time by paradoxically using an antique term: we are coextensive with the universe, and our minds are isomorphic with the thinking of the universe, which the Sufis call the mind of God. Holding a belief is one thing; experiencing it in practice in one's being and letting that realization transform one beyond recognition, is another.

There is just that step we need to make. It means letting go of self image, mental assumptions, of wallowing in whatever assets have been secured, and then freewheeling on the strength of a sheer, anticipated vision of how things could be if we would be if we allowed the universe to fall into place in a novel pattern in us.

Our Many-Faceted Personalities

Perhaps the secret of fostering personal growth is in realizing that our personalities are structured into multiple personae illustrated in an oversimplified way by the Dr. Jekyll and Mr. Hyde story. An apt example could be the potential pending varieties of mutations within a seed, needing just the right catalyst (in cell biology, an enzyme) to prime the desired mode into actuation.

Secondly, one needs to bear in mind that we exist and function at several levels, which one might designate as the multiple dormant tiers of our being awaiting the flash of our awareness to spring into activity. It is our ignorance of these potential dimensions of our being that lock us into our inadequate self images in which we get straightjacketed. The catalyst priming these many splendored potentials is the act of intelligence rather than that of consciousness. By that I mean self-generated self awareness, rather than the kind of experience based on observation and the interpretation of the data observed. It is self discovery instead of experience.

The reason why introspection is so deceptive is that we split ourselves into two purely fictitious parts: the observer and the observed. This split sets up an artificial boundary within our wholeness, which is just in the mind but does not exist in reality. No wonder that if we so proceed, we can never discover our potentialities, nor identify with them and allow them to unfurl. Instead, we remain hemmed into our assessment of the input from our face in the mirror, or our performance in life (successful or unsuccessful), or our disenchantment in our personality, or our inadequate self image, or our uneasiness about our ponderous conscience, or our lack of sparkle. But is it not the role that we are called upon to play in our lives that draws our attention to certain idiosyncrasies rather than others, and thus makes us discover them in ourselves?

For example, being in a situation of service will bring out the serviceable persona in us—being a father or mother, the affectionate and responsible persona; being a business man, the alert and well organized persona; having to fight even if for justice, the aggressive persona; a lover, the caring, perhaps the passionate persona in us; a musician or artist, the sensitive inventive persona; a spiritual teacher or seeker, the ecstatic, idyllic persona, etc. We have all of these personae in us. When succumbing to temptation, circumstances will trigger, almost compulsively, the Mr. Hyde latent in all of us; if inspired and elevated, the Dr. Jekyll.

In addition, the role one assumes as one meets or speaks to different people may cause one to switch surprisingly from one of those latent persona within oneself to another persona in sudden leaps and bounds. The same person, so gentle with a child, may behave aggressively whenever faced with a neighbor, and then prove convivial with a friend. The Good Samaritan may act meanly to a relative. The same person, solicitous with a person looked to for a favor, may prove hostile to a person who is dependent. Besides, one's attitude toward the same person may undergo amazing reverses: the lover's passion may turn to treachery; respect may sour to contempt. An actor or actress may discover a variety of very different personae in accordance with the role played. Moreover, he or she may find it easier to depict a clearly distinctive character rather than a rich composite personality. The greatest of human arts consists in integrating the multiple and extremely varied potential persona within our inheritance, which is precisely what Jung means by the integration of personality.

Then there are those who put on an act, for example, turning the charm on or looking fierce, or putting on their downtrodden look whenever they know they are observed. This then is the real mask, an artifice which may make it difficult for them ever to display or discover or manifest their true being. We are primed by our awareness of our potentials, and spurred by the challenge of the environment. The balance between these depends upon the extent to which we adapt to the environment, or to which we act upon the environment.

This is where our free will comes in. Irrespective of what the outer circumstances wreak upon us, we may choose the brand of personality amongst the infinite variety of potential personalities latent within us. What is more, we may mutate the qualities inherited. Creativity of the personality is comparable to composing variations on a theme which we may fluctuate inventively. Here lies our choice. To operate a choice, one would have thought that one would have to know our latent personae and that therefore self discovery would be a prior imperative. But our choice lies in choosing the role we want to play. Then the challenge we take upon ourselves will release the appropriate latent quality which we thus discover. Surprisingly, we enjoy more freedom in choosing the role we wish than most of us realize. If indeed spirituality lures us forward in the evolutionary process, then we progress by discovering our freedom and using it.

So much for our cosmic dimension, but how about our transcendental one? Here the bounty at our disposal is infinite! We are normally only using a minute fraction of our potentials at the higher levels of our being. What is the difference between our cosmic dimension and our transcendental? They are like the latitudinal and longitudinal vectors in our navigational reckoning. They are interdependent and not two distinct realities. If one says one inherits from the whole universe, one tends to assume that we are referring to the physical cosmos: the fabric of the stars, of the galaxies, the radiation of the Big Bang, the orderliness of a crystal's molecules, or the disruption of the harmony of the spheres in a solar or galactic storm, or the voracity of a wolf, the diligence of a bee, the playfulness of a monkey or the sensitivity of a butterfly. But in our transcendental dimension we also inherit the planning, the thinking of the universe, the creativity, the ecstasy, the psyche of the universe, the will, and, in fact, what we mean by the soul of the universe. And by the words "soul of the universe," what we are designating is what we mean when we discover the traces of it as our divine inheritance.

Note that in order to discover the more transcendent dimensions of one's being, observing the body and personality and even one's consciousness objectively, without identification (as Buddha taught), will cause one to shift one's self awareness and sense of identity higher up the scale of values or spheres of existence. But this is so only if one observes detachment by not identifying with the object of one's act of consciousness or with one's consciousness. To detach from identification with the object would allow the activity of intelligence to take over from the act of consciousness. Such is the method that will lead us to discover our divine inheritance.

The Interface of Spirituality and Psychology

Psychologists accuse those who work as spiritual guides of teaching the "spiritual bypass," that is, failing to deal with psychological problems and lulling adepts into a metaphorical Shangri-La, while neglecting important day to day issues. This reinforces people's temptation to escape rather than to face and unravel real life situations, and it often results in producing otherworldly dropouts from society.

Conversely, some psychologists get burned out by recurrently administering the same therapy with exasperatingly little change in the patient. Why? Some patients, although they ask to be cured, unconsciously do not really wish to be cured, because they experience the therapist as one who is robbing them of their justification for not having become "what they would have been if they could have been what they might have been."

We, as spiritual guides, are fostering creativity rather than therapy. One might ask. "Should not therapy come first before rebirthing?" This seems logical but it is important to give a person something to live for to offset reticence at being cured. The pull of the future is more motivating than the clutches of the past, and there is nothing more stimulating and motivating than creativity. If the human being is a holistic phenomenon, then the metaphorically creative levels of one's psyche are essential to the organic wholeness sought after.

Most of the party-line psychologists would lose their credibility if they were to prescribe the kind of practices fostered by spiritual groups: breathing practices, the mantram, visualizing the aura, grasping one's eternal being beyond the idiosyncrasies inherited from one's ancestry, and modulating consciousness in the cosmic and transcendental dimensions. But these are techniques which foster a correction in the psyche by working on the energy flow of the life field. These techniques help the adepts to overstep their self image and encourage a creative blossoming of latent qualities.

Actually, some spiritual guides and psychologists are exploring areas of mutual complementarity and enrichment. Fundamentally, spiritual guides and psychologists are dealing with a human need embodied in the struggle for self esteem and culminating in the unfoldment of one's personality, which is an expression of the evolutionary drive. Basically, the crux of the issue is that people's self image is simply a notion, a purely imaginary projection, constrained by the very fact that consciousness in the human being is focalized as in a lens and judges things from a localized vantage point. Therefore, the problem facing psychologists revolves around the fact that people get stuck in their fictitious self image, which blocks the evolutionary process from fostering a blossoming in their personality.

If we apply the paradigm of the seed, striving to manifest more and more of its bounty in the plant, the clue lies in grasping more dimensions of our being beyond the scope of consciousness in its middle range setting. This is where spirituality does make a contribution to psychology. Briefly, our being extends through several levels of reality. Transcendental and ancestral idiosyncrasies intermesh and overlap, particularly at the physical and psychic level.

We are encouraging people to earmark their eternal core being, irrespective of what they inherited from their ancestors, in keeping with the words of Jesus, "Be ye perfect as your heavenly Father is perfect." Notably, these more transcendental factors of our being aver themselves to be more impersonal or cosmic, or to dovetail with those of other beings. One may consider oneself as an inverted cone whose base is coextensive with the totality of the universe, and whose apex (which we usually imagine ourselves to be) is the convergence or funneling of all this bounty. To sift this quick of one's being, unravel it out of the humanly inherited factors and re-fertilize one's psyche through its creative power is the work of spiritual guides.

One can trigger this by self transcendence: observing one's body and mind objectively without identification. This seems paradoxical because, as already seen, our core being, irrespective of ancestral inheritance, does intermesh with our inherited characteristics in both the psyche and the body. However, thanks to the dimming of one's identification with the physical and psychological factors of one's being, during the self-transcendent experience, a sense of *déjà vu* emerges in the consciousness from some impersonal level of the psyche's memory. One feels, "this is really me." The emergence of this genuine core of one's being has an overwhelming effect upon the self image and presents a new challenge; namely, reconciling and integrating the oceanic feeling of one's cosmic identity with the constraining self image.

Thus the need branded by psychologists as self acceptance is met by spiritual guides by placing one's shadow self (attributed to one's inheritance) at the service of one's core being as a "bridge over troubled waters," and by interfacing and intermeshing with it, thereby transmuting the shadow self. Rather than considering the shadow and core being as two factors of one's being, one may consider them as two poles of the same reality.

It becomes obvious that spiritual guides and psychologists would gain much by working together since the factors they are dealing with interact and intermesh inextricably.

Reconciling our Psychological Needs with our Spiritual Needs

Here lies the crucial issue for those who harbor an imperative nostalgia for the sacred, yet honor their responsibility in our human society in the world.

We may acquiesce to our need to involve ourselves—with people, with situations—to manipulate the fabric of our Planet and to find fulfillment. We may achieve mastery by taking responsibility, upgrade our support system in the physical environment, improve ourselves physically and healthwise, unfurl our human potentials, nurture our intellect, cultivate our culture, our music, our art, to enjoy entertainment and relaxation and jokes, to discover hidden and perhaps unavowed aspects in ourselves by identifying with the person enacted in the human drama.

However, we may become increasingly concerned that in the course of this involvement, we easily and unconsciously get inveigled into constraining situations, not only circumstantial but in our way of thinking, which affects our attunement, and which evidences the impact of conditioning upon our free will. Our sense of suffocation, of frustration can become desperate. That which once delighted us avers itself to be a prison. Our need for freedom becomes all-consuming, compulsive.

At first shot, we tend to jump perfunctorily to the conclusion that our prison is our environmental and social circumstances; that to grow, we need favorable circumstances, just as a plant may need just the right sunshine and water and quality of earth to flourish. We suffer if our need for the sacred is waylaid by the sacrilege of worldly ways. We feel that we are missing out on something quintessentially important in our life: awakening, enlightenment. But what do these words mean? Are they clichés of our mind? Are they projections of our wishful thinking? Let us be wary of words, of doctrines.

We may well have created these circumstances (as we imagine a spider confined to its web), before we had this breakthrough of realization, albeit there may be cases where it appears that the prevailing circumstances are fortuitous, irrespective of our choice.

Many a soul in their yearnings for freedom, have escaped from what they thought was prison while failing to recognize that the prison was in their thinking.

As our outlook changes, our sensitivity is sharpened. The grossness, the selfishness, the worthlessness of so much that is avidly pursued in the world, the facetiousness, the ruthlessness of some, the insensitivity to the suffering caused—these wound our soul to the core. Modern technology has made our lives in the world more comfortable and practical, while more challenging, albeit at the cost of much defilement, pollution, and unfair competition wreaking destitution on the unadapted. At what point does need become greed?

What at first seemed worthwhile now avers itself to be trivial. The support system takes over, so that our purpose in gaining insight, unfurling potential qualities, our attunement to the divinity of our being, gets lost from our view. This is what everything was about! The futile, misconstrued game played itself out. As this gradually dawns upon us, our suffering seems to need to exasperate itself to a paroxysm of pain before we either do something positive about it or simply go under, wallowing in self pity. We ask ourselves: what am I doing in life?

As soon as we realize that we are ourselves party to all of this—that surreptitiously it has spilled over in us while we were inculpating others—we realize that the prison is in our having failed to spot this. We had been denigrating ourselves unbeknownst to ourselves, on a hunch that "something was wrong," unwittingly intuiting that it eroded our spirit. We had failed to see this until the burst of realization struck us. We had been contriving to escape from circumstances, whereas we failed to acquiesce that we were trying to flee from aspects of ourselves that we dislike and had been denying, albeit unconvincingly, and which are our real prison.

Consequently, we make a decision to not participate in what arouses our wariness, our aversion, our abhorrence. Can we live the life of the world without belonging to it? Instead of "seeking another kingdom," can we bring the sacred right into the profane? Can we handle ugly situations beautifully?

Here one encounters the danger of falling into a still more pernicious prison: vanity in our sanctimoniousness, which traps us in our ego, and which is the ultimate misconception. What we call "me" (the ego), is only a fraction of what we are. If we earmark and identify with a fraction of ourselves without including the whole picture, we distort the picture. Under the glare of awakening, that phantasmagoria exhausts itself. The way out of that prison is to extend our identity beyond what we think is our self.

Suddenly we realize, "I am not what I thought I was, whereas I was thinking and behaving according to what I thought I was!" It is by shifting our consciousness and sense of identity in the transcendent dimensions that we first grasp unity: beyond matter, beyond the subtle body, beyond form (imagination), in the realm of pure light, beyond consciousness, beyond the seeds of existence—awakening beyond existence—then reversing and seeing unity in diversity—in the seeds of existence, and then in existence.

True exaltation of the spirit resides in the fact that it has come to earth and has realized there its spiritual existence.

Encompassing all beings, we see God as a potentiality, striving to emerge in each fraction of itself.

The eternal is to be found in the becoming. It is a virtuality actuating itself in each fraction of the totality, which is what we are ourselves, and also the "others."

But to believe in the metaphysical concept that "all is one" is not good enough. Experience eludes the meshes of the knowledge that tries to scoop it up. Reciprocally, will knowledge spur us to experience? To experience what we know?

The breakthrough of realization will make us beautiful; and if we have been able to lift the veil that buried our own beauty, we see the beauty in others behind that same veil. When they discover themselves in the mirror of our soul, the chances are that they will undergo the same awakening process that we have gone through ourselves.

At this point in our forward march, we stumble upon the ultimate realization. Is our quest for freedom not the ultimate selfishness of the personal ego that we confused with the Self? Is not that erroneous notion of ourselves the ultimate prison? Is our quest for freedom not itself an expression of the ultimate concern of the personal self?

Discovering our real Self, which is what we mean by the Oneness behind the fragments of the One, opens the door of the prison. The way out of that prison is love. It is here that we are tested in our love and compassion, which is a gratuitous act of our free will—perhaps the ultimate freedom from the want of the self. This is enabled by avoiding criticism of those who are still immersed in "the ways of the world," who are struggling, self-destructively, incongruously and blindly. People need to go though their trips, be replenished or disappointed, disconcerted or devastated. We must know that we cannot spare another from follies by dint of having overcome our own. These are the pangs of birth. Our latent perfection and that latent in others, which we ascribe to God, is striving to break through our imperfection which we ascribe to ourselves and others.

As soon as we have ceased to fret about our own suffering, we become sensitive to the sufferings that spark the arrogance of other people toward us. When we see how they overcompensate for their vulnerability by possessiveness, we love them and would wish to help them in their covert distress. Laughing at our own past stupidity while bemoaning the suffering it caused acts as an alarm signal to those still in the quagmire.

In India this is termed "indifference"; it is really finding freedom in ourselves from being disturbed by the attitude of others. The consequence is the peace that is not born of the escape from prevailing conditions, but which is the catalyst of benevolent action arising out of the peace within. We need to watch that our equanimity is not reliance on a doctrine rather than having been achieved personally by meeting a struggle chivalrously.

We find that there is no end to the demands of people: they will want us to help them achieve their selfish ends, they may wish us to support their ambition, their power trips, to flatter them, feed their vanity, bolster their self esteem, overlook their foibles, have patience with their follies, understand their incongruities, corroborate their judgment of others, or to commiserate with their sorrows for failing to attain the satisfaction of their desires. Perceiving our innocence, people may deceive us, to pull us on their side in their conflict with another person. We must be careful lest by our good will to fulfill their demands, we find that we participate in their covetousness and sometimes concupiscence, or at least reinforce them. We do not want to become dependent upon their dependence upon us.

Every new outlook that frees us from perfunctory assumptions will change our relationship with others, and thereby alter the circumstances.

Suddenly the same world that we despised appears beautiful. We see the struggle for perfection in imperfection, the transparency of beauty trying to pierce the veil of ugliness; we see the immaculate present within its very defilement, order within disorder. "That which transpires through that which appears" is already present in that which appears; it is not elsewhere, it is not "other." It is in the legendary past of a pre-established harmony, and it flashes in the future as an intention: it is "infinity in a finite fact and eternity in a temporal act" (Prentice Mulford). It is the everywhere and always in the here and now. The existential is not an illusion veiling reality, it is the reality embedded in actuality. The purpose and fulfillment and reality of the blueprint of your house are in your house. The cosmic code does not precede the existential universe; it is organizing itself and thereby discovering itself in the "here and now."

Therapy

Most of us struggle in our lives to meet responsibilities, to upgrade our condition and that of others, to fulfill a worthwhile objective, to partake of the heritage of our civilizations. And sharing in the destinies of our Planet, most of us are to a smaller or larger degree subject to being pummeled and battered. Pummeled and battered in our sensibilities, our self esteem, our self confidence; challenged in our values, our philosophies, our beliefs, our performances or skills.

Our targets tend to lead us into a narrow purview. Sometimes they even lock us in a bind, obsessively masking the relevance or meaningfulness of our motivations in terms of a wider purview. We may reach a point where we realize that we are bypassing the major issue: that something went wrong. That which draws our attention to this realization is suffering. One did not realize that one was unhappy with oneself, with circumstances, with one's way of thinking or behaving. One is causing others suffering inadvertently because one is disgruntled, disenchanted. The warning has sounded!

Our good-wishers will say: you're pushing yourself too much, relax, take it easy, give yourself a break, perhaps a holiday, and forget your homework while sharing convivial conversations.

One has not realized that the reason that one finds it difficult to be peaceful is that one secretly despises that lazy person chronically lying on the beach, compulsively eating chocolate cakes and aimlessly chatting about trivialities.

Or the therapist will enjoin: get in touch with your feelings: are you happy? If not why not? You may respond: I really have no time to decide whether I am happy or not, nor do I know whether I am or not.

Reader, you have identified the workaholic. Unmistakably! One has become obsessed with one's will at the cost of one's emotions. The personal squeezes one into one's trip at the cost of what it is all about.

While appreciating the power that one gains by achievement, the objective that one sets out to accomplish limits the power. The more impersonal the objective is, the more dedicated to service, the greater the sovereignty that is gained. This way of looking at things sets priorities—fulfillment over achievement. Fulfillment defines a broader spectrum and implies that one's being enhances itself in the pursuit of the objective rather than in sacrifice for the objective.

This is where meditation comes in, if rather than pursuing stress reduction it fosters self discovery and self unfoldment. But you may ask: where does therapy come in? Therapists are teaching us to be kind to ourselves. Spiritual guides are teaching us to be kind to our soul.

Pain in the body or the psyche is a warning signal. Our programming is drawing our attention to something that needs to be dealt with. First it needs to be acknowledged. It may be telling us that our present course is not proving to be fulfilling, and inviting us to consider a change of tack. Perhaps our pain spells our response to that of another or others; therefore it is telling us that our present course does not match our need to be of service.

Where there is pain, there is damage; it could be damage to the psyche, which affects our self esteem, and then our efficiency or effectiveness. Where there is damage, there is a need of therapy. Wherever possible, the patient needs to be protected from the stressful agent, which admittedly is not always easy or even feasible.

Most importantly, one needs to be apprised of that built-in programming with which we are gifted. The cosmic power of regeneration might be trusted, and we might lend ourselves to its therapeutic effect. This is where faith comes in, which has proven decisive in healing. It requires a commitment on our part to avoid letting ourselves into a recurrence of the trauma, or, paradoxically, obsessively seeking the trauma, as in an addiction.

No doubt the spiritual contribution to the therapy does consist in balancing the thrust of the personal will by giving vent to an impersonal will, called "passive volition," as illustrated in meditative practices. There is obviously a place for both, or they may even balance or combine; in fact they are the poles of the same thing.

The better informed strata of the population have learned from an interface between the world's spiritual traditions. The interface points to two complementary solutions that for the sake of simplicity one might find illustrated in first Buddhism, and second Sufism.

The first solution evidences the need to shield oneself, to protect oneself by, as Buddha says, placing a sentinel at the doors of perception. This does not mean shutting the door to the input from the environment—both physical and psychological—but filtering that input, including that of one's own psyche.

The spiritual factor highlights the excellence of qualities in our being, which we tend to overlook when dissatisfied with ourselves. The dissatisfaction stems from our underplaying our resourcefulness. Simply overlaying our foibles with pride in our divine excellence would prove to be a clear case of an esoteric school "spiritual bypass." Nor would considering the voidness of the self, or of the world prove any more helpful.

The operation of the built-in repair system of the psyche is of an identical nature with that of the regeneration of body cells. Unless overstressed, the enzymes governing the replication of the DNA by the RNA and vice-versa will correct mistakes, like self-correcting spelling software. Even so, any distortions in our psyche may get ironed out by our faculty of replicating our real being in our personality—that real being that remains unscathed by the distortions. Thus our psyche can be restored to its pristine glory if we so decide.

The operative factor here fostering the repair process is confidence, and even an intuitive grasp of one's eternal being. No doubt one needs to protect the conviction that one gains by grasping it from the psychic environment, because this is where our self image is based. Here detachment avers itself a safeguard.

The counterpart is not seeking refuge in one's eternal being, but rather working on one's self image. This is done not so much by ironing out the distortions, but by positively reconstructing it the way we want it to be. Now that is creativity.

Rather than unclutching from the environment in an ivory tower, which is often the way of meditation, the creative person fosters the interaction between the perfect model and the environment. This is the art of the composer:

capture something of the trend of the time, but add a positive and original lead.

Here the party-line psychological approach would foster building a strong personal self. The spiritual factor would consist in fostering the convergence of the transcendent dimensions of one's being into one's ego consciousness so that one's creativity gains a cosmic stature.

The Sufis say God creates and recreates God's own self in and through us, in the measure that we reverse our vantage point and grasp the divine operation in us. Clearly these two approaches, rather than being contradictory, are complementary.

Healing the Wounds of the Psyche

Pain is a faithful companion that collects more of its kind on the way and does not let itself be fooled by our facetiousness. Yet pain wearies when we give ourselves over to glorification. In fact pain is a host at the center of the cosmic drama that extends the cosmic celebration to the existential realm.

Its lineage may be traced to what Dr. Stanislav Grof calls the perinatal stage of our life's trajectory in nebulous strata of our memory; however, fleeting memories of our prenatal uterine sojourn may sometimes break through from the unconscious. Nature protects us somewhat from the memory of the trauma of birth by blanking out consciousness, so that we embark upon our terrestrial episode with a (relatively) clean slate. But this is where it starts: childhood memories—vaguely erased, yet sometimes erupting with uncontrollable force.

Of course, there is no way of cataloguing these, since the scenarios of our childhood background vary so greatly; sometimes from the sublime to the horrendous, depending upon the case. It may be somewhat innocuous—a toothache, an upset tummy; or worse: being left unattended by one's parents, perceiving quarrels or even violence—

being frustrated from one's wish, or confined, or unjustly treated, or punished, or abused, or derided. Whether actually trivial or traumatic, these impediments assume in our childish perception huge proportions.

Mother Nature was putting us through the apprenticeship of pain in preparation for possibly yet greater trauma as we grew to adulthood. Later, upon reflection, one may come to realize that just as muscular stress (within certain limits) tones the muscles of our body, so does psychic trauma toughen our mettle. This is providing trauma does not exceed certain thresholds, after which it can prove to be psychologically depleting. Yet it is good to bear in mind that the threshold between stress and over-stress shifts according to one's determination and realization.

Doubtless a traumatic event, however past, leaves a mark in the psyche—most likely a wound which if not tended is likely to fester and even grow disproportionately out of hand. Physical wounds offer us an apt model for what happens to the psyche: the way is open to bacteria, even viruses. The difference between bacteria and viruses: bacteria are attacked by the immune system; viruses are more insidious, they take over the very programming of the host cells and deplete their attackers.

Just as a timorous person is more prone to be mugged than a valiant character, since our wounds constitute our weak spots, so people, unconsciously perhaps, perceive this weak spot. And if adversely disposed they will aim their attack right there; and if not, life will somehow find a way of doing this to one. Alternatively, thoughts and emotions accruing from outside and then ingested and incorporated, may infect the wounds, manifesting as bitterness or despondency. Painful thoughts may haunt one obsessively if not dealt with.

How does one affect a cure? In medicine two methods are availed of:

a) administering a foreign product that attacks the bacteria—rarely able to attack the virus;

b) enhancing the organism's own defense system.

Likewise with the psyche.

What healing processes does meditation have to offer? Positive thoughts auto-suggested in meditation themes provide a most apt antidote to the negative self-defeating thoughts triggered by our reflections and our psychological trauma. These will sometimes counter the negative thoughts forcefully, and effectively protect the psyche from further infection. The sheer repetitiveness of a meditation theme as a mantra, conditioned by its association with a sound sequence will act as a protective dressing smeared with a balm upon one's sensitized heart.

Where the wounds are more deep-seated, affecting the overall structure of the psyche, then it is incumbent to call upon our psyche's inbuilt immune system. Indeed nature does provide us with a degree of inner resilience against upsetting impressions, thoughts and emotions. This ability is affected by the traditional indifference illustrated by the imperturbability (*vairagya*) of the Hindu anchorite (*sannyasin*).

The strategy devised by our smart programming is to refuse admission to unwanted elements, based upon a differentiation (*vivea*) between self and nonself. In other words to refuse admission to our sense of identity. This can be true even when this sense of identity is extended to the zones in the environment which are usually considered as lying beyond oneself, but bear an affinity with one's nature. Certain meditation practices extend one's sense of identity to everything in which one discovers attributes akin to one's own, and thus lead to further reaches of self discovery.

This sense of recognition has been replicated in artificial intelligence. It rests upon a more advanced, and therefore more subtle, process than the commonplace subject-object relationship based on otherness (the I-It relationship of Martin Buber). This is identity based on resonance, similarity. In practice this is a blend between absolute identity and difference. For example, two gongs may have certain frequencies in common and others dissimilar, but owing to the similarities, if one strikes one gong, the other will start vibrating in resonance. This function built into our psyche allows us to enrich our personality with elements in harmony with our being. They have something in common with our own nature, yet differ in certain respects; on the other hand there is a turning down of any response (indifference) with regard to anything that is too foreign.

Also our programming needs to consider that our heredity is a hybrid, consequently extending to our zone of identity while setting certain limits: for example, to cross-pollinization and breeding based on similarities versus incompatibilities. So our genetic programming provides the organism and indeed the psyche, with some accommodation by which it can ingest elements in which the heterodox features may even outweigh the homeostatic ones. This is exactly where we are at risk to make a compromise and accommodate elements that prove toxic, harmful, and destructive to our being.

Let us bear in mind that since this defense mechanism of the body and the psyche is inborn, it does not depend upon the feedback of experience. The defense mechanism is genetically determined, so there are vast differences of innate susceptibility accountable by heredity. Actually we need to account for pre-conceptual features: in the parlance of esoteric lore (let us call it meta-psychology), we differ in the particular composition or admixture of qualities. The qualities are our divine inheritance, called *ayan al thabita* by the Sufis; and it covers a vast range. This is predetermined.

It its incipient stage, therefore the immune system acts as a deterrent repelling harmful intruders, and likewise with the psyche. However, once in function, the system adapts itself to the environment. If the intruder manages to gain access within the organism or the psyche, the organism or psyche learns how to attack it, ultimately defeating it totally by killing it or eliminating it. The genetic code that exhibits much stability throughout our lives to provide a template for the structuring of our tissues, does mutate greatly in respect of the immune system. The ability of the individual to respond to a particular antigen needs to be tailored to the nature of that antigen. Even this is foreseen in our planning, so that it may be held that the wherewithal to resist harmful psychic elements is written right into the pool of our divine inheritance. We are provided with a psychic defense system highly adaptable to what seems to be unexpected trauma.

The macrophages first neutralize the disturbing element by engulfing it, then disintegrating it; precisely so does the psyche when its function has not been impaired by over-stress, both emotional and mental. But given the stress of our lives in our present day civilizations, harmful psychic elements tend to gain access into our psyche, and our defense mechanism gets over-stressed. This is where psychotherapy and meditation—optimally a judicious combination of both—will prove to be the ultimate resort when disturbing thoughts have become ingrained and persistently obsessive. Mercifully the challenge of the assailant will enhance the immune system.

In the psyche, the antigens need to be reinforced by a concerted volitional act, since in our civilizations we have turned down the autogenic psychic defense mechanism actuated by the myths of old. Certain methods of meditation are devised precisely to trigger archetypal psychic forces that effect recovery. The organism and psyche know how to self-heal if we know how to let them take over. Our will acts as the catalyst triggering off an unconscious, cosmic will, if we know when to let the transit take place. This rests upon an act of faith: to enlist the action of those archetypal factors of our being, we need to honor our higher being.

The Critical Issues

Our self esteem is the real issue in our lives. This is usually precariously suspended on our own fallible assessment or that of others. The fact that on this thin thread of a mind's notion hangs our performance in achievement, our prospects of unfurling our personality, and our joys and pains calls for serious soul-searching and some restructuring of our thinking. For here lies the critical issue.

In our present day civilizations the struggle for survival has become so desperate, the distress of the destitute so appalling, competition so ruthless, and emotions so callous, the clue to material survival has become psychological survival founded upon our self respect. Thus the key to fulfillment is a function of our self image.

Realizing how crucial our self image is, it is the more amazing that it is really a projection of our inherent creative imagination. Our performance in life, our success or failure, is suspended upon an act of imagination! So the question becomes, how do we work with our self image in order to upgrade it?

We are touching upon the very crux of psychology, and yet we must also include and honor our spiritual dimension. It would be a violation of the holistic paradigm to neglect or underestimate the value and role of this transcendent dimension of our psyche. Our self image is the product of scores of unassociated factors, and it gels easily into a tenuous Gestalt which resists change. This process is insidious. It can even become compelling and obsessive, and may ultimately lead to self defeat.

The clue is then to earmark the essential ingredients enmeshed in the particular admixture that is our personality. This is not easy since this is an enormous spectrum. After this we need to identify with these, that is, really convince ourselves that they are latently present within us and can be unfurled, reinforced, nurtured, and protected as they grow.

A perfunctory probe of our idiosyncrasies will evidence the degree of our parental, ancestral and even evolutionary inheritance, as well as the imprint of our culture, upbringing, schooling, and social environment. The transpersonal elements in our psyche are more difficult to earmark, and are inevitably inextricably intermeshed with the ancestral ones. To cull these, one needs to apply methods of modulating consciousness into its transcendental setting. This is just exactly what meditation is about.

At this stage, it gradually occurs to one that indeed one does inherit from the genes of the entire physical universe, including the stars, the galaxies, and cosmic rays. One inherits from other dimensions of the universe as well, such as: the thinking of the universe, the emotion of the universe, its programming, motivation, hopes, expectations, fears, precarity, disappointments, and more generally, its magic.

If the way you interpret the term God is the universe as a being endowed with a body, mind, emotions, consciousness, will, etc., then truly one might say that we carry within us the divine inheritance. Seen holistically, this would also include a material inheritance as transmitted bodily through parents, for indeed our bodies are formations of Planet Earth and made of the fabric of the universe, including the sun, the galaxy, and traced ultimately to the Big Bang. And if we recognize that the universe is not just a physical reality, we will realize that we also inherit from the personality, consciousness and will of that being whose body is the sun. This is the being the Sufis call Prince Huraksh, and who was looked upon by Suhrawardi as an archangel. By expanding the envelope, we would discover our inheritance from that being whose body is our galaxy, the Milky Way, and whom the Sufis consider as a super archangel incorporating the psyche of Prince Huraksh and many more, including yours and mine.

And if this sounds disconcerting, there is more, because we have to include the clusters of galaxies, and ultimately the whole of that being whose body is the physical universe.

This indeed makes sense of the term divine inheritance. Most importantly, what does it take to be able to experience this? The theory will not suffice. Perhaps the clue resides in the fact that while the peripheral and readily retrievable storage of our memory only covers data inputted since our birth (generally after a year or more), the ordinarily unfathomable depths of our unconscious store a host of data that never ceases to overwhelm psychotherapists, and especially those carrying out research in the unconscious, with utter dismay.

Are We Being Tested?

Are we being tested? I have yet to come across someone who does not feel that life is testing him or her, although I am sure there are people who do not think that way.

Some people ascribe the test to God, others to the blind hand of destiny, others to the people in their lives who are giving them a bad time, or who are opposing them. Some feel tested by those they have to serve, or by the health of their own body, or by their inadequacy. But can one really say that our fate is preordained? If that were so, there would be no room for free will.

How aptly do the words of Christ, "Why hast Thou forsaken me?" apply! Al Hallaj, who was tested in the extreme through torture and crucifixion, said, "Thy abandonment of me is a proof of Thy love, for Thou testest most those Thou lovest most." I would propose as an alternative, "Those Thou valueth most," just like a school teacher will give more difficult tasks to the better pupils.

Be it as it is, there seem to be degrees of tests. One tends to believe one's test is just about the worst possible one. Perhaps one of the tests where one's ability is challenged to its limits occurs when one is endeavoring to love a person one dislikes. There may be several reasons for disliking a person. The most obvious one is if that person acts cruelly or ruthlessly towards other people or oneself. The extreme case is torture, physical or psychic, harassment to the point of mind bending, or confusing someone in one's conscience to the point of torment, like making someone recant, or through intimidation or persecution.

The second reason one may dislike a person is often related to the first one; that is, when that person pursues self interest and disregards the wellbeing of another, or unjustly flouts the right of another.

The third reason is blatant dishonesty in the pursuit of that person's own interest. Pursued in the extreme, this behavior might lead towards incriminating another for one's own misdeed and getting away with it, particularly by using bribery, coercion, extortion, blackmail, or foul play. This kind of psychic coercion can work very subtly, surreptitiously destroying another's psyche without the other realizing it. The other tends to give in from sheer mental or emotional exhaustion to a stronger ego, especially if he or she does not have the clarity to nail the hoax of the arguments. Confusion and uncertainty are compounded when these acts are ambiguously mixed with an occasional generous thought and word, perhaps even materialized in an act serving as a screen that seems to vindicate all the less tasteful actions.

One should add to this list a disagreeable person, simply bad tempered, unpleasant and inconsiderate, often someone nurturing a grudge or convinced that he or she has been wronged.

The cases just quoted are obviously extreme; sometimes one can see better by magnifying. There are, of course, degrees of this. The opposite is probably also true: one is oneself guilty of precisely the same attitudes and so there is a double reverberation, thus escalating the psychic tension between two beings. More frequently, those features are more accentuated in one person than another, but present to some degree in both. Consequently, there is wear and tear on the psyche, particularly of those exercising these features less intensely. Conversely, the ascendency exercised by the one excelling in one or more of these features upon the one less so inclined is detrimental to the ego of the former, and is reinforced by the tolerance of the less aggressive one, a tolerance that is tantamount to a condoning.

Obviously, one cannot endorse these attitudes. When they are chronically reiterated, one condemns them in one's mind. Can one judge an action without being judgmental of the person? It is indeed difficult to dissociate the actions from the person, and consequently it becomes most difficult to like the person. Can one dislike a person and still love him or her? Here comes what I believe to be the ultimate test. Pir-o-Murshid Inayat Khan says, "We are tested in life in our love." That is the rub. That is the message of Christ.

But I think one needs to combine love with detachment, not just love and not just detachment. Surrounding oneself with a zone of silence is a necessary protection, if nothing else, for the psyche, with which one cannot argue logically or ethically, and which registers resentment beyond one's conscious control. Pir-o-Murshid Inayat Khan once said that you can only turn your cheek if there is a buffer protecting the heart; that the heart might love irrespective of the treatment from outside, then one would be acting instead of reacting.

Therefore, love is the prime action. I believe this is the most difficult thing in the world; everyone is tested in exactly this way. This test is more important than *samadhi* or even *samadhi* with open eyes, because it transcends understanding.

On Resentment

I am aware that by challenging people to find room in their heart for those who have offended them, I am arousing in many an obstacle to their wholehearted enlisting of the teaching because many feel that I am asking something which they feel they cannot do. This fosters in many an even worse sense of inadequacy than was already there; so that, instead of helping them, it is placing them in a bind. Confirming that this is the message of Christ still does not do it.

A similar situation arises when one is told by religious authorities that one is a sinner, blowing up one's sense of guilt beyond the tolerable level. One's self image is already bad enough—nothing is gained by making it worse. This may indeed aver itself to be the hitch in spiritual prescriptions: "shoulding" people and thus making them feel uncomfortable. While the intention is good, it does not generate realistic help.

In contrast the psychotherapists propose self acceptance—which would mean that, while one has difficulty with forgiving someone who has done one serious harm, in particular by wounding one's psyche, or while one is struggling with resentment against a person with whom one is continually brushing shoulders and who brings out the worst in one, one feels that one needs to be open to work with it because resentment makes one feel most uncomfortable and festers like a lingering wound, continually bugging and undermining one. Paradoxically, resentment is often surreptitiously linked with guilt: guilt for having allowed oneself to be slighted or abused. Add the guilt of failing to forgive to this, and it becomes intolerable. Most often this guilt feeling is unjustified and can be dismissed by the conscious mind; however, the unconscious brooks no argumentation.

Resentment avers itself here to be written right into the programming of the psyche. It deters one from being the enabler who gives license to a person to do one harm, or for that matter harm somebody else. Therefore with the exception of those cases where the violence or threats of the aggressor have put one in a bind, it is more healthy to recognize and admit failure in having given vent to one's anger, thus unmasking and disarming the culprit, rather than covering up one's resentment even from one's own view because one does not like being cantankerous. Bereft of one's defense system, one is not only vulnerable, but is facilitating malevolence.

Now to deal with both one's resentment and the guilt is difficult to substantiate, because on one hand, one may be indicting oneself unjustifiably, and on the other the mind provides every argument to acquit one. Subliminal feelings need to be unearthed gradually and with enlightened supervision to avoid overstressing by disorienting our already precarious self image. In short, one's resentment or anger or rage needs to be released cautiously from the unconscious. That means identified, recognized, and then skillfully processed by converting rage into outrage—first healing, and then regenerating. If not, it may erupt dramatically, leaving the psyche devastated and stymied.

How does one heal a physical wound? Starting with first aid, one needs to protect from further irritants, which includes infection. Likewise one needs to be sheltered in a protective and supportive psychological environment, feeling cared for. In these circumstances, the regenerative process gets on its way, gradually rebuilding damaged tissues. Similarly, damaged elements of the psyche need to be rebuilt skillfully and painstakingly, and of course it will take its necessary time.

However, sheltering is only half the battle. The regenerative forces of the body expend energy and may require an extra boost; even so with the psyche. Ultimately it is ecstasy that avers itself to be the energy of the psyche. While it might be more conservative to say enthusiasm, ecstasy is the superlative, enthusiasm quickening itself *ad infinitum.* There can be no doubt that it is by admiring something beautiful, or contemplating or accomplishing a valuable deed, that one's bewonderment ardor is aroused. It may be by glorifying the splendor manifesting as the universe, whether or not personified as God, that one sparks one's spirit to ecstasy.

How does one bring oneself to be high when circumstances are disenchanting, at best low key? This is where spirituality affirms itself to be a tonic for the injured psyche rather than a sedative, because the act of glorification unveils the divine status of one's own being—the sense of sacredness that triggers self validation, which in turn permits personal creativity. Since the self image is a totally inadequate image of the psyche, a notion, and therefore is of the nature of imagination, one can work with it creatively.

What is more, the infirmities of the psyche can be diagnosed through their traces in the self image. Pain is the alarm signal that there is some lesion which manifests as a distortion of one's real being. Yet, curiously enough our true being can be retrieved out of this distortion unscathed, exactly as the voice of Caruso, so badly distorted by the recording technology of his time, can be retrieved from the old records. The difference with the psyche is that while the record registers the past, the psyche need not just reinstate its pristine state, but can improve on it. While the template is impervious to any defilement, the psyche is ever recurrent.

The hitch is that one often obstructs this regenerative process by failing to believe that nature has the property not only of restoring itself, but of mutating, and likewise the psyche. And it takes a trauma to set the evolutionary process into brainstorming new ways of being. According to physicist Ilya Prigogine, the evolution from more rudimentary to more sophisticated structures in nature requires a breakdown of the stability achieved in states of equilibrium. He calls the structures thus arrived at, thanks to the disruption of the status quo, dissipative structures. It is the vision of how things could be that saves the structure from irreversible disintegration.

Therefore one needs to not only lend oneself to the regenerative process, but also welcome the strong, sometimes dramatic pummeling of the forces of the cosmic drama upon one. Eventually not only bygones get more and more into bygones even though they may still linger in the twilight of the lighted up area of consciousness (at least one develops the ability to live with the scars), but also one learns to put pain to good use. This is the great art. Many of the handicapped learn to adapt themselves to their disabilities, and some even compensate for their inability with enhanced acuity, as for example a blind piano tuner—or, like Brahms, to capitalize on pain, using it as a catalyst to enhance inspiration.

What can meditation propose at this stage? In the first place, if indeed emotion calls for a conceptualization of the problem and the conceptualization escalates the emotion into overacting, one can gauge the wisdom of the *rishis* about questioning one's assessments, thus avoiding that the emotional charge slips off the handle. The danger is that under the emotional overstress, the thinking gets awry and the psyche runs amok into unrealistic fantasies.

But the crunch of the matter is that by putting conceptualizations on hold, one releases a whole different dimension of thinking: the intuitive mode. One substitutes feed-forward for feed-back. One scans the events from the vantage point of the programming rather than trying to infer the programming from an analysis of the events.

We are talking of a noncommonplace mode of understanding called transcendent cognizance, not based upon the feedback of experience, but upon the properties of our own thinking which functions on the same principles as that of the thinking of the universe, except infinitely less adequately.

Some psychotherapists disentangle their patients from their conceptualizations by asking them to say how they feel rather than what they think about their problem. The added advantage here is that the focus is now in the heart.

Of course it is true that ultimately one is tested in one's love. It is one's love that has been wounded, violated, desecrated. There has been a betrayal of the pure love of the early days. The innocence has been sullied. Love has soured into a paradoxical love-hate syndrome. Here lies the acid test. Can one love a person whose actions or behavior has devastated one, or that one condemns, or abhors?

Does one have the strength to scan one's mind to provide excuses for them, mitigating circumstances to ease one's wrath? Such as: they were badly brought up; they are spoilt brats; they are struggling for self esteem, and I am the scapegoat; their genetic package was flawed. Combining these would require a difficult coordination of left brain/right brain activity. The danger is that in trying to do this, intellectually the left brain takes over right brain functions, so that one does not really love, but tries to believe one does because one is enjoined to.

The answer would therefore be for the right brain to take over, so that there is no need to try to provide an excuse for a person. This is the unconditional love. One's love for one's child will overcome any criticism or admonishing in one's mind. Such is the power of love—it triumphs over the mind. Where the right brain prevails, one does not have to provide mitigating arguments, one zooms on the good points of a person. People who manage this become very charismatic and have the makings to be successful in life by mastering the art of dealing with people, rather than dismissing them from one's heart. And what is more, by dint of some ironical divine wit: here lies the secret of being high!

Furthermore, it is helpful to grasp clearly the distinction between struggling to control things or not trying to control but letting a sense of orderliness and sovereignty operate, where one's higher self takes over. For example, it is realizing that Planet Earth feels and thinks through one or rather in one, that Leonardo da Vinci's inventiveness or Bach's attunement, or Einstein's insight are features of the thinking and feeling not just of that being that is Planet Earth, but also of that being that is the universe and which some call God. Precisely the same is true of *our* thinking and feeling and willing, except that it gets limited, sometimes distorted by being funneled down.

This is why people find it difficult to forgive. No matter how much one wills, one cannot overcome one's resentment and heal the pain by one's own personal effort. In fact the will can put one in a bind by causing one to hate oneself for hating another and not being able to avoid it.

Resentment degenerates into hatred and gets transmuted by heroism. You cannot tell yourself, or, for that matter, anyone else, that you or they "should" be a hero. One volunteers one's heroism when the call for service is sounded, or one does not. Giving vent to the latent hero in one is ultimate fulfillment. It elicits one's need to see and fulfill a purpose in one's life. What is more, in releasing this need, one is honoring a dimension of one's being that one treasures as representing a higher value. This is where meditation will ultimately help one overcome resentment, after processing it.

But it is giving vent to actuating one's role in life in dedication to service that triggers the discovery of the more transcendental dimensions of one's being, heretofore unknown and latent. This is discovering by doing. The confidence gained by the discovery of these strata of one's being upgrades one's performance. Often, dedicating oneself to service will prove to be therapeutic in overcoming the side effects of resentment.

There can be no doubt that the key to safeguarding one's self image from further inroads lies in considering it holistically. This includes the more cosmic and especially transcendental dimensions of one's being, where one's self image is crowned in something of the nature of the splendor that is behind all creativity and which is trying to manifest and actuate itself in the universe. Then one must reconcile this aspect, which is latently present in the depths of one's being, with the inadequacy born of having the support system of one's personality made of the fabric of the evolutionary process occurring on Planet Earth. This confirms Pir-o-Murshid Inayat Khan's aphorism regarding reconciling "the aristocracy of the soul with the democracy of the ego."

Thus, honoring the divine status of one's being proves to be the ultimate lifebuoy. It keeps one afloat through the crisis in one's self esteem facing resentment triggered by self pity, and thus rescuing one from sinking into the bitterness of hatred with its epidemic of violence and the resultant cruelty wreaked upon one's fellow beings.

Love

Yes, we all nurture wounds deep down. When lovingly tended, these may simply leave a scar. Somewhere in our psyche is the chipped pottery, or as Shams Tabriz says, "The palace in a ruin." It is also the masterpiece in the making. The flaws in an antique are a guarantee of authenticity and may carry their particular charm, if not too devastated. That ongoing work of artistry that is our personality is worth all our efforts in working with it, for the same pain that can blemish our personality can act as a creative force, burnishing it into an object of delight.

Our personal version or concept of pain acts destructively upon us when we wallow in it and fail to see the pain of the one we think is causing us this difficulty, particularly when our anger prevents us from working things out with the other. Pain is never an isolated situation; what we look upon as our pain is our participation in a network of pain that may well extend to the whole humanity. The sting of pain is in the isolation in which we tend to enclose ourselves in our own self pity: our self-inflicted loneliness, which refuses to see how the other feels or felt.

As we dig more deeply into our own and the other's conscious and unconscious motivations, each concealing and sometimes precipitating another motivation, we come to realize how ignorance of each other's intentions builds up into a totally phantomized mountain of misassessments, one resting upon the other. As one touches the bottom, where it hurts most, one realizes that the worst pain is caused by being misunderstood, or by misunderstanding the other. Communicating with one another will disclose one's real intentions reciprocally.

Where the probe exposes an intention evidencing a disregard for the other, love is outraged by a feeling of betrayal. The usual outcome is a devalidated self image: one had suspended one's self esteem so precariously upon being loved and the default of love has let one down! Of course, interests cannot always be in sync; people may entertain conflicting aspirations. But love is standing by one another supportively, guarding each other's pride. When admonishing, one should take heed that the thin thread linking you both reciprocally is not unduly stressed. Its only resilience is the power of one's love.

In this nebulous context of our understanding, our love for the "other" becomes easily jeopardized, eclipsed, and even undermined momentarily or irretrievably. This is where only a deep soul understanding of another's feelings can save the slender thread of love from being ripped by the weight of judgment. It is true of course that it is one's love that causes one to overcome one's biased judgment of the other in the first place.

Relationship then avers itself to be a thing of beauty, irrespective of or beyond the personalities building it up. It has a meaningfulness for the universe, built on the sublimation of the mutual pains and joys gained through a respectful and loving exploration of each other's feelings, motivations, ideals, hopes and fears, and need of truth and freedom. When we handle ourselves beautifully in adverse circumstances, they become testing cases upon which each one builds trust in the beauty and meaningfulness of life.

Unconditional Love

There are those with whom we resonate quite naturally by the gift of affinity, or those dear to us whom we admire even if we do not see eye to eye with them. But we are challenged in our capacity to love by those whom we find difficult to love, or who make themselves difficult to love, whose personality we criticize, or whose actions we condemn, those who have treated us unjustly or even abused our confidence. In fact this is precisely where dislike or simply incompatibility escalates to the point of culminating in resentment. It is resentment that constitutes the veil separating us from our celestial counterpart and will block access to our celestial home in the hereafter.

Should one remain encapsulated in one's ego self image with one's love oriented towards the personal dimension of the loved one, one's human love is bound to be vulnerable. One is on tenterhooks as to whether one is still being loved; one may be trying to validate or prove oneself in the eyes of the loved one; or one's love may easily get tarnished by criticism, resentment, or a battle of egos. This is where the wisdom of the perennial spiritual lore bespeaks another dimension and a further all-encompassing perspective, removing the impasse. It consists of including those dimensions of one's being and that of the loved one which one had failed to countenance.

> **The false ego is that which that ego has wrongly conceived. It is not that the false ego is our ego and the true ego is the ego of God. It is that the true ego which is the ego of God has been reduced to a false ego in us.**
>
> **Hazrat Inayat Khan**

By the same token, one opens to a perspective whereby one sees how everything and every being are interconnected. This is traditionally called the divine point of view—let us call it trying to see as one imagines the universe would see—everything in reciprocal context rather than in the content of one's personal grasp.

According to the Sufis, the loved one becomes the mirror in which one sees oneself, in all the dimensions of one's being in which the bounty of the universe converges.

> **Behold the world entirely comprised in yourself. The world is man and man is a world ... . The heart of a barley seed conceals a hundred harvests. Behold the world kneaded as dough, the angel with the fiend, the cherubim with Satan.**
>
> **Mahmood Shabistari**

Of course, the more sensitive we are, the more idealistic, the more we entertain a nostalgia for beauty, unaware, usually, of the fact that this is the way in which our intuitive sense of the divine perfection, of which we are an imperfect exemplar, is disclosed to us in form.

The dervishes highlight the dichotomy: splendor (as beauty) and power (as majesty)—"masculine" and "feminine" archetypes.

> **When God manifests His glory to a man's heart so that His majesty predominates, he feels awe (*haybat*), But when God's beauty predominates, he feels proximity (*uns*)... . There is a difference between one who is burned by His majesty in the fire of awe and one who is illuminated by His beauty in the light of contemplation.**
>
> **Hujwiri, Kashf al-Mahjub, tr. Nicholson, p. 376**

This is why the personal dimension of love is associated with beauty and majesty, in their more overt expression in their physical form, but more so in their subtle mode.

This is to be grasped in the splendor that transpires through that which appears, rather than in that which appears. In its more advanced mode, it is the beauty or majesty of a human personality.

But to grasp it in another, as indeed in oneself, we need to come to terms with the fact that we are many-tiered, and that these many-faceted effigies of our being are intermeshed. Moreover they change rapidly in accordance with our thoughts and attunements. Furthermore, let us realize that the deep core of our being remains immaculate within its own defilement. Should we identify with it, we will grasp beauty transpiring across ugliness

Consequently one will have understanding and compassion for the desperation or compulsiveness in a person who is awkwardly and counterproductively struggling for self esteem at our cost—or ourselves at the cost of another. Should one overcome the constraint of one's personal identity, and also that of the loved one (thinking that one is a "condition of God" will have that effect) then, instead of being the target of our judgment, the personal dimension of the loved one becomes the stepping stone leading to the One who represents one's ideal. That is the One whom one really loves.

When this stage is attained, love outreaches its personal dimension and, prevailing over the personal joy and pain of personal love, sparks ecstasy.

Actually, one is really searching for one's self in the loved one, only to find that it is the Divine Beloved, Self-disclosing by manifesting and actuating in the loved one, that helps us to find our real selves.

For the Sufis, our quest to know "who we are" is our response to the divine nostalgia.

The Hadith Qudsi says:

I was a secret treasure and I loved to be known.

It does not say: I wished to be known—therefore the motivation was not the curiosity of knowing, but love.

For the Sufis, the original impulse setting off the momentous process of existence was love, and the mystic's love for God is simply the response to God's love.

And God in divine perfection turned towards that which was in God's own Self: the attribute of nostalgia. This attribute was also a form within God's Essence. Imagine you saw something beautiful in your essence and you were enchanted by this feature in your essence!

> **Having thus radiated, He spirited a person *Huwa, Huwa* (Himself). He considered it for a time amongst His times. Then He saluted this effigy for a time amongst His times. Then He spoke to this human prototype, and complemented it on its good appearance. Then He rejoiced about the good tidings, reaching beyond everything that is knowable or not-knowable. Then He lauded it and glorified it and appointed it as the elect.**
>
> **al Hallaj, Kitab al Ishk.**
>
> **Cf. Massignon, *The Passion of al Hallaj*, Princeton, 1982.**

If indeed love is the magical trigger that sets off the explosion of life as the cosmos, it remains the mysterious imperative spurring our human endeavors, evidenced by the scruple of creative minds for perfection. It points to our ponderings concerning the meaningfulness of our lives, our strivings, our frustrations, our disappointments, our disenchantment, and perhaps our re-enchantment. Moreover, the power of unconditional love gives us the resolve to uphold a person's pride while acquiescing to their flaws and follies. The great paradox is that, by loving one's ideal of God espied in a person, one helps that person to honor his or her real self. Therefore it is love that makes God a reality.

Dreams

Throughout the United States, people are getting together in groups to discuss and interpret their dreams. This is a symptom of our times. We have become more realistic than before and seek to harvest aspects and dimensions of ourselves that we know nothing about or preferred to overlook. We sometimes send a pressing message across the borderline from the uncharted reaches of the unconscious into the pigeonholes of our mental constructs. These have a disquieting effect upon our projects and challenge our rationalizations, for the unconscious harbors an entirely different mode of thinking from the usual, encompassing wholeness. That which is deemed as incongruous by the middle range thinking of our day consciousness acquires meaningfulness.

Interpreting dreams with our commonplace logic, particularly considering the temptation of tendentious thinking, may prove dangerously misleading. Freud's attempt to haul unconscious elements to the surface is not without its drawbacks. A deep sea fish emerging at the surface would be bloated and could not feature or function any more according to its nature. Therefore, I would discourage the layman from playing the apprentice sorcerer, and leave the skillful task of interpreting dreams to the trained professional therapist. However, we have a more constructive recourse: dream therapy or, better still, promoting creativity in our dreams as a complement to diagnosis. I am referring to a technique explored and applied in Vedanta and also Sufism. Rather than draw unconscious motivations to the surface of the conscious, one thrusts the light of consciousness into the nebulous unconscious depths.

One of the many activities of our sleep life is simply digesting or regurgitating the residual impressions of the day. No doubt the unconscious can accomplish most of this work more efficiently than conscious volitional action. In like fashion, the motions required to type or play the piano or drive a car are automated. Nature always seems to find a way of insuring an economy of means. But when one makes a mistake, one has to deautomatize the process in order to imprint a correction. Clearly this could be applied to the dreaming process. But could there be a way of exercising an impact on one's dreams?

How about reverie? We call reverie the state in which we are suspended on the threshold between diurnal (day) consciousness and paradoxical sleep (sleep with dreams). We know that if we shift slightly into sleep, we have no impact on our imagery and if we slip back into diurnal consciousness, we have some handle and incentive in the exercise of our imagination. We can steer it. Depending upon how close we are to the threshold, we may enjoy having more sway over the flow of imagery or find ourselves overwhelmed and willy-nilly invaded by it, not unlike steering a ship in a heavy sea.

Nidra Yoga is the art of maintaining oneself at the threshold, which means that one is keeping the door open between the diurnal and the sleep state. One remembers one's daytime mode of thinking and how things appeared when one was conscious of the material world, while on the other hand, one is aware of one's dreams. By maintaining the continuity of the Ariadnean thread of consciousness, one is able not only to remember the pictures projected in one's dreams, but also the multidimensional personality that one assumed. What is more, one is able to influence one's dreams, and so sow seeds in the deep recesses of one's personality that will eventually germinate in a tangible way. This would offer a means of fostering creativity under cover of the unconscious. Our conscious mind would have discounted the possibility of developing superlative qualities and would therefore be blocked.

A new technique teaches people to learn languages while listening to music. The language curriculum is imbedded in the music subliminally, so that the pupil is never consciously aware of it; yet when the same words are said aloud, they are recognized. Besides residual impressions of day experience, one may recognize several tiers in the dream world: unconscious or unavowed fears or wishes, features about oneself that the unconscious seems to aim at pointing out, or resolutions of problems one failed to see. Probing into the elusive layers of our dream world, we will discover vestiges of impressions that tell us of other spheres of reality in which our psyche is immersed, yielding a cryptic hint of what they could be like. Among these, one may spotlight the emergent process of self creativity. To grasp this eruption of unconscious elements, it is useful to intuit the way the soul sees itself projected in our personality, rather than try to glean something of the nature of the soul as viewed from the vantage point of our personal self image.

Under the label "soul," I earmark little known dimensions of our psyche which appear as more stable than the better known aspects of our psyche—perhaps even eternal. The secret of affecting this is first to reverse time, and then to invert time; that is, first a retroactive mode of thinking, recalling reminiscence further and further back in time, then shifting one's thinking into a dimension of time not generally understood. One shifts the setting of one's consciousness from thinking of events viewed in their sequence, to grasping the know-how gleaned from the events and deleting from one's mind the contingent circumstances. This is called in computer language, "input processing" in which the substrate of the experience is eternalized as information. One likes to refer to these levels of our being and of the universe to account for such phenomena transpiring in dreams as premonitions, hunches, visions of celestial beings, or the landscapes of the soul described by numberless mystics. These impressions of a nonverbal, pre-logical, spaceless and timeless nature appear to evidence an *a priori* level of knowledge, in which the soul grasps archetypes whose exemplifications constitute the subject matter of our middle-range mental activities. Here is the level of meditative activity taking place in dreams.

The parallel between the cryptic psychic activity conducted in sleep and meditation has been painstakingly elucidated in the *Mandukya Upanishad* and in descriptions of visionary experiences left by Sufis such as Shahabuddin Suhrawardi (*maqrul*), Avicenna, Najmuddin Kubra, Farid-du-Din Attar, and numerous others. Imagery presents the advantage of bypassing conceptualization. The self-actuating formative processes originating in the deep sleep state transpire as special forms in the dream state. The dream process projects aspects of one's self into landscapes, and even into beings that appear as other than oneself in the dream scenario, sometimes as animals, or even cars or planes. Inversely, the prevalent circumstances are sometimes so much part of one's self image that one fails to detect the fact that these are circumstances impacting one from the psychological environment. Hence the ambiguity of our dream experience calling for skilled expertise. Using therapy or creativity rather than diagnosis, one may train oneself to work with these landscapes, even as an artist might be given an unfinished painting to complete or even to alter drastically.

How does one proceed? Let us remember that all creativity is a crossover between "listening in" to the birthing process of the universe emerging in oneself, and the way one customizes this universal emergence by dint of one's own incentive, inventiveness and exploratory drive. An example of this would be found in a group of musicians improvising. If each were expressing individual fantasy, without listening to the others, it would result in a cacophony. If each were to toe the line to a leader, they would not be personally creative. But if each would be sensitive to the overall mood of the group as such, and at the same time contribute personally to the richness of the whole, they would be demonstrating a creative model.

Now, let us see how this would apply to working creatively with the human personality. It would involve one thrusting the searchlight of consciousness into the dark unconscious—like Orpheus—to intercept the tender shoots of qualities still in the formative process before they emerge into the personality as idiosyncrasies. Then reverse the process and apply one's will to auto-suggest to the unconscious will to shape these as one would like to have them, rather as one might cultivate flowers or breed animals by bending the formative process so that they depart from their state in the wild. This is culture: where the human creativity acts as an extension of the divine creativity, carrying it a few steps further in the evolutionary drive.

In order to effect the first step, one needs to learn how to turn one's consciousness within, as it were—to discover an inverted space.

A Dream in a Dream

Several components of your being are trying to speak to you in your dreams. Or is it that what you think you are is interrogating your deeper self, only to find that the layers of your being are part of a many-tiered puzzle in infinite regression. Will you ever reach the elusive depths? Untold obstructions block your access. Yet those thwarted pieces of your being beg for recognition, cry for expression—to play their role in fashioning your being. Imagine what we are missing out by neglecting to listen in!

Thoughts, emotions, and images are jumbled like radio waves in the atmosphere, or like eddies on a lake. To your day thinking, you only express a slither of what you imply. And what you imply eludes your own awareness. Maybe it's the job of the shaman among the wiser minds around you to earmark a flash of the emotions behind your words, your semantics, the effigies of yourself which you project in your narratives, the myths concealed behind your reality. But the wise are rare and far between, and one is indeed privileged to have any such wizards around. So one is left with the alternative of falling back on the wise person mysteriously lurking within one's dreams or aroused in rare moments of vivid lucidity.

The forced tempo of "real life" estranges one from dreams. Our longing for life to be a dream come true is condemned to the wastepaper basket of utopia except—except—if one is prepared to fight for it at the cost not only of great strife and stress, but pain to oneself and others, and of course incurring the scourge of being labeled a freak. On the other hand, society marshals people within the limits of the common denominator called the "norm," which operates as a salutary safety valve against whimsical, incongruous aberrations. It is the correspondence of our dreams to our everyday life that guarantees their relevance and saves our creativity from the entropy of erratic fantasizing.

A whole barrage stands between the deep yearning of one's soul and the "real world": our involvements, the desires of our bodies, of our hearts, of our minds, our likes and dislikes, our vulnerable self image, our upbringing, our conditioning, sheer survival. One tends to slip down to the lowest common denominator, the path of least resistance. One would no doubt find it easier if chances opened up to give one an opportunity to prove oneself to be a hero. But they do not come to us in that way, so we need to create those opportunities.

In your pensive ponderings, scan yourself, and confront your motivations with the power of truth to eliminate insidious self deception and justification. But while revealing its secret, step by step when cross-examined, by virtue of its need to parade a masquerade of validation, our psyche covers up the deeper frustrated motivations conspiring in our soul. Unless you succeed in piercing this smoke screen in meditation (or hypnosis), it is in your dreams that some clues to these deep springheads of your soul may erupt. Images, effigies, scenarios blurred or distinct may project themselves on the screen of your dormant mind with sufficient force to buffet your memory when waking up. The chances are that our interpretations of them are afflicted by wishful thinking or sheer conceit or dusky misgivings.

In deep meditation, turning within, you may be able to spot a deeper motivation that your psyche will concede—

the cause spurring the cause. Turning upwards, you may grasp lots of different values, sometimes at loggerheads, sometimes reinforcing one another. Is it your quest for beauty? Is it your pursuit of excellence? Is it your honoring truthfulness? Is it your concern for compassion? Is it joy? Is it peace? Is it love? Is it accomplishment? Is it wisdom? Enlightenment? Freedom? These may conflict and not tolerate any compromise. Your soul may be pummeled, pulled in opposing directions as in a tug of war, or etiolated in a challenging quandary. In no way could you expect to solve the riddle you are faced with, because everything is important, everywhere you see priorities and priorities of priorities.

Your dreams may however prove to be good counsel because they bypass the mind's commonplace rationalizations. The key is accessing your dreams through your meditations. Meditation skills may be devised to autosuggest to yourself a pilgrimage into your dream world.

But watch out for the emotions lurking behind the imagery of your dreams' fleeting incongruous effigies. This is where the message incubated in your dreams explodes with the greatest thrust. Gauge its compelling urgency, its insidious forcefulness. It may catch you unaware, not realizing the importance of the emotional need it conveys to you. The emotions of the heart are imperative and cannot always brook their inability to adapt to real-life situations. But the nostalgia of the soul is overwhelmingly compulsive when unmasked, and arouses a challenge to the status quo of one's life and the established order routinely built over years of dedicated hard work, perhaps because it affects one's self validation so deeply. This nostalgia erupts in every recess of one's mind, and sparks the emotion of the heart which delights in rising from the personal emotions and responding to its more cosmic source.

To access the emotions at the soul level, the ordinary dream will not suffice. It takes the tour de force of awakening from your dream into a "dream within a dream." You dream that you are dreaming of images, while realizing that these are mere projections of your creative mind. But at the level where you are, there are no forms, no metaphors, no mental constructs—just ecstasy and realization.

Attaining Peace

There is no doubt that desire brings one down into the body, mind, and personality, wreaking upon one dependence and uncertainty, which are inimical to peace. One cannot reach one's higher self without having found *rida*, a satisfied state, a state free from longing, pining. Otherwise, one is pulled in two directions. There is turmoil and ambiguity.

The circumstances in life in the world reinforce desires, especially bodily desires for modern comforts and permissiveness. One becomes addicted, whereas the wilderness has a decongesting, detoxifying effect. Peacefulness comes with the recognition that it takes time to mature spiritually, just as it takes time for a plant to grow or a fruit to ripen. It cannot be forced. Furthermore, time and forbearance are needed to painstakingly unravel the knots in relationships.

Where there is truth, there is peace of mind, giving one serenity. If something is not quite right, much as one might justify it, somehow one gets sapped from within and feels uneasy and jittery. If you agonize over your problems, it is as though you were pulling on a knot instead of unraveling it. Unraveling requires patience, perseverance and an indomitable spirit.

There is a Greek legend according to which a village treasured a mysterious knot. It was predicted that whoever was able to unravel that knot would conquer the East. Alexander tried, but in desperation, cut the knot. This was the famous Gordian knot. Alexander showed the same precipitation in penetrating the East without ever conquering it, though governing the countries he crossed.

Slashing a problem, mutilating its niceties will not resolve it any more than tugging on the knot. The knot is relationship, which is actually part of a tapestry, a network of inter-relationships, each related to each other. It is easier to tie than untie. When the knots become tangled, one easily becomes devastated, frustrated, or angry. In one's impatience, one makes a hash of something, which, if dealt with painstakingly, would carry the evidence of beauty. (When one's hair is combed, the strands run parallel to each other, oriented meaningfully, in concert. They do not cross one another. The strands of hair are still relating; the relationship has become harmonious.) One does not have to forego or abandon a relationship. It is still there, transformed, pacified, and maybe transfigured.

Pir-o-Murshid once said, "The relationship between two people is like a bridge through which God meets God, like the hands of a child trying to clasp the arms of a doll through the windows of the doll's house."

As one finds peace within, especially during a retreat, one gains trust in the power written in all life. This power can right, restore, even redeem, and ultimately resurrect the crises or collapses which foster fluctuations within situations that might have become sclerosed in us or remained mental binds. One learns passive volition at a soul level. That is why the Prophet Mohammed said, "Return pacified." Therefore, in order to reach the eternal cosmic vortex of one's being, one needs to sort out one's situations in life.

How can one reconcile the absence of desire that makes for the peace which enables one to grasp one's eternal being, with Murshid's teaching in Sufism that every desire originates in the divine desire for fulfillment in manifestation?

The soul in its human condition is like a bird. Most have to descend to the earth to fulfill their bodily needs. Some fowl like turkeys and chickens are so earthbound that they hardly can fly at all. Hawks catch their prey on the ground, falcons in mid air and then perch to consume it. Some, like the stormy petrel, will stay on wing for weeks, perhaps months, only diving briefly for food. If one exhibits the features of the legendary *Simurgh* by identifying with one's real being after having passed through the death of the ego, one can dwell within the haunts of men and communicate to them something of the states and spheres one has experienced. Those witnessing this will be inspired and illuminated to their own sense of *déjà vu*. Every person has the capacity of intuiting existence beyond body, mind and personality.

The knot may have resulted from having tried to pull in two directions, pursuing objectives that are incompatible. One is trying to reconcile the irreconcilables, a set of terms I often use. What this stands for needs redefining. It blows the trumpet of a challenge. It reflects the attitude of someone who is pursuing mastery at all costs. One of the dangers with mastery is overstress. The danger lies in displaying reckless optimism. One forces the issue by a *tour de force*, rather than letting the natural forces flow unfettered, only to find that use of force was unrealistic. Some irreconcilables cannot be reconciled. It could be like throwing a challenge at fate, involving others irresponsibly. Of course, it could feature genuine heroism and stoicism, but one must guard against the temptation of an ego trip. To allay this, Pir-o-Murshid teaches balance. Do not overstress, but with the power gained by one achievement or obstacle overcome, you may test yourself with something a little more stressful.

The terms I so often use refer to words of St. Augustine: *conjunctio oppositorum*, the union of the opposites. Scientists call it complementarity. For St. Thomas Aquinas, God is static and dynamic at the same time. The present day holistic view is that we are both transient and eternal, part of the totality and carrying the totality potentially in us. Pir-o-Murshid says, "We are divine perfection suffering from human limitation."

We can have, at the same time, the greatest pride in our divine inheritance together with the greatest humility, because of the limitation that we impose upon that perfection. It is difficult to reconcile these in ourselves; therefore, it certainly is a challenge. But the acceptance of the limitation, which is a surrender rather than a challenge, brings us into balance. First a little pride and a little humility, then a little more on both sides as one gains the power to handle the dichotomy.

Chapter 7

Addiction and Freedom

Meditation as a Factor in Addiction Reduction

The escalating number of case histories on recovery from addiction confirms that medication, while undoubtedly effective in reducing and even removing the physical withdrawal symptoms, most times leaves the patient high and dry, emotionally depleted, in a kind of moral limbo. The reason is that a therapy limited to the physical processes fails to address the deep psychological motivations behind the craving, whether it is alcoholism, drug abuse, cigarette addiction, masochism, sadism, overeating, sexual perversions, or the quest for trance.

These motivations present themselves as an antinomy: on one hand a need for an emotional high, in the hope that it may lead to access a more cosmic and transcendental and nobler dimension of ourselves—and indeed of the universe—than our commonplace one; conversely an escape not just from the platitudes of the humdrum daily routine of most people and the ensuing low-key emotional attunement incurred, but from the despair attendant upon the sense of powerlessness to control one's life in which most people find themselves jammed.

The same applies to meditation, which paradoxically offers a very complementary therapy to the medical one required for effective addiction remission. The craving for an emotional drug-free opiate indicates a desire for an escape from a sense of inadequacy in dealing with one's responsibilities.

For this reason, the Sufis seek an emotional high "in life" rather than beyond life by advocating modes of meditation that aim at awakening in life In fact, the key issue is our desperate need for the sacred, both in and beyond the universe, including ourselves. Failing the fulfillment of this need, our self esteem is eroded.

What do we mean by sacredness? An example: one is forcibly aware of the sacred when one is humiliated: a violation of the divine status of one's being; the same applies to the outrage aroused in us when the divine status of others is defiled and profaned.

Our sense of the sacred is inextricably linked with our concept of God. One needs to grasp that one's higher self is coextensive with that aspect of God which the Twelve Steps recovery program calls the Higher Power. It may be helpful to visualize a model: think of radial lines that have a center in common, or alternately apply the holistic paradigm. Furthermore one needs to shift between the cosmic and the personal dimension of oneself (one's nature in contradiction to one's character). Since we limit God by our conceptualization of God, it is important for us to explore how our human psyche actually projects its experience of the "superlative" in terms that are meaningful to it.

The notion of God conveyed by the unconscious is embodied in (i) the archetype of the nurturing mother, our evolutionary underpinning, (ii) the archetype of the father, our divine inheritance, (iii) the archetype of the child within, our recurrent rebirthing, and (iv) the archetype of the alter ego, the enriching cross pollination with "other than ourselves."

The transference to the actual mother, father, child-within and partner is most times fraught with fulfillment or frustration, or both simultaneously. Dependence upon these must, in the very nature of things, be followed by severance with the ensuing sense of loss. Alternately one feels a need to free oneself from this dependence, in both cases in order to find one's own self-actuating self whereby one arrives at a healthy mature relationship.

Sufism therefore values both the fulfillment and enrichment attained by involvement, and the invulnerability and overview gained by freedom from involvement. Sufis, most particularly, foster the great art of cross pollination between the two.

For the Sufis, our need for involvement in life with people and in circumstances, is the way in which the divine nostalgia works through and *as* us to build a beautiful world of beautiful people. Craving is considered to be a distortion of the divine nostalgia for existentiation, where the divine impulse has been lost to sight. And our need for freedom from dependence upon the existential underpinning of our lives, exemplified in asceticism, evidences the conditioning to the more advanced modes of the programming of the universe. We participate in this by our incentive in "fluctuating the orderliness of the universe from a state of equilibrium" (Ilya Prigogine). If perpetuated, equilibrium would stifle the evolutionary advance. The Sufis illustrate the quest for freedom as a participation in the divine act of unification. In doing so, the know-how gained by experience at the existential level is recycled into the programming of the universe.

Dr. Stan Grof's research reinforces our hunch about the pain and sense of loss in the severance and weaning from the mother, or alternately the frustration because of a paucity of nurturing. Thus frustrated, the child's resort to the father is obstructed by the fear of ego loss under the constraint of authority. Moreover, to find fulfillment in partnership, the adolescent needs to attain a certain degree of self actualization. Hence the need for dependence is transferred to a surrogate prop or crutch: alcohol, psychedelic drug, tranquilizer, cigarette, or otherworldliness that addresses one's need to find a relief from the strain of taking responsibility. This dalliance with one's powerlessness betrays complacency.

One comes to the realization through the Twelve Steps that one is fooling the body and mind by failing to acknowledge that one's crutch is self defeating. One is then ready to uncover within oneself the dimensions of one's being from which healing may be mustered.

The Sufis recognize four dimensions of healing energy:

1) an earthly dimension which operates a repair process, restitution to the originally unimpaired state (homeostasis)

2) an inner dimension from which a regenerative force emerges which will revitalize the cells of the body and the emotions of the psyche

3) a cosmic dimension from which energy may be availed of from the environment

4) a transcendent dimension from which a paradoxical energy, acting as a catalyst releasing latent energy, may quicken one's being in a sudden flash of instant healing. This is called the Holy Spirit.

Let us now examine more closely the four archetypes of the unconscious referred to earlier, and outline the corresponding meditation practices with a view to exploring the manner in which they may effectively help in the addiction recovery program.

The Mother Archetype

Our resort to the mother archetype evidences our need to be both shielded and nurtured owing to our sense of powerlessness and inadequacy, or at least owing to our sense of the limits to our personal power or capabilities. Our dependence is compensated by the quality of dependability embodied in the mother archetype: reliability and stability against excessive turbulence or uncertainty. This stability also requires and encourages an enhanced sense of practicality, the importance of ensuring the practical underpinning of our enterprises, with the inevitable quest for material comfort.

Mother Earth—nature—presents an essential feature ensuring homeostasis: the tendency for the reinstatement of a state of equilibrium that has been disturbed, a repair faculty written right into the system. It is conditioning and habit-forming, which is an essential factor in learning. By the same token, the disadvantage of this stability could be excessive conformism, traditionalism, even fundamentalism. Paradoxically, adherence to traditional modes of worship safeguards and fosters the attunement to the sacred in age-old ceremonies.

It follows inevitably that the religious practices enlisting the importance of the mother aspect of God are embodied in earth rituals, such as that of Persephone, sometimes leading to orgiastic rites as in the Greek mystery cult of the Maenads.

Yogis harness this telluric energy in the Kundalini practices whereby the upward surge of nerve impulses from the bottom of the spine is fostered. This is called kindling in neurology, reversing the more usual energy flow of nerve impulses initiated by the will which generally flows downwards.

Typical meditations illustrating refuge in the mother archetypes are achieved by practices enhancing an oceanic sense of oneness with the environment or the universe at large, which the French poet Rimbaud called *participation mystique.* The astronaut Rusty Schweikart related his experience in a space walk: "You are out there, no frames, no boundaries... your identity is with that whole thing."

In the Buddhist practice, liberation from dependence upon the physical, mental and psychological underpinning of our being is achieved by clearly distinguishing between the observing self on one hand and the body, thinking, emotions and psyche, on the other. One systematically withdraws one's identity with these elements by considering them as "other" than oneself and by identifying with pure consciousness. The next step is withdrawing one's sense of identity from personal consciousness to an impersonal "I." Clearly, by freeing oneself from the limitations of one's notion of oneself by dependence upon one's existential underpinning (the mother archetype), one awakens into cosmic identity. Cosmic identity is not, however, to be confused with transcendent identity, as found in the *arupa-jhanas* of Buddhism and in the Yogic *samadhi*. Therefore it might be defined as self transcendence.

In contradistinction, the Judeo-Christian-Islamic traditions, and of course Tantra, include the body and psyche as integral aspects of our total self, but distinguish between those elements in us that we should reject and those that we may make good use of but which need to be transmuted.

The Father Archetype

The quest for the father archetype fulfills the need to discover the archetype of the exemplar. It evidences our innate hunch regarding transcendence, which the French mathematician Henri Poincaré describes as our intuition that there always is a number greater than the greatest number we have envisioned so far and this in infinite regress. The same applies to time and space and accounts for our sense of perfection.

The practices illustrating the quest for the father archetype envisioned as "beyond the beyond" are typically embodied in the Yogic search for *samadhi*: awakening beyond the existential realm by unmasking the hoax of our mind games, upgrading the commonplace conditioning of our middle-range thinking by substituting a more sophisticated software that exhibits cosmic and transcendental dimensions more in keeping with the thinking of the universe. Rather than taking for granted that one awakens out of the sleep perspective into diurnal (day) consciousness, Shankaracharya advocates awakening out of the perspective of diurnal consciousness, first into the dream perspective (orthodox sleep), then into deep sleep (paradoxical sleep) where the object of consciousness, whether perceptual or imaginary, has fallen out of focus. Consciousness evacuated of its content evaporates, giving vent to the awakening of intelligence which is actually the ground or seedbed of consciousness.

It offers direct access to the thinking of the universe without reference to its actuation in existential experience. One discovers that if, for example, the physicist is able to make sense of the programming of the universe, it is because human thinking is isomorphic and co-extensive (that is, of an identical nature with and holistically enmeshed in) with the thinking of the universe. Isaac Newton said "I think after God's thinking." This is transcendence, not to be confused with self transcendence, encountered in Vipassana, where consciousness has spilled beyond the boundaries of the notion of the self but has not petered out.

Typical involvement in the father archetype may be found in people who have difficulty in taking responsibility and need to be guided or enjoy being dominated, even sometimes by a despot (which accounts for typical political incongruities), and also in quite a few cases of guru worship. This may equally be encountered in excessive value or credulity attached to belief systems based on religious authority or institutions. God is looked upon as irascible, fate as irrevocable. The result is fatalism and the downplay of personal initiative.

The father archetype appears thus as threatening to the ego will. This inevitably manifests in resentment for authority and a defiance of orderliness; one dethrones the father. The result is slackness, slovenliness, permissiveness, even unruliness and hooliganism, culminating in a lack of self respect. However a Higher Power is yielded to when there is no alternative, when every effort of one's incentive has failed. This spells surrender—the return of the prodigal son.

By some ironic paradox, that which ventured to challenge the divine will (ascribed to fate), avers itself to be one's vulnerable puffed-up display of masquerading personal power, actually masking one's fear of exposing one's inadequacy under the smoke screen of addiction. This personal evaluation of one's inadequacy, vulnerability and fallibility is based upon one's having convinced oneself that one is powerless to control one's life. Both assessments are of course relatively fallacious because they are based upon (i) one's failing to grasp what is being enacted behind one's problems; (ii) one's identifying with one's personality rather than grasping the cosmic ground of one's being attained in the appropriate meditation; and (iii) one's looking at things from the personal vantage point rather than either extending one's consciousness into its cosmic dimension or awakening beyond the act of consciousness into the realization grasped by the act of intelligence attained in the transcendental modes of meditation.

When confronted, the Trojan horse of make believe and self deception sustained by the illusion meted out by the drug, admits to having been a ploy. When fully broken down, this subterfuge will yield to an awakened respect for the sovereignty of the orderliness behind the programming of the universe, which manifests as the divine operation embodied right into one's own higher will.

Resolution may be arrived at by integrating ego personality with the ground of one's personality which the Sufis ascribe to divine inheritance. We have difficulty in achieving this because of the obvious incompatibility between the splendor of our eternal self, and the inadequacy and sometimes paucity of our personal idiosyncrasies. Pir-o-Murshid Inayat Khan addresses this need "to reconcile the aristocracy of the soul with the democracy of the ego."

Resolution may be attained by availing oneself of the virtues of passive volition, that is letting the divine operation have its way while at the same time asserting one's will. This would tally with Ilya Prigogine's "fluctuating the equilibrium of the orderliness behind the universe," rather than "doing one's own thing" without regard for that orderliness. It would be like a yachtsperson or hang glider pilot harnessing the wind to the pursuit of an objective. The art of achieving this consists in clearly discerning the difference between the personal dimension of one's will and a more cosmic and sovereign dimension of that very will. This is mastery rather than just stubbornly forcing one's will upon situations willy-nilly.

It would also mean integrating the perspective of awakening beyond life with that of awakening in life, which is transcendence with the oceanic feeling of being holistically enmeshed with all things. Ideally this would mean being clearly aware of the nature of the physical phenomena surrounding one and experienced in the very cells of one's own body, and equally of the reality of the circumstances and situations affecting not just oneself, but humanity. One would be aware in the global environment at large while at the same time grasping what is enacted behind the scenario of life, intuiting the programming behind the events, letting the thinking behind the universe transpire in one's thinking as in *samadhi*, while at the same time grasping the values at stake, the personal issues involved, and unmasking the mind games and their guile and sham.

The Archetype of the Child Within

The child within proves to be our saving grace when, alone in suffering from a poor self image, we pine over our profligacy. When confronting ourselves in all truthfulness, our acknowledgement of guilt may lead to a sense of having profaned the child within. This is a frequent occurrence in alcoholics and other addicts, and appears irreversible. The converse may well occur: namely the feeling of having been defiled by an inappropriate act of another person upon one, as in the case of rape.

There seems to be in psychotherapy a tacit assumption that in these cases the child within has been damaged. Attention needs however to be drawn here to an analogy: the voice of Caruso which was very distorted by the bad technology of the time can today be retrieved owing to our high technological advances. This points to the fact that the voice is still there within its distortions, even as eddies on the surface of a lake maintain their integrity though intermeshing in wave-interference patterns.

Here lies the saving grace of the child within against our self-made sense of opprobrium. The child within is still there unscathed, covered under multiple sheaths marked by the spillover wreaked upon us by our adaptation to the environment, and also the mortgage of our maturity.

To earmark the child within, we need to peel off the accumulated sheaths. In order to retrieve the voice of Caruso, sound technicians had to reverse the distortions. This would mean owning up to dishonesty and thus opening up to public blame, giving up any contrivance to use guile in self interest and thus appearing ingénue to our smarter fellows, and eschewing any feelings of dislike or hatred for people who may well be obnoxious.

We may discover this archetype still present in the depths of our being in the clear eyes, the innocence, and the propensity for compassion, and the trustfulness of a child. This may encourage us to trust ourselves to make a fresh start, from scratch as it were, and to make a pledge that opens a new chapter in our lives. Our spiritual legacy eulogizes the child archetype as being immaculate, exemplified in the immaculate state of the Virgin Mary, or the mother of Buddha or of Zoroaster.

The Sufis ascribe it to our celestial counterpart or subtle bodies, the quintessential core of our psyche which like as a mirror can never be tarnished by the impressions upon it. The meditation practices aiming at the discovery of the child within consist in learning how to turn within. As we hold our breath after inhaling as we withdraw our attention from the environment and from our psyche, we discover the emergence of a fresh blossoming of qualities trying to break through in our personalities—a rebirthing. Moreover we discover a fresh dispensation of vitalizing energy that dynamizes the cells of our body and our minds.

Of course the child in us needs to grow up to maturity: in the existential drama, the angel becomes the master. Therefore at puberty the adolescent sheds off the child within like the snake of its skin, because the paucity of the child's discrimination makes one badly adapted to the challenge of real life. Here lies the moral of the Parsifal legend. To mark the passage from the angel to the master, he sins: he kills the swan—the symbol of the immaculate. For this he is banished, and has to learn to discriminate between that which is appropriate or not. His encounter with the very epitome of evil in the Queen of the Night brings him back to the father archetype represented by the Grail temple, not just as the prodigal son, but as the hero, the knight, the controlling master.

The way to get control over our fate where we previously felt powerless is therefore fraught with the overcoming of whatever it is in us that causes our devalidation of ourselves, and which we are trying to escape in addiction.

Resolution between involvement in and weaning from the child archetype is illustrated in the combat between Jacob and the angel. As the light dawned upon Jacob, he realized the angel was his celestial counterpart, his own higher self to which he was not owning up.

Resolution once more requires bringing together the effigy of the child within and that of the master, envisioned as two superimposed images, both bearing a striking resemblance, yet one being a distortion of the other.

The corresponding meditation practices consist in a catharsis, exemplified for example in the "theosis" of the Hesychasts. It is a kind of cleaning out of one's thoughts and emotions, working with one's aura of light while identifying increasingly with one's celestial counterpart, and thus purified.

The Archetype of the Alter Ego

Involvement with "other than oneself," whether in a personal relationship or partnership in general, or with nature or the universe at large, evidences the value of discovering oneself in another oneself who is better able to actuate the qualities lying dormant than one has achieved so far. Plotinus said: "That which one fails to discover in contemplation, one seeks to experience outside oneself." Hence the perennial quest for the alter ego—*anima* of one's *animus*, or the *animus* of one's *anima.*

Moreover the latent resourcefulness lying dormant within the seedbed of one's psyche emerges by being called upon to meet the challenge from "outside." Hence the need to achieve in life in one's partnership with others.

It means, however, that one's self esteem may be precariously poised upon proving oneself to oneself, and particularly to others. One becomes overly susceptible to criticism, and most vulnerable. The outcome of this is inevitably dependence, whether material or emotional. If one is not a match for the ego of the partner, an over-transference of one's ego in another ego arises, to the extent of finding self validation by satisfying the needs of the other. This is tantamount to becoming dependant upon the dependence of another upon oneself.

It is the quest for liberation from dependence that prompts the ascetic, the hermit (in India the *sannyasin*) to leave the world, to abandon possessions and seek the solitude, to practice austerity by severe discipline, to emancipate oneself from the susceptibility of personal emotions in order to become invulnerable, and to pursue peace rather than joy with its mortgage of pain. The consequence is aloofness, remoteness, the introspective mode.

What would be the resolution of an effort to reconcile these two irreconcilables? There is a saying of the Sufis: "Renounce the world, renounce yourself, and then renounce renunciation out of love." The challenge would then consist in involving oneself with people and circumstances, without letting oneself become emotionally dependent, loving irrespective of whether or not one is loved. This is unconditional love, loving a person who makes himself or herself most unlovable. A good example of the actual application of this resolution would be interdependence rather than dependence—self actualization in a creative way while networking, sharing. This would require triggering off in others one's vision of perfection, which was virtually present in them although they may not have been aware of it.

A further resolution would consist in connecting knowledge gained by experience and the intuitive insight gained by turning within. This is achieved by learning by doing, acting upon the environment or circumstances to confirm one's hunch, rather than merely interpreting occurrences, and by active looking: casting one's glance upon things rather than using one's eyes merely as passive organs of perception.

The corresponding meditation consists in filtering out the grosser and deleterious impressions from "outside," and sublimating or distilling those that are somewhat compatible with the subtle effigy of one's being. Moreover, rather than trying to reinstate one's pristine celestial state, brainstorm the way one wishes to be, and what is more, transfigure the effigy thus fashioned into the body of resurrection.

A further meditation practice consists in cultivating qualities present in oneself in an embryonic state by exploring their relevance in dealing with problems. Meditation thus avers itself to be a rehearsal for life.

Social Freedom

We are witnessing in our time the bursting forth of the forces of freedom in many fields. Dr. David Bohm (perhaps among the foremost scientists of our time) once defined freedom by two analogies:

One was the difference between the behavior of molecules at low temperature constrained within a clearly defined pattern, or the same at high temperature, fluctuating unpredictably. The other was a ballet whose choreography may be strictly configured, or the same ballet where the dancers are able to enjoy a certain degree of incentive within the overall pattern.

I like to illustrate the same in a group of musicians. If they play according to a composer's score, the scope of their initiative is limited as compared with a situation in which they improvise. But if each were doing his or her thing, it would be a cacophony. J. S. Bach revealed the secret behind his music by pointing out that each voice had its own area of freedom, but each had to constrain its incentive in the interest of the whole. The balance between the restrictiveness imposed by the whole upon the parts, or the inventiveness of the parts overcoming the autocratic imposition of the whole is a delicate one. The guide lines vary according to our sensitivity.

Another example in music: having been exposed to the pressure of a gruffer civilization than that of our ancestor of the 17th century, our ears have become tougher. We can stand dissonances that would have made Mozart cringe. The consequence has been the opening of a greater range of possibilities for modern composers. However, the challenge to their craftsmanship is proportionally greater, and tends to exceed their ability.

Another leading physicist, Ilya Prigogine, shows that it is the fluctuations from an order whose equilibrium is offset (in what he calls dissipative structures) that explore new possibilities. The newness would be unforeseen if the older order was observed. Creativity is within the individual inventiveness. On the other hand fantasies that do not resonate at the scale of the community are automatically weeded out. This is because if everyone did their thing it would be chaos, and the collectivity would suffer. There would be an opening to abuses in which the stronger would victimize the weaker. This is the reason for the observance of the law enacted in concert with competent socially minded people.

The above models illustrate aptly our problems in the world at large, in politics, in morals, and in our belief systems. As civilization advances, the constraint of our social institutions may suffocate our creativity to a point of exasperation for those caught in the "prefigured ballet." On the other hand those who try to challenge a despotic order run the risk of being martyred. Situations may, however, arise where the pressure of the despair of the oppressed is strong enough to embolden them to take the risk of being immolated for the sake of overthrowing the despots. When the decks are clear, the jockeying for power once more releases the instinct of domination, hopefully now checked by the collectivity.

Freedom of the Individual

At the scale of the individual, one may distinguish several kinds of liberations:

a) freedom from the assumption that the physical world is as it appears;

b) freedom from our assessment of circumstances, especially those in which we are involved.

c) freedom from being caught into the perspective of others;

d) spiritual freedom: freedom from dogma, or theories, considered as simply more or less enlightened viewpoints;

e) freedom from dependence upon circumstances for one's joy;

f) freedom from bodily pain or the fear of death—the latter giving one a kind of psychic immunity;

g) freedom from one's self image;

h) freedom from one's sense of individuality,

i) freedom from the quest for freedom, which spells voluntary involvement;

j) freedom to involve oneself to free others.

One is always running the risk of forfeiting one's freedom by one's co-dependence. If one is not wary, another person may make one dependant upon their dependence upon one. One may yield to the will of the other out of weakness, but often out of pity or compassion, to avoid a row, or simply out of kindness.

If one's self esteem is staked upon one's "goodness" rather than one's wisdom, one will easily fall a victim to this psychological trap. And the escape gets more and more difficult, since the pain caused to the person one is enabling, if one were to decide to wean them, becomes greater as time goes on.

It is often an angelic nature who falls in the grips of a domineering and egoistic person—or gets close to it, as illustrated in the Parsifal legends. Incidentally, the fear of co-dependence ought not to make one unkind and simply selfish in pursuit of one's own well being, impervious to the needs of others. Incidentally too, one ought not to confuse co-dependence with interdependence, where two people balance their mutual dependence in full conscious consent and dedication.

Escape? or Creativity?

What contribution does our spiritual dimension offer our human problems? Circumstances are not always favorable. Most people are afflicted by hardships, frustrations, misfortunes, even misery and catastrophe. Therefore, hail to the good moments! The yearning for escape from those circumstances, if one perchance entertains such daydreaming, could simply lead to ruthless unkindness (generally only to slip back into a similar pattern) or to unfulfilling isolation, or to the otherworldliness of an ashram.

Do you ever experience that yearning for the serenity, the nobility, and the ecstasy of "another kingdom"—only to find, as Buddha said, "There is a place which you cannot reach by going anywhere"? "That kingdom" is meshed in "this kingdom," being subliminal to our existential universe. Consequently, clues to "that kingdom" may transpire through what appears in our life circumstances. These clearly represent another dimension than the one paved by our daily life struggles, therefore we need to find the route accessing its reaches through our meditation practices.

Let us explore what light the spiritual overview may throw on our assessments of our problems.

If you train the light beam of your eyes and your consciousness to espy what is trying to transpire from behind whatever appears, wherever you turn your eyes, the splendor of the universe in all its bounty and at all its levels will reveal its potentiality. It will do this whenever you listen, or feel, or taste, or smell, or love, or wonder, not only in a dawn in the high mountains, in a cathedral or a Beethoven symphony, in human ingenuity, in the scientist's mind probing outer space, in the eyes of a baby, or the prowess of a hero, but also in a resentful victim of abuse, or the millions in distress, in those who are disenchanted and embittered and floundering in our sometimes cruel society. Oh, marvel! It is also in you, lying in wait to be aroused by being awakened. We discover the splendor latent in our own being through the object admired, and it reveals to us our own beauty. But to have eyes that see "what transpires," our eyes need to be active rather than passive.

> **All that man considers beautiful, precious and good is not necessarily in the thing or the being, it is in his ideal; the thing or being causes him to create the beauty, value and goodness in his own mind.**
>
> **Pir-o-Murshid Inayat Khan**

We must look further. To paraphrase Verlaine: two prisoners—one sees the bars, the other the stars.

Our prison is our horizon, our self image, the outreach of our realization, our discontent, the measure of our ability to love unconditionally people who make themselves difficult to love, our addiction, our self pity, our inadequate ploys to protect our vulnerability by a puffed-up front, briefly, our own ego.

To be disenchanted by the humdrum of the life to which we have been conditioned by our civilizations; to find our responsibilities confining, the challenge of opposition and competition stressful; to find the support system for survival leaving too little time for spiritual practice; to complain at being let down by acquaintances; and especially, to be disappointed in what situations do to our personality—these can only prove counterproductive.

> **Unhappy is he who looks with contempt at the world, who hates human beings and thinks he is superior to them; the one who loves them thinks only that they are going through the same process that he has gone through.**
>
> **Pir-o-Murshid Inayat Khan**

Check to what extent you are affected by prevailing circumstances to ascertain to what extent this hampers your freedom to be yourself.

> **A person asks himself how all he sees affects him and what is his reaction to it all. First how does his spirit react to the objects or the conditions he encounters, to the sounds he hears, to the words people speak to him. Secondly see what effect he himself has on others when he comes in contact with them. One should learn one's condition, the condition of one's spirit, of one's mind, of one's body, one's situation in life and one's individual relationship with others.**
>
> **Pir-o-Murshid Inayat Khan**

We may think that we long to escape from unfavorable circumstances, but if so, we most likely fail to see that we are unconsciously trying to escape from the way we were in the past that contributed towards creating those very circumstances. Turn within and ask yourself introspectively where your decision triggered off those circumstances, and to what extent the fortuitous situation that you ascribe to fate could have been called upon surreptitiously by something in your nature that needed to surface to heal or overcome. This may not be the case, because randomness upsets the programming of the universe to offer scope for a further degree of orderliness.

We find that our resentment rivets us to the past. Somehow we lose our real self by identifying with the person afflicted by external conditions.

The only way to free ourselves from our past is to reconnoiter our fears and our motivations to protect our psychological vulnerability. We must admit that we have been falling back on our ego's strategies, admit to having a cantankerous, disgruntled nature due to our frustration at being unable to retaliate, or to being loaded with self pity. We are flawed by relying on the inadequate ego rather than relying upon the rich pool of resourcefulness latent in the seedbed of our personality. Thus we could evolve.

> **By independence is meant self-sufficiency: that what they can get from their own self they must not look for outside. That is the principal motive of those who are striving for self-attainment, because it is the means of overcoming the sorrows and troubles and woes of this life. One sees a constant striving in the life of the adepts to make themselves independent of outside things as much as possible. On the other hand worldly people think it progress if they can become daily more dependent on others. Every step we take is towards dependence; and the more we depend upon others, the more we think we are progressing. In the end we come to such a stage that for what the soul needs, what the mind needs, what the body needs, we depend upon others.**
>
> **Pir-o-Murshid Inayat Khan**

Moreover, one so longs to turn the tables on time to undo one's iniquity, the harm done and the pain wreaked upon others. Could good deeds ever compensate, or give absolution? If we have changed, does it change the past? Indeed, the past has changed, our resolutions are retroactive. One learns by trial and error.

The key is to try and prefigure "how I could be." Our nostalgia for "the way things would be" if we became "how we could be" will redeem us from our past by opting for our next move on the chess board.

Give vent to this longing for our projections of a state of awakened awareness and unfoldment, concretized by the creative power of our imagination. It will arouse latent faculties lying in wait in the seed bed of our personality

All depends upon the expanse of the environment we embrace: our commonplace lives with its "storms in our teacups," or the trivia and drama dispensed by the media. Or, alternatively, we could embrace the creative visions of the "explorers of meaningfulness," or even the expanse of our own being as it customizes more and more of the inexhaustible bounty of the many-splendored universe of which we are a part.

We can only enhance our way of being by exploring beyond its confines. To achieve this, imagine as we meditate how things would look from the antipodal point of view, the divine. What if the universe (God) finds fulfillment in being liberated from its (His or Her) virtuality by being existentiated as us? Conversely, is it not that nostalgia of the universe (God) which sparks our realization of our need to actuate the universe (God) as ourselves by our personal incentive?

Rather than resorting to escape, which arises out of your personal perspective, you will find in your meditation personal fulfillment in the way the universe may reveal itself to you as yourself, in the unfurling of your personality. Think that you are transforming the universe into yourself by dint of your creativity, which is triggered by the awakening of your realization. The wider and loftier that scope, the richer your creativity.

If you greatly improve your personality, you will find that circumstances now need to adjust to your new being, or alternatively, your circumstances will not disturb you that much (like the elephant that gets use to the jiggling of chickens).

Instead of trying to escape the prison, expand its walls, like Marcel Marceau in his mime, so that it is no more a prison, by including the higher dimensions of your being, like overtones in a musical tone, without which the tone would sound flat. Our social circumstances will prove confining unless we see it is our domain, and work at embellishing and brightening it with those "higher octaves" of our being.

To make this quantum leap, you will need to ride the tide of evolution; you will venture to access a wider orbit than the *samsaric* repetitiveness of the commonplace: the spiritual dimension. This does not mean to elude your life's situations, but to include them on a wider octave, like the comet which has not lost its contact with the solar system and its planets, but which connects these in the perihelion, nearest to the sun in its orbit, in a wider loop than the scope of the planetary orbits, with that mysterious nebulous cloud at its aphelion, farthest removed from the solar system.

To escape, on a tangent, from the repetitiveness of the samsaric wheel we have generated, we need to hoist ourselves in a very elongated elliptic orbit, like that of the comet, polarized by an ever more advancing vertex, and lured by extra-samsaric dimensions, without losing our connection with our earthly personalities.

We now know that comets may be the originators of our solar system, emerging out of a nebulous cloud in that little known area of space-time which the Sufis call Adam, the cloud of unknowing, and which continues to rain upon us, and feed us with its ionized gases and stardust by sublimating itself. Yet its gift to us denizens of the solar system is not without a life-threatening risk to itself. If a comet allows itself to be caught by the gravity of Jupiter, it will immolate itself to give its life over to the solar system, as was the case with Comet Shoemaker Levi 9 in July 1994, or it will crash into the sun, as Comet West did in 1976. Moreover, a comet is invariably perturbed by its passages near larger bodies.

If you espy this originating cloud of unknowing lying at the edge of the outreach of your consciousness, in infinite regress, you will find that it dispenses recurrently renewed vitality and bounty to the existential underpinning of your being, but will, however, annihilate you if you let yourself be overstressed.

Likewise, the celestial counterparts of our being suffer by their investment in our earthly personalities, yet they ferment them, ripen them, and sublimate them by overarching them. By evolving, we are setting in motion in ourselves this further latent dimension of our being: "the evolutionary drive," which is inviting us to find our place in the scheme of things.

Chapter 8
Creativity

Awakening and Creativity

Awakening and creativity are the two poles of life's activity: the universe discovering itself in each extension of itself, and the universe existentiating itself as it mutates by fostering inventiveness in each extension of itself.

Let us think of ourselves as extensions of the universe rather than fractions, and the universe as the being we call God. For example, the live cell is not really a component of the body, but the expression of the whole program of the body (the DNA). Likewise, we are an expression of the universe as a whole and therefore of God, rather than a fraction of that universe or a creature. It is our realization of this in the course of our activity that is the first half of what we mean by spirituality. The second half is manifesting and existentiating the program—that is, the mind of God—in which we participate or to which we contribute by our creativity. The Sufis call the first God Consciousness and the second manifesting the manner of God.

One could describe awakening as what would hypothetically happen to a live cell if it discovered the code of the whole body and was able to see itself as an expression of that code—and, to push the argument in infinite regress, if it could reach into the thinking of the universe and see itself as an expression of that thinking. Or one could describe it as a villager on a world tour. Or simply an astrophysicist discovering the galaxies. Or, better still, an astronomer on a spacecraft who becomes a space-person. But one has to bear in mind that what one is discovering is actually the reality of which one is an extension. One therefore discovers one's cosmic dimension.

But creativity is one step further: it is discovering possibilities that have not yet manifested in the universe by actuating them, just like an aircraft creates its own path rather than following an already constructed highway. Or, better still, the space engineer who discovers the mathematics that will chart the optimal track for the spacecraft. Or an electron that finds a further shell for its orbit around the proton when existing shells have already been occupied. Where do those shells exist if not in an inherent harmony governing physical phenomena? They are not material things like roads or tracks in the desert.

We must be wary of thinking of this harmony as "preestablished" as Leibniz did, but rather as being invented step by step as the practical need arises. This is what the Sufis mean when they say that God had to existentiate Himself in order to discover Himself—that is, existentiate what He could become (which possibilities are inexhaustible) by becoming it in us, rather than manifesting what He already is (which is the religious dogmatic view).

This is why I believe the Sufi teachings represent the spiritual dimensions of the scientific paradigms of our time. Ibn Arabi calls the human "the created creator" (rather than the created creature), and Hazrat Inayat Khan emphasizes human creativity as being an extension of the divine creativity. Of all works of art, he gives priority to the art of personality. By discovering a new way of being, one contributes towards the advance of the harmony that is the software of the universe. We are the being of God discovering unforeseeable possibilities within Himself by concretizing that which has never been done before. This means prefiguring the new perspectives by inventing the way as one advances, finding new ways of being by customizing the advancing trend of the harmony of the universe in one's personality. This is called pragmatic knowledge as compared with proto-critical knowledge: knowledge gained by experience rather than theoretical knowledge (sometimes called transcendent knowledge).

And Ibn Arabi says, "By discovering God's consciousness in my consciousness, I confer upon God a mode of knowledge, and by grasping God's nature behind my nature, I confer upon God a mode of existence." It follows from these propositions that by recognizing God's consciousness focalized as my consciousness, I confer upon God a mode of existence because in the light of God's consciousness, I can earmark God's nature transpiring through my personality, and consequently actuate it. Reciprocally, by actuating God's nature in my personality, I confer upon God a knowledge of God's being that adds something to the knowledge that God had of Himself prior to projecting Himself into existence as me.

Hazrat Inayat Khan describes the transcendent knowledge as the state where human consciousness reaches into the divine conscience prior to the existential condition, and pragmatic knowledge as God's awakening through human experience. By emphasizing the empirical knowledge, I do not mean to discount the transcendent one. Wisdom is the interface between the external knowledge of the soul and the know-how gleaned by experience. Of course, the Sufi view and the new paradigms of science are mutually cross-pollinating and excitingly promising for the future of human thought. As evolution proceeds, human thought advances like a tide, untiringly breaking into new horizons.

In practice, what does it mean for the individual? Being more luminous, joyous, aware, sovereign, life-giving, loving, compassionate, and honest than the universe has produced so far. Is that possible? Why not? It is our ignorance of our divinity that is our limitation. We are not just the plant we think we are, but also the seed, and not only does the seed expect to reappear at the end of the cycle of the plant, but it carries within itself infinite possibilities of splendid mutations.

Ecstasy In Action

"O, to sparkle my soul with ecstasy!" Is this not the plea sounded by so many, asking me invariably the same question, "Pir, how does one get high and keep high through life?" (Need I say, without the artifice of drugs, for an artifice they are.) In a rather awkward attempt at candidness, I pride myself by preluding my answer with, "I wish I could" and then blissfully proceed to tell people how to do it. Well, life is only worth its wager if it is spurred by dreams, even if but a few ever come true.

Speaking with U.S. entrepreneurial managers successful in their field, what struck me was that unless fired by an enthusing objective or challenged at the edge of their ability, they tend to slump into boredom, disenchantment and lackadaisicalness, and they lose their grip. In fact, for the upgoing businessman, life must be a venture to keep the adrenaline flowing and to stretch energy to its breaking point. The venture that spurs people on is making dreams come true, whatever the dreams are. They could be materialistic ones, according to one's scale of values.

This is what Hazrat Inayat Khan meant when he eulogized some of the tycoons he met in the "New World," including Henry Ford. "Why has one been sent upon the earth if one cannot look at the earth for fear of being called a materialist? Those who make spirituality out to be something like this make a bogeyman out of God. In fact, spirituality is the fullness of life."

I am cheered to discover just how socially oriented that dream is, in more cases than one might have imagined. A productive job from a managerial point of view is a job which, while giving the initiator lucrative dividends, gives jobs to many others also, thus helping them to fulfill some dream of theirs. In fact, to enlist people's support in one's venture, the payment of wages is not enough. The great art of leadership is helping people with similar dreams who themselves would not have the initiative or wherewithal to fulfill them, thus helping one to fulfill one's own dream. This can only happen if these dreams match and reinforce each other.

I never cease to be amazed by discovering to what degree there is a basic commonality behind the maze of differences between people's aspirations: love, beauty, convenience, self esteem, justice, adventure, creativity. Unfortunately, many of these basic urges get distorted and even turned upside down in an incongruous and counterproductive way by disappointment or failure, or by having been the victim of injustice or humiliation or browbeating. You see, ecstasy is total involvement, taking the plunge for better or for worse, relentlessly coping with the odds, dauntlessly riding the tide of adversity and starting again if one fails or slips, believing, against proof of the opposite, in the values pursued, appraising the splendor and meaningfulness of life, facing the squalor and injustice wreaked upon humanity by those who lost that belief and who contrive to draw all around them in their doom, sardonic sordidity, defeatism and self destructiveness. Dreams are intended to come true. Their fulfillment is what they are about.

Usually, defeat is due to having failed to see the connection between the ideal and the hard facts, to unravel the Gordian knot connecting reality to actuality, linking metaphor to the nitty-gritty. The next stage after the dream stage consists in seeing how you get from "here" to "there," step by step, each step clearly envisioned, and to forestall anything that might come in between, waylaying one. This is crucial since failure begets failure and has a devastating effect upon one's self esteem.

Life becomes a venture when taking the risk of being innovative, which is what creativity is about. In fact, the human spirit lives on creativity and dies in conformism, routine, and toeing the line. Ecstasy is the magic out of which life is born, the wand that opens doors into unpredictable perspectives. It is simply fulfilling one's zest for life with all its wonder, if one can take life's pain without self pity, its attacks without bitterness, and its inevitable setbacks without discouragement. Ecstasy is the intoxication in which creativity thrives, the motive power in that supreme faculty inherent in the human being—creative imagination—the ability to anticipate, to prefigure, to imagine how things could be if they would be as they might be.

Ecstasy is triggered off every time that one rises above oneself, every time one frees oneself from a constraint in one's circumstances, in one's way of thinking, emotions, or self image. It is triggered every time one discovers the cosmic bounty and inexhaustible innovativeness invested in one—in fact, when one discovers the creator in one, as oneself. Ecstasy lies in waiting in anticipation of the delight of sniffing out the richness of diversification dormant in the unexplored drabness of many people's lives. For example, a snow-covered landscape may appear bleak until one discovers the enormous wealth of crystalline patterns in the snowflakes under a microscope. We could exploit the bountiful richness hidden in our lives if we could first earmark it and then make something out of it. Creativity is the thrust of ecstasy discovering unexplored richness and making it an actuality in our lives.

Embodying States of Consciousness Reached in Meditation

The Celestial Celebration on Earth and the Human Drama

There are moments when our minds are stirred by a compulsive need to explore uncanny levels of our being that inspire in us a sense of wonder. We touch precariously upon the unknown. At those magical moments we know that what we are experiencing is real. At least the nebulous scene was touched with a tenuous sense of what we ascribe to reality. Yet we do not know how to convey these impressions to others, let alone to ourselves in a lucid fashion.

Such precious moments fill us with awe and delight. If we have qualms about what our civilizations have done to our beautiful planet, perhaps such moments confirm our hopes in the continuing possibility of a wondrous effulgent world. Unfortunately those fleeting impressions pass before we are able to secure a handle on what actually transpired. But we may perceive in this unusual encounter the answer to an imperative, in fact possibly desperate, need for the most precious of all gems: the gift of the heavens in our otherwise trite lives.

Much as we would feel moved to recount the experience from the rooftops, it would be foolhardy to spell it out to those who may even repulse such an experience as hallucinatory and fanciful. If a zephyr of beauty has brushed across our world, let us not expose it to those who would besmirch it.

Truly enough we have a valid argument for the scrutiny of our questioning mind: Yes, come to think about it, there was that *déjà vu!*—a remote sense of something familiar—something to assuage my mind's doubtfulness. Yes, I have witnessed the likeness of the very same luster that gleamed across those heavenly landscapes in the eyes of that child whom I shall never forget.

Why did it trigger off a sense of *déjà vu?* Because matching experiences set up associative processes in the mind. Was that not something to cleave to in my temptation to yield to my skeptic leanings? A glimmer of a reminiscence of having witnessed on Planet Earth something of the nature of the celestial realms flickered on the horizon of my mind?

In similar vein, listening to a choir may have evoked a wisp of *déjà vu*. The composer was attempting to convey a feeling of the atmosphere of the heavens in a sacred celebration. Conversely, lofty *human* emotions may open to the composer vistas of heavenly splendor. For example, in his soul-searchings inspired by his love for Clara, Brahms touched upon a higher level of his being. It came flooding in as a flurry of notes, melodies, and rhythms. In so doing, he built a bridge giving us access to unknown strata of ourselves. To make this miracle happen, one has to allow oneself to be uplifted, moved to the very core of one's being, by an intuition that bespeaks a splendor beyond the apparent world. Does it not seem unfortunate that we should let ourselves be confined to a slice of our being (the physical and mental) when our total being actually fans out in a vast spectrum?

In their musings, people in a contemplative mood have sometimes culled clues as to the nature of these spheres. Then, in the wake of those who have trodden the no man's land, come the philosophers who build systems to account for the testimonies of the mystics. In the scriptures of all religions, the references to celestial spheres are legion: they are often codified in intellectual cosmologies, angelologies, etc., to be stored in the archives of our minds. These may offer the advantage of providing us with a topography of the uncharted reaches, the landscapes of the soul. This topography has been particularly elaborated by the Sufis.

The Sufi Sheikh Ahmed Ahsa'il points out to the existence of a level of our being he calls *Jism A*, our celestial body which communicates the nature of our Supercelestial being *Jism B* down to our subtle body (or effigy) *Jasad B*.

Can you identify with this template behind the structure of your mind, which he calls *Jasad B*—an archetypal level of our understanding? Thus through the mediation of our higher bodies, the cosmic programming provides for a practical means of communicating something of the nature of the heavens to the earth.

Conversely, our subtle mind/body (*Jasad B*) and celestial body (*Jism A*) ensure that the feedback of the know-how and wisdom we have gained by our interfacing with the physical and psychological environment encountered on earth, will become part of the divine programming. We could well envision ourselves after death, distilling the impressions of the earth, transmitting their gist higher up to our super celestial being. Imagine the prospect offered of being able to occupy oneself totally to being creative. Imagine creating out of the interface between the many splendored planes, beautiful and meaningful structures like an artist or a musician!

It is important that we learn to work with ourselves to translate the impressions transpiring through from lofty levels of our many-tiered being into our personality. These may eventually even gel into our physical atmosphere, perhaps even countenance.

Of course the ultimate work of art is the human personality. *Here we are the artist, the fabric, and the work of art.*

No sooner do we pay attention to our deep need for this precious food for our soul, than we awaken covert unconscious memory which suddenly erupts. We remember what seems to be our eternal being. At least it seems eternal in comparison with our personality that changes so rapidly. Can you remember the countenance of your eternal face?

Reverting back to our physical body, we cannot fail to be devastated by the contrast. We have a feeling of having incurred defilement in the course of our descent through the spheres. On the other hand, in comparison with our existential frame, our celestial nature seems embryonic. Obviously, owing to our incarnation, we have matured and enriched ourselves through the interface and osmosis with the physical and psychological environment. Our latent qualities have unfurled, and we have distilled wisdom out of the know-how gained by meeting the challenge of life.

At this point, it is a gratifying thought to realize that our celestial counterpart is still present within the very configuration of our physical frame, interspersed with its defilement just like the pristine voice of Caruso is still present within its distortions owing to the bad recordings of the time. Imagine a holographic slide in which two similar yet different images are superposed—one blue, the other violet. You can toggle from one to the other. By dint of your will power and creative imagination, you can correct and reverse the distortions in the blue one to approximate to the violet, while honoring the maturity evidenced in the blue one. You are able to confirm that you can ally wisdom with innocence.

Having captured a hunch of the nature and even features of your angelic being, can you see how the attunement of the celestial spheres tends to configure your psyche, and even your body (at least the expression of your face and your deportment)? To be creative, we need to customize consciously and willfully that which the universe is doing beyond our compass. This means that we need to be inspired by the splendor that is continually endeavoring to seep through the very shaping of things, and at the same time take into consideration the drama on earth.

While acknowledging the shocking accounts we are continually assailed with of the greed, the cruelty, the deceit, the grossness, and the vulgarity that come through or try to come through our humanness, could we still be appraising the incredible wealth and bounty gained by dint of incarnation? By the people, by our civilizations, by our cultures and our technologies, by the thoughts and emotions aroused in our encounters, interrelationships with others, with beings of all kens and at all levels? The nostalgia, tenderness, perseverance, faith, idealism, realism, loyalty, caring, sacrifice, imagination, compassion, generosity, honesty that breaks through in the human venture is overwhelming and warms us to the values gained on the Planet.

Of course such a bounty cannot be achieved without conflicts, disruptions, disasters, chaos. Orderliness does not beget change, rather it encourages complacency. Change requires involvement, courage, venture, risk of a disaster, risk of humiliation in defeat, deprivation, suffering to the point of being the victim of a terrible ordeal or calamity. Modern physics points to the fact that to evolve, which means to change, living systems have to "fluctuate from equilibrium." Our incentive shifts the software of the universe. Indeed free will unleashes forces beyond one's control or knowledge.

The dramas and fiascos on earth that we cannot fail to be involved with are due to the fact that, according to the Sufis, God's motivation in the whole process called creation is to bequeath His or Her ultimate asset: free incentive. To understand how this comes about, can we place ourselves in the antipodal perspective to our usual one? Suppose that you were to bequeath the best of your assets out of love. Since indeed the most treasured resource in life is free will, the Sufis ascribe to God the foremost quality *rahmaniat*—magnanimity. So let us consider our free incentive which is the very springhead of creativity as the ultimate divine gift.

Unfortunately the price of that act of generosity is that, by the very fact that the totality gets funneled down into each fraction of the totality, the many-splendored bounty potentially present in the totality gets constrained and limited. Each expression of the totality that is ourselves sees and assesses things from our personal point of view. Consequently greed, rancor, conflict, hatred, violence, and profanation crowd in; or alternately simply apathy, resignation, sardonic irony—being low-key. One needs to protect oneself against the abuse of that very free will. Willy-nilly we are involved in the drama.

How do we uphold the values from our celestial inheritance in the middle of real life situations? We are at the crossroads between heaven and earth. How does the celebration in the heavens of our souls interface with the drama in our psyche? How do they interact, intermesh, then gel in our personality? To what extent do they match or are they pulling us in opposite directions? Are we doomed to have to compromise in order to adapt ourselves to the commonplace, or can we uphold our ideals in the middle of it all, while still honoring all the values garnered by human endeavor, sometimes at the cost of hard strife? Can we remain high, radiant, aware and joyous, while meeting situations instead of escaping them? The clue is what we touched upon in our discovery of our heavenly inheritance. In this perspective it is clear that in the handling of ugly situations (with selfish or unfair motivations of people around us) there is an option offered us between reacting in the same vein, giving vent to our resentment or concupiscence, or applying those values that we cherish as they come through us, such as magnanimity allied with sovereignty, truthfulness allied with compassion, beauty allied with rigor, wisdom allied with innocence, or alacrity with serenity.

Or are we fooling ourselves? Are we justifying our own handling of situations on the misleading adage that the end justifies the means? It is the means that constructs the end. Recognizing our humanness without trying to justify it, yet honoring our celestial inheritance, can we get these two poles of our being to cross-pollinate? That is precisely what personal creativity is about.

How do we celebrate the betrothal of heaven and earth in our personality? Dare you see things from two complementary perspectives at the same time? Have you ever, while climbing the high mountains, surrounded by evanescent clouds lighted up by an array of most amazing hues, watched a storm raging in the valley? And hiking in the valley, have you been shattered by an alarming outbreak of thunder and lightning while capturing evanescent blue patches of sky as the dark clouds rushed by above? Both perspectives are complementary, depending on where you are—your vantage point.

I am sure (or at least hope) that you experience moments when the forces of life are aroused with a vengeance and you give vent to the lightning and thunder bursting forth in your own being. One's frustration as one meets opposition to one's commitment in life will ignite anger. In this scenario all the forces of violence, unkindness, rancor, and hatred are rife. To succumb to them is just too easy. Here is your chance to fulfill that covert wish that you may be entertaining of being a knight. Violence is energy. It can be harnessed by catalyzing a creative act. This energy might just provide one with the push to achieve precisely that for which one had not been previously sufficiently motivated.

We are endowed with the option of becoming a new person. We do not have to be what we have always been. We can even shake off the conditioning of the past and our forestalling of our future prospects.

But evolution proceeds by leaps and bounds. It takes an outburst of energy to bring about a change—a quantum leap—a total departure from the past. It takes the pain and glee of the drama on the earth to open a clearing in our sky revealing the splendor of the heavens, and thus sparking change.

The power thus wrought will erupt in your will. In fact the clue to a radical change is in resolve—making a binding pledge to change.

Creativity

An idea dawns upon the horizon of your mind. Are you moved to grasp it as it flashes at you, or do you let it pass by? If yes to the first case, if indeed, the idea is sufficiently potent, you are a creative person. It may be a catch word on an advertisement poised to draw your attention. Maybe someone said something that sparkled your spirit. Maybe you were moved by solemness, suffering, a plea for rescue, or by a heroic deed. You may have captured a mood, a mode of being, from the landscape or the skyscape that spoke to you of a mysterious meaningfulness and many-splendored attunement behind all of this. Maybe someone's prowess emboldened you, and set a whole tidal wave of psychic energy rushing into your adrenals. Maybe you were tickled by a humorous thought or witty remark, or by a curious constellation of events, like the monkey grasping, in a flash of insight, a feasible link between that nut outside the cage and that stick inside. Perhaps you feel that the surprising synchronistic concatenation of totally unexpected encounters and impressions is trying to impress cryptically upon you a message whose meaningfulness consternates your mind. Maybe you are spurred by a self-generated thought impinging impromptu upon your mind, or a feeling of nostalgia or unaccountable anguish, or passion, even holy passion, or cosmic wrath.

The idea could be crystallized in a single word, or you may think of it as a topic; in fact, it is a seed thought. It could be an elusive emotion that gets spirited away if you try to hold it without harnessing it. Most frequently, the idea sparkles an emotion.

If these prompts were not meaningful enough to marshal your energy, if you did not feel stirred by them or did not believe you were up to making something out of them, possibly you lost a chance in a million of manifesting your latent creativity. If you rise to the occasion to which the loaded idea now challenges you, you will be discovering a resourcefulness in yourself that you had never suspected. The idea/emotion served as a catalyst for self discovery. Now it's your turn to play ball. The idea /emotion may constellate galaxies of related seed thoughts interrelated with impelling emotions. If you remain stuck with the thought / emotion without germinating it, it will be stillborn. After you have responded to the input from outside, you need now to cross-pollinate these metaphors with the metaphors that emerge from inside. The feedback loop has spurred the software of your psyche, rather, that of the universe! One idea/emotion will conjure another in infinite resonance, inviting you to endless variations. You are fluctuating the order of the universe!

Yet at this stage, "How do you feel?" is more important than, "What do you think?" All creativity is born of emotion. All the levels of your being are affected from the soul downwards and the body upwards. Do you sense the flutter of your soul as you gently touch upon the magnificence of the mind of which your mind is a ripple in the universe of thought behind the universe of atoms and galaxies and bodies? And do you feel the eddies of the thrill of the spirit reaching right down into your heart—even your heart of flesh—making it beat faster? Yes the heart needs to be shattered and overwhelmed, not just the soul, so that the divine intention carried by the incredible planning of the universe may be updated and fed back by you, through you.

You have become as a creator, the laboratory of the divine experiment in creativity. If you react this way to the winds that pummel you from out there and everywhere, you are a creative person. You have plugged into the matrix of all potent ideas/emotions that get actuated in this splendid universe of ours. Yours is the pursuit of excellence. Your productivity will not only aver itself to be a projection of a significant aspect of yourself into the observable existential realm, but will indeed unfurl the potentialities lying latent in your personality. It will confer upon you the charismatic self image of the accomplisher: self esteem and self confidence. Your life will open up; the mists of despair and despondency will clear.

This is the experience of discovering God in oneself; one's divine heritage in the form of the All-possibility that moves the universe as wheels within wheels, universes within universes, minds within minds, souls within souls, hearts within hearts, worlds without end.

A Palette Full of Colors

Imagine you are the artist of your personality. Your personality is your work of art. You are working on it.

To start with, it is not completely your canvas. You inherited it from others; or rather it has passed through many hands, each contributing more features. However, even before you got possession of it, you had had some hand at it, since you had influenced the previous artists in some remote way. But now, you are solely in charge, except that you have to watch how people influence you in fashioning it.

You have a well endowed palette at your disposal; displaying a whole flurry of shades. Your eye falls upon a vivid green that yields an impression of vivacity. You remember reading in a book on Sufism that they use a mantram in Arabic to help trigger that quality; vivaciousness—a life-giving force. It is called *Hayy*. Upon gazing at that lush green, you feel recharged and electrified. You feel so full of a life-dispensing power that you could cause the buds of flowers to open up and cure the sick. You daub it on your canvass over some of that nondescript brown, giving it a new gloss. You have dynamized your personality. In fact, you are prancing around your room like a leopard in his cage in want of an outlet for your newfound energy. The color will stay, unless of course you spoil it again by one of those dreary moods that come on when you are unguarded.

Now your glance notices that lovely sky-blue. Yes, the sky on your canvas is just too depressingly cloudy. It does not mesh with the bright green you have refurbished your canvas with! There is a clarity about that blue that makes more sense of the green. You hear that blue stands for a kind of immaculate sacredness. That is why the dress and aura of the Virgin Mary are traditionally painted blue. The Sufis depict the Holy Spirit (*quddus*) in the same way, ascribing this epithet to the angels. It is *ingénue*, cannot stand any artifice, eschews sophistication. You daub it too on the canvas, clarifying your sky with a diaphanous effulgence. All of a sudden, your whole painting lights up.

Can you keep the color? Can you will it to be indelible? Someone comes in the room telling you that she had seen the broach that you had lost on another woman's neck (or was it your pet tie on another's neck?). You are furious. You look back at the canvas: the blue of the sky is smeared. Within a split minute it has been spirited away, it has got murky by your selfish, resentful mood. You try again, promising to guard against ugly thoughts, however justifiable.

Now somehow the lovely golden hue on your canvas strikes your attention. It has a royal quality about it. The glorious golden incandescence has the immediate effect of making you glow. You feel powerful, cosmic. In fact, you now surprise yourself sauntering across your room with a haughty demeanor, head high, bubbling over with self confidence. You figure yourself as the ambassador of that Being whose body is the universe and sets the pace of evolution by overcoming chaos by orderliness and incongruity by meaningfulness. You are in charge now. As you unwittingly visualize utopic beings manifesting sovereignty, as one would imagine the three wise men, you ponder upon all the reasons why you did not develop that wonderful quality as they did (unless of course you are convinced that you are a master—in which case, I apologize). You figure out that maybe it is because you gave in to compulsions, personal gratification, addictions. Daubed on your canvas, the golden hue confers a sumptuous sheen upon the whole picture. But you soon discover the need to prevent it just being a gaudy glitter.

In fact you wonder whether it would not have been better to have first smeared on the gold as a background, assuming that gorgeous radiance would transpire through whatever color you superimposed upon it, conferring upon your painting a rare quality. Assess what this means: effacing details on the picture and starting again! And you are not sure to reproduce what you effaced! Yet somehow you are heartened by the thought that if this is to be your painting rather than that handed down by those ancestral people, you are given a chance of updating it the way you like, if you can. It may be an admirable one, but you will wish to make something other of it—imprint it with the hallmark of your special idiosyncrasies. For example, if the outlines were too rigid for your liking, you would want to bring in more fluidity, adaptability. Or you would prefer more contrasts. But you do not wish to lose its pristine positive features, all the invested thought and nostalgia and values of all those to whom you are beholden, maybe heavenly beings too. It occurs to you that all you have to do is to retain a mental picture of it, and take the plunge.

So you take courage at heart and wipe out the picture, lay on the gold and start again from scratch! Reflecting upon what this means in terms of your personality, you realize that all you built up in your being or all that you inherited from your ancestors was precarious if it was not founded upon a masterly spirit of determination, discipline, and personal overcoming. Moreover you realize that if you had just added more punch to your personality without it having been deeply grounded in your being by dint of sheer mastery, it would have proven to be a collage, an element that does not mesh with the other aspects of your being. Your personality needs to be organically constructed in sync with all its other constituent qualities.

Now of course the red zooms out stridently at your retina from your palette. It captures your glance forcibly. It would be very tempting to spurt dashes of red all over the canvas randomly—give it some pep! The effect however would be sloppy, incongruous, like that of a person with bouts of uncontrolled anger interspersed with inveterate weaknesses—a flawed personality. Yet, not without a remote reference to the red scarf to the proverbial bull, the color red does arouse, to put it mildly, a certain vehemence in you. You feel more ready to confront challenges, unmask fraud, flay hypocrisy, and unveil a coverup. You burn with righteous indignation for the falseness, guile, manipulation and deception around you. You feel like righting the wrong, vindicating the innocent. The dervish in you is aroused. The password of the dervish is *Haqq*: the truth.

Yet too much red, especially in the wrong places can look hideous, unseemly, uncouth, even vulgar and disturbing to sensitive civilized beings. Truth ruthlessly doled out without being blended with compassion can prove to be cruel, even unwisely destructive. A warm orange would seem to blend nicely with the fierce red as for example in a lovely dawn.

Now, in an otherworldly mood, the many-splendored array of hues on your palate merge in a kaleidoscopic way; somewhat as in a rainbow, yet differently, because they are intermeshed, mutually transpiring through each other in a gossamer effect. How uncanny! Are you living an alternate experience? Just tired? Or mesmerized? Or is your psyche carried into a peak experience by your bewonderment at that marvel of color—the marvel communicated by color? Perhaps after all, the color is just the medium, the device, but what is coming through is more important; it is pure splendor—the splendor out of which the universe is fashioned and which the universe is briefed to display. Every time you give expression to the higher dimensions of your being on your canvas, remote echoes of the cosmic celebration in the Heavens manifesting as beauty in nature and as excellence infuse your mind. You have touched upon the keystone of creativity: ecstasy. The signature tune of the dervish is *azim*, ecstasy arising out of glorification.

If it is excellence that you seek, know that beauty is born of glorification, and so is your personality if you wish it to display the splendor behind the universe, or rather the splendor trying to transpire though what appears as the universe.

Music as a Training in Harmony

"What we call music in our everyday language is only a miniature which our intelligence has grasped of that music or harmony of the whole universe which is working behind everything and which is the source and origin of nature...the music of the universe is the background of the small picture which we call music. Our sense of music, our attraction to music, shows that there is music in the depth of our being. What does music teach us? Music helps us to train in harmony. Man, being a miniature of the universe, shows harmonious and inharmonious chords. Vibrations can be changed by understanding one's life—understanding the rhythm of the mind."

Pir-o-Murshid Inayat Khan

Have you ever stirred in your sleep as a melody came to you as from nowhere and bid you to awaken to write it down or at least remember it in the awakened state? This happened to Brahms, out of which his 4th Symphony unfurled:

It was only after having resolved his frustrations and found a way of joy while accepting the constraint of the situation that Brahms was able to give expression to the joy of love. But compare with Tomaso Albinoni's uninhibited sentimentality, heartwarming but rather facile and unsophisticated, in his Adagio in Sol Minore:

Have you ever felt frivolously trifling, nonchalant and carefree? Mozart translated this mood into the dancing notes of a famous tune:

Let's try it out ourselves: drop your reserve for a moment, give your responsibility a break for a while and just let yourself in for a burst of the joviality that you have been holding back—let it take over.

Have you ever felt facetious, flippant, pert, dallying with a burlesque edge, probably as a reaction to people taking themselves too seriously, or against heavy sanctimoniousness? Dimitri Shostakowitsch reacted to totalitarian stiffness and stuffy formalism in his Symphony No. 9:

Have you ever just thought of a melody, quite spontaneously, to give expression to a bout of energy? Beethoven did this in the first beats of his 5th Symphony, giving vent to the emotions roused in him by his admiration for the verve and heroism of Napoleon in his younger unspoilt days.

Notice the scanned, crisp rhythm here, expressing venture and aggressivity in comparison with the sweet and alluring rhythm of the first quotation, which expresses the delight of love?

We all know how easily we yield to the forceful impact of the environment, both physical and psychic, by reacting rather than acting upon the environment by dint of our self motivation. A lesson in dealing with life's situations can be given in the language of music. In the slow movement of his fourth piano concerto, Beethoven teaches us to call a buffer between that impact and our emotional attunement. This he does by refusing to play ball, and calling a zone of silence, turning within in the stillness of an inverted space where all creativity emerges—thus setting his own pace upon the environment. The impact of the environment is reduced to functioning as a catalyst, triggering our pent-up potentialities:

Obviously Beethoven is depicting himself as the pianist and the world as the orchestra. Notice the contrast between the staccato of the orchestra with the poised legato of the piano:

Supposing you drift into a mystical mood, you will find yourself shifting your improvisations from the major mode to the minor: and if you continue, thus turning more and more within, you will fluctuate even further from the minor mode, exploring subtle nuances of emotion. This is what the Indian musician is doing, exploring unchartered areas of tone and rhythm while improvising.

Note the departure from the minor mode. Note the effort to reach the dominant note by a process of escalation:

Stravinsky ventured upon a novel mode in the Symphony of Psalms. Have you ever felt dreary, drab, low-key—ever tasted of the blues? Have you ever found yourself wrapped in a mysterious melancholy—a nebulous gray mood, like a lake in the mist concealing the unknown, the non-determined? Get it off your chest by burning off the mist so that it may rise as a curtain upon the dawning of a diaphanous light:

Claude Debussy portrayed the malaise and ambiguity of his time in a way that speaks of the soul searching in each of us, exploring the unknown, in the Cathedrale Engloutie (the sunken cathedral.) Note the wealth of pastel intonations:

The next step he made in Clair de Lune; here he is describing something like clearings in the woods in the moonlight:

Reflecting his time, Debussy could never allow himself to come so clearly in the sunshine as did Bach in an untold number of compositions. A pertinent illustration of this advent of the Divine presence upon the earth is to be found in the beginning of Bach's Christmas Oratorio:

Have you ever felt free or freed, unfettered, liberated, unflappable, having shaken off a load, or having pulverized the walls that were hemming you in, or cast aside the harness imposed upon you by your friends? (Bach describes something like this in his Concerto for Four Harpsichords.)

Now you are streaking across space eerily like a ripple of unbounded energy. Sometimes the verve of the situation is expressed by a sense of urgency. Hasten, hasten, says the bass voice in the following passage of Bach's St. John Passion:

This sense of urgency is well known to us all—is it not? A further example of this mercurial verve is to be found in some of the choruses of the St. John Passion:

The urgency with which Bach calls our attention to a cosmic event on earth has attained probably its ultimate expression in the beginning of the same work.

Note the sharpness of the notes sung by the choir while the orchestra builds up into crescendo waves.

In contrast to this annunciation, we have an apotheosis in the Gloria Patri of C.P.E Bach's Magnificat. If you play this sequence, you will find that one apotheosis builds up into a further apotheosis, and so on until the final resolution.

emerged irrespective of their know-how—just an impulse to express the emotion felt at the time, first in rhythm, then in tone.

Notice the repetitiveness of the rhythms in every case quoted here! Just start by expressing your emotion as a rhythm. Once the rhythm has set in, there may be fluctuations in the rhythm. The melody seems to emerge from the rhythm—check it out. You will find that, lo and behold, you can compose!

Could you this time give expression to, not just unbridled joy which remains confined to the person, but cosmic glorification? Have you ever felt moved to the foundations of your being by an impelling urge to express glorification when you are faced with the sudden realization of the splendor behind all of this we call the universe? J. S. Bach expressed this in, amongst untold examples, the Hosanna of his B-minor Mass:

Notice the breakthrough of energy affirming the certainty gained by faith by dint of repetition, while rising undauntedly like the arches of a cathedral.

How different from Stravinsky's plaintive alleluia in his Symphony of Psalms!

It is difficult for the modern denizen of our Planet to nurture the effervescent optimism which sparkled the spirit of the early Church, releasing the emotion of fervor unrestrainedly.

Have you ever been daunted by the struggle for meaningfulness in our day and age against soul-killing realism or even the metaphysical anxiety upon sardonic reflections on where we are heading—where it will all lead to if we continue on this tack? Prokofieff's ponderous soul, searching on the edge of war and peace in the Peregrinus of his Alexander Nevski, reflects these misgivings we are all feeling:

Have you ever overcome a foible or an addiction or freed yourself from a debt? Have you noticed how as a result one could pace with poise and majesty and with an air of sovereignty and determination? Bach expresses this masterly pace in the Passacaglia in C minor for organ:

The pace is manifested by a continuous advance marked by a syncopated rhythm, indicating the alternation between the left foot and the right foot.

The purpose of life is like the horizon. One thinks one can see it, but as one advances a further landscape has become one's horizon. If you cannot read music, you may buy the tapes or records of these excerpts which will help you understand my commentaries; or ask somebody who can read music to sing the melodies to you.

Old Wine in New Bottles

We think and feel differently today from the way our ancestors did in many areas, not only owing to the advances in technology, communications or science, but in terms of our philosophy of life, of our sensitivity to dissonance in music, and unrealism in art. We have moved quite a few steps in areas unexplored and even shunned by our ancestors. In no way could we build a cathedral like Notre Dame of Paris or Chartres or Cologne, nor would the ornate structure of Milano Cathedral or the filigree niceties of the more stylized Indian music tally with our sense of clear lines and functionality.

If we care to take an analytic look at the evolution of architecture, we will realize that the new emerges as if of necessity out of the old, like organic life out of the inorganic. The new Coventry Cathedral was planned so that the ruins of the outdated cathedral are still in view, somewhat organically integrated. In an effort to bridge the old and the new, in Ted van Leer's and others' compositions, medieval folkloric tunes lead into the rock and roll style, spanning centuries with ease. Composers demur at the thought of composing anything of the caliber and maturity of J. S. Bach, yet Stravinsky in the Symphony of Psalms brought something of the mettle of the masters of the past through, monumentally.

Yet in the areas of spirituality, particularly religion, most of our cultures are medieval in their thinking and jaded in their emotions. For the sake of clarity, let us at least get a basic confusion out of the way: spirituality must not be confused with religion—nor, necessarily, religion with spirituality. At best, religion is institutionalized spirituality, calcified into dogmas, rituals, and partisan allegiances. If the major areas of our cultures can be updated, cannot spirituality be updated by extricating itself from its religious underpinnings? Of course! And what is more, this is what we are about. Pir-o-Murshid's ideas were challenging to the established thinking in his time; the full implications of their relevance only come into perspective in our time. When asked what I would do when I was grown up, he said, "He will spread the message to the intellectual audiences of the future." That was the language of the time.

Today we would say that the awareness of people in the 1980's who are interested in spirituality requires an updating in keeping with the thinking of our time. This is precisely the material of my brainstorming. Humans have landed on the moon. We can think of Planet Earth objectively as seen from outer space, instead of thinking of outer space as seen from the Planet Earth. Science has provided mystics with several paradigms which serve as practical models to represent experiences that mystics could not explain before: the holistic paradigm, inverted space and new vistas in psychology, which fascinated Pir-o-Murshid.

Sometimes we are saying what our predecessors were saying but in a new context, which means that implications with regard to our present way of living and thinking need to be woven into the picture. Being out of context reeks of an anachronism. Recently, Coleman Barks presented a rendering of Mevlana Jelal-Ud-Din Rumi's poetry, which is, to say the least, unsettlingly challenging and uproariously provoking. Would Jelal-Ud-Din have thought this way if he had lived in our time? There is no way of knowing. Yet somehow, just like our bodies are those of our ancestors, converged and mutated, so with our minds. Our minds are their minds that have moved with the time. The Bible is appreciated by some in a modernized version.

Pir-o-Murshid lived much closer to our time. Could his words bear the trauma of Coleman's rewording? How would Ulm Cathedral look if one replaced some of its naves by modern modular units? How would Pir-o-Murshid's thoughts be rendered in our modern idiom? What ideas would be catalyzed by those thoughts in an innovative and inventive way?

Instead of saying, "The mind of God," one would say, "The mind of the universe," as I have been expressing it. Instead of saying "divine emotion," one would say "emotion in its cosmic or transcendental dimension." Instead of saying, "Our divine inheritance," one would say, "The transcendent dimensions of the person looked upon as the whole person," that is, by virtue of the holistic paradigm of our time. Instead of "spirit," one would say, "energy in its subtlest form, operating as a catalyst." Instead of saying, "Make God a reality," one would say, "Actuate the resourcefulness programmed into your psyche, which is cosmic and impersonal." Instead of saying, "The hand of God" or "the divine intention," one would say, "The software of the universe."

Quite frankly, I prefer Pir-o-Murshid's own words, although the above renderings sound very much like the way I speak and think. He said, "If it is not the coin of the day, let it be rendered an antique." There is room in our day and age for Notre Dames, for plainsong and square dancing and Bach and Schumann, without doing what Kosmos did to Bach's three part "Invention in Solaris." But there is also room for "Solaris" too. So there is room for Murshid's original words, and also Pir Vilayat's rendering.

It is not just a matter of linguistics; there is a shift in values in our time. For example, today we are wary that there may well be a touch of masochism in saintliness, or sadism in mastery. Predictably, Pir-o-Murshid had pointed out that the act of the policeman punishing the boys who had beaten up a dervish was better than that of the dervish inviting them to beat him for his foibles. Murshid said that mastery is not desirelessness. It is not checking or frustrating impulses, but harnessing them. He wondered whether the *rishis* in the Himalayas would have the philanthropic dispositions of many American businessmen, and he wanted to show how one could bring spirituality into life in the world. There is no doubt that his thoughts were novel as compared with the traditional spiritualists. Yet the thoughts and beings of the Hindu *rishis* and Christ and the Sufis found a new life in Pir-o-Murshid in their relevance to modern life in the world; so his thoughts live and blossom in us.

The Dance of Joy

A million galaxies are a little foam on that shoreless sea.
We came whirling out of nothing scattering stars like dust.
The stars made a circle and in the middle we dance,
Turning and turning, it sunders all attachment.
Every atom turns bewildered,
And it is only God circling Himself

Rumi
Fragments, Ecstasies, tr. Daniel Liebart,
Omega Publications, Inc. (1981)

Thy music causeth my soul to dance; in the murmur of the wind I hear Thy flute; the waves of the sea keep the rhythm of my dancing steps.

Through the whole of nature I hear Thy music played, my Beloved; my soul while dancing speaketh of its joy in song.

Pir-o-Murshid Inayat Khan
Notes from the Unstruck Music: from the Gayan of Inayat Khan, Omega Publications, Inc. (1988)

To be happy, to dance, we need to be beautiful, and to be beautiful we need to validate ourselves. It is just in our ability to love those who make themselves most difficult to love that life tests us in our love of ourselves—because, often unbeknown to ourselves, it is our self esteem that is at stake.

The bottom line is that, as Pir-o-Murshid Inayat Khan pointed out, "we are tested in our love." Yes, this is precisely what is enacted in life. It is admittedly difficult to keep one's joy—the dance of one's soul—high when dealing with a cantankerous person, or an unkind person or a domineering or manipulative person, or a person who exhibits a pattern of trying to draw one into a conflict.

Our spiritual progress is determined by our ability to harmonize with our social environment; but how can we harmonize with people who would only be well disposed toward us if we give in to their egos, thereby forfeiting our own values and responsibilities? This is assuredly the great art of life: being able to cumulate authority, and kindness, and joy—and insight. People are awkwardly vying to validate their vulnerable self esteem by affirming their egos—maybe at our cost. Maybe it is the only way they know to fulfill this need. Maybe they justify it in their reasoning as standing up for their opinion.

Understanding is the first step to forgiveness. One can entertain understanding, forgiveness, and love, even respect, while standing by one's commitment in life. Forgiving someone who hurt a dear one is much harder than forgiving hurt to oneself. Moreover, some cases are so outrageous that one questions: how is it possible in this case? Yet forgiving is the key to joy and to that authority that is not powered by the despotism of the human ego—having room in one's heart for those who offend and betray one.

As for guilt, if we are honest, it leaves us no escape. Remission? To acquiesce to divine forgiveness, we need to forgive ourselves. Making a pledge to never repeat the offense and making amends will help.

God has mercy and forgives your sins.

Qur'an

To give joy to others, we need to find joy in ourselves. Therefore to dance now, we need to dance the dance of joy over the thorns under our feet, while rejoicing that we have been transformed by exploring our shadow and thus being able to confront it. We rely upon our ego to ensure our psychological defenses; it features our crutches. To wean ourselves we need to validate our self esteem by including in our self image the celestial levels of our being.

We are inexorably immersed in the very selfsame process whereby life transforms the dung feeding the seed into a beautiful flower—moreover with the bonus of a perfume. Does not the seething clash of warring clouds resolve in the luminous fireworks of lightning? Is it not significant that, as the universe evolves, matter in the form of the human body serves the awakening of higher levels of being? The pain of childbirth opens up a peep into the heavens revealed to us through the eyes of a babe. We learn that the ordeal of those tortured in concentration camps erupts in a breakthrough of ineffable ecstasy as death rescues them from their executioners. The example of heroic beings may help one. It can help to make the transit into "life after life." A revered friend once told me he had been tortured twice during the Second World War, once by the Nazis, then by the Soviets. In his ordeal, he kept feeling sorry for those who were causing him agony in body and mind because he saw they were brainwashed, and consequently he could forgive them. He said all he had to do was to get into the consciousness of Christ being tortured by the soldiers of Herod.

Forgiving makes the difference between burning up in the fire of the psychological hell of acrimony, or exulting in the splendor and clarity of celestial effulgence.

Have you ever been graced by a dream revealing the abandon of the heavenly dance of jubilation when, by forgiving the traitors who betrayed them, heroes are crowned with the beatitude of saintliness?

Chapter 9

Mastery, Service and Leadership

The Basics of Pir-o-Murshid Inayat Khan's Teachings Regarding the Ego

The primary process upon which Pir-o-Murshid bases the training of mureeds revolves around his adage "make God a reality, so that God is no more just a belief or concept." To make God a reality, one needs to "awaken the God within." It is realistic, rather than based on a belief system. It means discovering and identifying with the holistic dimensions of our being—our divine inheritance—rather than limiting ourselves within the constraint of our commonplace self image.

Somehow to validate ourselves against self doubt, we may unconsciously resort to a deceptive strategy; being defensive may lead to being sanctimonious, overbearing, self-righteous, or arrogant. This is a very dangerous syndrome often found amongst people dedicated to a high ideal or purporting to be "spiritual" who incur the risk of stumbling between the horns of a dilemma: the ideal versus reality. This leads to incongruity, inconsistency, ambiguity, a mismatch in our self image between parading make-believe self validation while floundering in the abyss of self denigration.

Therefore, the first step is *muhasibi*, self examination, matching our motivations with our objectives, and our objectives with our values.

We ask ourselves why we are doing this or the other thing and what our motivations are in our relationship with another person. Somehow our attitude towards people, and consequently our way of handling people and situations, is a function of our own self image which is ordinarily deceptive. This self image is commonly a device used, probably unconsciously, to protect ourselves against the onslaught upon our self esteem by others—a strategy which proves ultimately counterproductive because it does not enlist all our resources. In our ignorance of the bountiful qualities of our real being, we resort to an inadequate strategy!

Investigate whether you are resorting to this strategy. Are you yourself presenting an imaginary self image to protect your vulnerability? If so, you may detect the same strategy in others. This representation of what is really only one aspect of our real being, with which we identify. This is precisely what Pir-o-Murshid calls the false ego. Murshid defines the "false ego" as a faulty self image. Our faulty self image shows itself to be an inadequate and misleading support upon which to establish our identity. Its consequent effect upon our handling of our problems may have disastrous consequences. It is a fraction of our being with which we identify, whereby we are not enlisting all our potentialities. The crucial issue is therefore unmasking the hoax of "the false ego."

One's defense system may in extreme cases be blown up to the extent of parading a puffed-up selfish disposition, oppressing and treading down kindred beings who themselves nurture an inferiority complex or at least a poor self image, and do not have the confidence to counter this assault on their vulnerable self esteem.

This is how this false notion of ourselves may develop: In our youthful trusting naiveté, we believe in our projections of ideal values to which we pledge allegiance. Soon we get hurt by people, wounded, disenchanted, rejected, disenfranchised. The need to provide protection against further assaults upon our vulnerability becomes urgent, imperative, compelling! What are the resources which promise to provide us with a shield? Where can we find a healing? Outside, in friendly, compassionate, reliable support from the brigade of dedicated helpers, counselors? Or inside—in our very in-built self-healing propensity? Our self esteem, our self confidence, our ability to make way in life is at stake!

Our programming equips us with several strategies. The commonest one is simplistically reactionary and fraught with primitive emotions. See if you can detect these strategies in yourself, then you can earmark them in others:

1. If abused or humiliated: anger, resentment that can escalate into hatred with its ensuing cruelty.

2. If oppressed or repressed by a despotic or tyrannical ego: either aggression, spite, or resenting having to yield, thus losing one's self respect.

3. In one's endeavor to validate oneself by vying in valor or emulation: feelings of envy or jealousy may be aroused.

4. If one grounds one's self esteem on one's vying with others in one's possessions: covetousness and greed may ensue. (A curious trick of the ego is that the egoist sees in every other person a pronounced ego. "Why has he got a higher rank than me?")

5. If there has been a pattern of being punished or disadvantaged by having owned up, or stood up for what one believes: a tendency of being devious, cowardly, or manipulative may ensue.

All these reactions (and probably many more) evidence our rather perfunctory and therefore inadequate efforts in dealing with the challenge to our being from the psychological environment. They may present themselves as a shield, a dressing, a parade, or a mask concealing or camouflaging our real being. The consequence of their effect upon our self image is confusing, contradictory, and incongruous. It could work both ways: it can bloat one's ego to the point of making one megalomaniac, judgmental and contemptuous, or on the other hand self-defeating and demeaning. It can lead toward sanctimoniousness or toward false modesty.

This ego feels vain when it says: "I cannot bear it. I am better than the others." And so one's weakness is presented as strength.

Failure to recognize these features in our personality as strategies obstructs the discovery of our true identity, which would help in overcoming or transmuting them. On the other hand, to remove these protective displays or crutches would trigger dangerous withdrawal symptoms: otherworldliness, helplessness, listlessness. Yet, they aver themselves to be counterproductive in the long range.

Since they are reactive, defensive, and therefore only engage a small, peripheral area of our psyche, to forestall the withdrawal symptoms that one would trigger by removing them, it is advisable to replace them gradually by enlisting the rich gamut of resourcefulness latent in our various inheritances. Removing them with the kind of will that we develop when identifying solely with this area of our psyche, "the false ego," can only cause conflicts and result in a split in our personality.

No doubt by our failing to recognize and own features in our personality like guilt, resentment, anger, jealousy, or covetousness, these qualities would simply conceal themselves in the unconscious and erupt uncontrollably, or make us feel mortified and frustrated. But if we become aware of the way the universe converges in us (as the ocean in a wave), which is what Pir-o-Murshid means by God consciousness, we would then muster a transpersonal will, in which the divine will would supersede the limited, egoistic personal will. This could be illustrated by plugging a battery into the charger.

Furthermore, it is in the nature of life to continually self-organize as us. To achieve this we are concomitantly dissolving at the jagged ends. This could be illustrated by a flower: for the fresh petals in the center to unfurl, the jagged ones at the periphery need to fall apart. One does not have to chase them away; they will disintegrate to give way to the new dispensation.

Pir-o-Murshid also presents an original concept of the will, which he illustrates by the yacht's captain harnessing the wind but directing its momentum in the desired direction. One could represent the wind as the self-organizing faculty written into the programming of the universe and our will, as we avail ourselves of this force, and yet bend it according to our personal initiative, which is what we mean by our will. In this case it is clear that we are not talking about the will of a fraction of our being, that has alienated itself from our whole self (which Pir-o-Murshid calls the false ego), because our will is a customized expression of the divine impulse, as illustrated by the wind.

More importantly, since our false ego represents only a small portion of the bounty of our being, by calling upon it to meet an undesirable onslaught upon our being, one is failing to actualize the virtual potentialities that lie in wait in the wider range of our being: the seedbed of our personality. Whereas if we place a buffer between the challenge of the psychological environment and ourselves so as to discover that bountiful underpinning of our personality, that challenge will act as a catalyst rather than an onslaught, spurring those latent potentials. One tends normally to evaluate one's idiosyncrasies based on one's self image. If one discovers wider areas of one's self image, latent potentials will surface.

This is the reason why Pir-o-Murshid attaches so much importance to becoming aware of what he calls our divine inheritance.

> **The fulfillment of this whole creation is to be found in man and this object is only fulfilled when man has awakened that part of himself which represents God Himself. The same God, so little of whose perfection manifested in the plant, arises again at the end of the cycle, trying**

to emerge as perfectly as possible in the midst of human imperfection. The one who is conscious of his earthly origin is an earthly man; the one who is conscious of his heavenly origin is the son of God.

Pir-o-Murshid Inayat Khan

Pir-o-Murshid points to the efficacy of meditation to downplay our false self image and therefore overcome the counterproductive strategy of the false ego, thus mustering all our resourcefulness by discovering the bounty latent in us.

The false ego is overcome through meditating upon the true self which, in reality, is God. It takes a powerful impact, involving our being in its very substance, to bring about a change so as to shift our identity from the constraint of the commonplace self image. This is where meditation culminates in prayer.

When they stand before God to learn, they unlearn all things that the world has taught them; when they stand before God their ego, their self, their life, is no more before them. They do not think of themselves in that moment with any desire to be fulfilled, with any motive to be accomplished, with any expression of their own; but as empty cups, that God may fill their being, that they may lose the false self.

Pir-o-Murshid Inayat Khan

Man is the most egoistic being in creation, who keeps himself veiled from God, the Perfect Self within, by the veil of his imperfect self, which has formed his presumed ego. In the beauty of prayer, by the extreme humility when one stands before God and bows and bends and prostrates before God's Almighty Being, one makes the highest point of one's presumed being, the head, touch the earth where the feet are. One in time washes off the black stains of false ego, and the light of perfection gradually manifests. One stands then face to face with one's God, the idealized Deity. When the ego is absolutely crushed, then God remains within and without, in both planes, and none exists save God.

In that state, called *fana-fi-allah*, when the soul is absorbed in God, we lose the false sense of being and find the true reality. Then we finally experience what is termed *baqa-i-fan*, where the false ego is annihilated and merged into the true personality, which is really God expressing Himself in some wondrous ways. This is the same also as *nirvana*, where the true reality of life is experienced and expressed by rising above ourselves.

> **If this limited self which makes the false ego is broken, and one has risen above the limitations of life on all the planes of existence, the soul will break all boundaries, and will experience that freedom which is the longing of every soul.**
>
> **Pir-o-Murshid Inayat Khan**

Mastery—the Effect of Retreats

As we plunge deeper and deeper into retreats, we become increasingly amazed at the effect of mastery on human transformation. The sheer determination that it takes to reverse the human machine, represents a remarkable victory of the will, with the result of unleashing intense magnetism. And it is this energy that shifts consciousness from its commonplace setting. Of course, meditation is the art of learning how to use the human focus of a universal will to mobilize that universal will in all its infinite scope. Eventually, the forces of life take over to set up a tidal wave of transformation. However, even though will acts as a catalyst, it is ecstasy (the energy of the psyche) that avers itself to be the driving force. People of great accomplishment have performed feats of mastery. If you are not making a success of your undertaking, the chances are that you are not in control of yourself.

Mastery is subject to much controversy in the Sufi Order and in general. Most psychologists since Freud warn that inhibiting impulses, frustrating desires, and withholding anger, will damage the psyche and make a person uptight, crestfallen and timorous. Promoting this view, a few teachers have been departing from the characteristic mastery of traditional schools to promote an epicurean permissiveness. The sluices are wide open, indiscriminately; everything goes. Public opinion is outraged.

In the nick of time, psychologist Carol Travers, in her book *Anger, The Misunderstood Emotion*, points to the danger of simply giving in to anger. She says that by so doing, one escalates anger possibly to the point of a tantrum; it takes over. One may become an irate, inconsiderate, and insufferable person.

Murshid took a balanced view of this problem. One is sometimes faced with the choice between wounding one's psyche by withholding an emotion, or blowing a delicate situation by behaving in an uncouth manner, showing a lack of sensitivity and refinement, rather like an elephant in a glass palace. This behavior can sometimes do violence to a person's self esteem. In this case, just as it is not always advisable to mollycoddle the body, but rather expose it to the seasons, even so the psyche will get strengthened by rough-handling it, provided one does not overdo it. However, while the ascetic orders practice detachment and desirelessness to effect liberation, the Sufis see the whole universe as the divine nostalgia for self discovery, the actuation of potentialities, proliferation, inventiveness and evolution.

If, as the Muslims affirm, *la ilaha illa 'llah*, "it is all one being since there is none other than God," then what we believe to be our desires are extensions of the overall divine desire, albeit narrowed down by the limitation of our personal perspectives and maybe distorted, possibly eviscerated. Rather than quash an impulse, Murshid advocates harnessing it as a yachtsperson harnesses the wind to blow the sailboat where one wishes instead of where the wind wishes. Rather than disperse the energy of anger in an explosion of fury, one could make use of that energy in an implosion: gaining an ongoing sense of dignity and sovereignty that imposes respect.

The trouble is that mastery easily becomes a feat of proving oneself to oneself or to others, especially when challenged. It is the stuff that makes the mountaineer, the athlete, the fireman, the hero, the yogi. Besides, people and fundamentalist institutions have a way of making one feel that one "should" do this or that. One finds oneself in a bind when pushing beyond the boundaries between stress and overstress. The bind is in the mind. One fears being humiliated in one's self esteem, reproved, punished, or even dismissed if one should fail. At a certain point, something has to give. If one has a vulnerable mind, one slips into schizophrenic behaviour; if a strong mind, one could have a heart attack or cancer.

A perspicacious person will notice that one is more vulnerable to overstress when pitting the personalized will against the odds, doggedly and stubbornly. One must regard the natural trend of the formative processes within us that prevail upon us to stop hitting our head against the wall and get into sync with a will of a more universal and impersonal scope calling for attention from within. One could easily slip into cussedly "doing one's thing" under the banner of mastery, unaware of its effect on others. It is because the dervish musters the will of which his will is the extension (what we call the divine will), that the mad elephant will obey him. If he were to apply his personal end of the cone, of which the divine will is the big end and his the small, the dervish would be killed by the elephant. Such is the divine power that sparks one when one discovers in oneself the same power that moves the universe.

Faith and Belief

Do not confuse faith with belief. Belief rests upon some kind of proof: I believe in this or that. But faith is like doing away with crutches. It is intuition, that inborn, inherent mode of cognizance prior to experience, which philosophers call proto-critical. What I want you to do is try to remember whether your faith flounders when facing trauma. I must have triggered off a lot of thoughts in your mind. Try to remember these because I'm giving the guidelines of what you can do with those thoughts. Open your heart to another person and tell each other some of those things that you hardly ever talk about to other people. Somehow there is a moment when one feels like opening one's heart.

You might try to recall the following elements: first of all, the event must have had some relevance to your sense of values. For example, I remember when my sister Noor and I had to decide whether we were going to be non-resistant or whether we were going to participate in the Second World War. It was a question of values. We had been brought up in the Ghandian idea of nonviolence. I suggested that if the Nazis had a lot of people at gunpoint, and you couldn't save those people without killing the Nazis, if you don't kill the Nazis, you are responsible for the death of those people. I don't know what the validity of that argument is. You could discuss that but this is a clear case where a situation is challenging your sense of values.

The second element is your motivations. You started off with a kind of plan of what you would do in your life. A child says, "When I'm grown up, I'll do this and that." You might have had to revise your plans, not because you were forced to, but because something clicked in you, all of a sudden you discovered the purpose which you hadn't seen before. Pir-o-Murshid Inayat Khan says, "The purpose of life is like the horizon; the further we advance; the further it recedes." I thought this was my purpose and now that event has totally shattered the idea I had about my purpose.

Illustrative is the story of a man known as the Lion of India, who was fighting the British to free India. He was walking the streets and there was a leper who asked to be taken to the water. The Lion of India didn't have the courage to do that because he was afraid of catching leprosy. Then, as he was walking along the way, he felt terrible about it and though, "I, the Lion of India, don't have the courage to hold my fellow man in my arms and take him to the rescue of the water." He walked right back and did it. Then he decided overnight that he was going to leave everything and build a leper colony. What he did was marvelous for those thousands of lepers. Now that's an example of a situation that might affect your programming. So try to remember those circumstances that changed your motivation.

The third element is—how do your feel? Did the situation trigger anger? Did it trigger hatred? Did it trigger resentment? Did it even trigger guilt? One can feel guilty for having allowed oneself to be victimized by someone. Guilt is not a very rational thing. So how do you feel? Do your remember how you felt prior to the event? And how did you feel when the event took place? If you're very perceptive, you'll find that there are certain emotions that draw one's soul downwards and have a kind of delaying effect. Somehow, one gets tarnished by the emotion. There are other emotions that make one rise; for example, an act of heroism will make one high. So, how do you meet that problem? Did it trigger a sense of wanting to battle against injustice?

That brings us to the fourth element: the dichotomy between the fight and flight reflex. We find that animals measure whether they can cope with an attack or whether flight is the best part of valor. If you decide on confrontation, it makes you strong; if you decide on not dealing with the subject, it makes you weak. So remember the event and remember how you reacted. Perhaps your instinct told you not to attempt anything beyond what you thought was your power and then, later on you regretted it and decided that if this should ever happen again, you would confront the problem instead of running away. The question is, did you at sometime in your life make a vow, a pledge of "I will?" It involves you in your honor. That gives you power; try to remember that. When you had that moment of euphoria, you suddenly realized that you were tested to the ultimate springheads of your being. The whole unfoldment of your being depended upon how you were going to deal with this challenge. If you goofed, well, okay, you are given another chance.

In the meantime, one does tend to deteriorate if one doesn't deal with the chances very positively. One sees people start life so beautifully, and then gradually they deteriorate in time. Then there are those who become more beautiful as life goes on. There are those who have lost the battle of life because they've been discouraged and disenchanted and haven't known how to hold the "rope of hope"—so that nothing can take away one's sense of meaningfulness and of the splendor behind everything. The photons in a beer can are as beautiful as the photons that are reflected in a snowflake. When we can see beauty in people whom we dislike or who make it difficult to love them, it's a triumph of faith over judgment.

Looking at how you were transformed, or let's say affected, by the trauma of the environment is only half of the task. The other half consists in seeing how a change in you changes the environment or circumstances. If we only work with the first half, then we look upon ourselves as the victims of fate. If you look upon the task from the second point of view, then you become competent in your ability to transform your fate. At first, it's not very clear because if we use our reason, it's difficult to see that we transform the circumstances. Do you mean to say that I called this accident upon myself? No, this accident was purely fortuitous. That's the way we think.

Remember the words of Jung, the psychoanalyst, who said, "If you don't confront your shadow, it will come to you in the form of your fate." Those are very important words because you can't see the causal connection. Jung was talking abut a totally different connection, synchronicity, rather than the very commonplace causal relationship that represents the lower functions of our thinking. From the moment that you can recall a situation in which your being had an impact on the circumstances, instead of you being victimized by the circumstances, from that time on, you will gain confidence in your ability to govern your fate. That's why for the moment, we're looking back and trying to recall a situation in which it is very clear to see how your decision affected the circumstances.

If you try to figure it out with your mind, you're lost; there's no point; you're wasting your time. You have to keep your consciousness very high, being always conscious of your eternal being. Then see how your eternal being has had to deal with all that you had inherited through your ancestors and the circumstances of your draw of life, and how gradually you lost contact with your real being and things went wrong. Now you have reintegrated your real being again; you're looking at things and beginning to see things clearly. One has to keep on working at it. Consider yourself as an instrument that you have to keep tuning all the time. One gets out of tune very easily.

Miracles Do Happen

Musing upon the importance attached by the Sufis, particularly Pir-o-Murshid Inayat Khan, to achievement, I am trying to figure out how these lofty theories would apply to living in the society of our day and age.

The commonplace way of life is relatively straightforward with its ups and downs, bouts of joy or pleasure, disappointments and despair. There are natural laws, of course: what you sow, you reap. If you put energy into life, work diligently, the likelihood is that there will be dividends. Slothfulness most predictably will leave one indigent unless one has one of those rare lucks of "making money as one sleeps," which also occurs. But a profit that one has not attained by one's efforts is likely to be irresponsibly squandered and what one does with one's assets may prove disappointing. The leading edge sought by the more progressive managers in our modern industrially oriented societies is the pursuit of excellence. That the pursuit of excellence is more psychologically rewarding than just cold calculated moneymaking or aggressive profiteering is the conclusion that a number of successful business men and women have reached today. In the end, it proves even more profitable.

Pir-o-Murshid attaches very much importance to achievement because it releases potentialities, which he calls our divine inheritance. Of course, a further step would consist in grasping the divine nostalgia for actuation—you may call it existentiation (not just manifestation) of the many-splendored universal potentialities longing for expression behind one's impulse. By linking up with the divine springheads of our personal motivations, life gains a whole other dimension. This is a typical Sufi way of looking at things, and it makes for creativity in achievement, since one is injecting a cosmic dimension into one's venture.

There is yet another step that lies still further beyond the commonplace, and therefore bypasses those middle-range laws of nature we just referred to. In fact, it looks as though there is a whole hierarchy of laws ranging from the middle-range laws to transcendent laws, difficult to figure out by our finite modes of thinking, something like synchronicity or the concatenation of causes in the modern systems theory in physics. The Sufi Ibn Arabi refers to a causal chain moving down in the transcendent-immanent vector of time, rather than the arrow of time moving in the process of becoming. These insights, evidencing other dimensions of human understanding, are most perplexing. The Sufis refer them as the "consternation of intelligence."

Since it is energy—whether physical or psychic—that triggers a project or program (software) into actuation, we are indeed speaking about power, but a power that makes a thing happen beyond predictability or likelihood (in the conventional way of assessing likelihood). This is what we call a miracle. The Sufis call this "divine power." At the ultimate levels, even the divine fiat is delegated, but only to the selfless and the dedicated, traditionally the renunciates. Pir-o-Murshid pinpoints the clue when he clarifies that, although achievement enhances one's personal power so that one may undertake greater challenges, the personal objective (that is, either the personal gain in terms of money or prestige, or even the practical format of that goal) limits that power. Whereas if one has renounced any concern about gain, or even just the fact of being successful, then the power one wields is infinite. This accounts for the fact that some renunciates or sages are ascribed the power of making things happen, sometimes quite miraculously—but it works for others, not for themselves.

Perhaps you belong to that clan of beings who are only successful when you are doing things for others. No sooner do you try to promote your own well being or pursue your personal wishes than it just doesn't gel. If so, you are amongst the blessed poor in spirit! Such altruistic sharing could consist in benevolent donations to hospitals, or study or rehabilitation programs, or research or competitions. Nowadays, a progressive formula is upgrading one's staff with advanced training. How this power works is most intriguing. There was the case of Baba Farid Ganj-i Shakar, one of our predecessors in the chain of the Chishti Sufis. He was known to open doors to people who were destitute. He asked a man who needed to look after his aging mother to give all his money to the poor. Within a week, he got a marvelous job! But a man who shirked responsibility and asked

Baba Farid to help him was instructed to repeat a few supererogatory prayers. It didn't work. Asked why, Baba Farid said, "The first man needed help to help another, whereas the other man relied on my power and did not believe in God from whom my power derives!"

The secret behind this power is a covenant of fealty on the same lines as the pledge of suzerainty undertaken by the vassal with respect to his sovereign in the medieval traditions of chivalry. In fact, the initiation in the Sufi Order is called *bayat*, which means the vow of serving as the ambassador of the divine sovereignty. Indeed, the sovereignty of a king depends upon his recognition by his subjects. However, reinstating things in their universal perspective, the Sufi Sahl Tostari says, "If you are the repository or warranty of the divine sovereignty, the *sirr ar robubiya* (the secret of his sovereignty) it is because God is the secret of that secret—*sirr-as-sirr-ar-robubiya*—since the power rests with God ultimately."

What this amounts to is that the strange divine power that makes things happen, the secret password that opens doors, is the divine sovereignty whose pledge is actuated by selfless service and kindness to one's fellow beings. This is all very perplexing because on one hand Murshid says, "To achieve, you need enthusiasm, whereas to meet adversity, you need indifference." That's the law which accounts for the fact that we are pulled in two directions by these two impositions. But to insert indifference into the pursuit of excellence, that is the ultimate tour de force!

You do not renounce the world but you renounce yourself out of love; you are in the world but not of the world. You become the instrument of the divine *fiat* to help those beckoning for help in their despair, and in so doing, you make God a reality in your being.

The Hierarchy

All surrender to love willingly and to power unwillingly.

Pir-o-Murshid Inayat Khan

When we talk about the hierarchy, we are thinking of beings like St. Francis or Buddha or Akhenaton—the numbers are infinite of these beings held in esteem not only by their followers, but by people at large throughout the centuries. Great beings are held in esteem not because of their position or office in the world, imagined by some on the model of our secular governments with all the bureaucracy and ego squabbles for power, but by the evidence of their selfless love and dedication to their fellow beings, and by their abdication of any claim to a position or use of personal power.

Most people find it difficult to handle power.

No sooner does one build an institution, than people are called to positions in which they are subjected to the temptation of exercising personal power, influencing other people, enforcing their will by dint of their official position. What follows are intrigues, quarrels, unkindness, backbiting, all the kind of things one finds in spiritual groups, just as one does in the rather selfish society we are living in. Great beings are people who have abandoned the values of the world, and because of that they deal with worldly problems in a different way, a subtle way.

For example, when Buddha, on his tour of Indian cities, visited his native town Kapilavatsu, his father, the king, sent a pompous procession to greet him, the crown prince. Avoiding this worldly recognition, Buddha was found with a group of monks begging in the back streets of the city. St. Vincent de Paul did the same when the President of the French Republic came to honor him. Gandhi refused the post of First President of the Indian Republic. Akhenaton relinquished many of the artifices of the pharaonic tradition.

St. Francis abandoned the riches of his ancestral inheritance and so did St. Clare, who walked bare-footed in the streets, in rags, and catered to the lepers.

This is what Murshid means by the aristocracy of the soul and the democracy of the ego. "The Murshid is there for the mureed," he says. One is there by the esteem held by virtue of one's realization, mastery, self sacrifice, dedication, service, radiance, and sacredness, not by virtue of a post or office in the hierarchy. One is only able to take that post when one does not wish for it. And then, for having lost one's ego, the divine power of love takes over from the despotism of the autocrats, which is so devastating to those who are struggling for self esteem and who lose self confidence by being undermined by people who purport to be superior.

No claim to superiority: such is the message of Islam marking the advent of democracy. The challenge comes when occupying the post to preserve it from the despots while upholding its sacredness. One must strive to live up to the divine status present in each of us while keeping the human touch. One must be able to love those who envy one or denigrate one or try to foul one, and also to accept the responsibility while unmasking the sham of any adulation and deference to the outer position. This is the aristocracy of the soul together with the democracy of the ego.

Leadership

Many people are disappointed or disenchanted in their lives because they have not found the purpose of their life, or have not achieved their projects. The consequence is self denigration which acts as a deterrent to any further strivings. Now these negatives vie together in reinforcing each other respectively in a vicious circle dragging one downhill.

If one still entertains a spark of positiveness, obviously one needs to break the vicious circle either by steering clear on a tangent: finding freedom in one's person; or tugging the circle into a spiral: the spiritual dimension.

1) The first step consists in getting very clear about one's motivation. To make it easier, since some have difficulty in being turned on by any motivation whatsoever, one might ask oneself: what would you like? or prefer? Actually you may well find that this alters as you evolve and is based upon the values you ascribe to things.

2) This consideration is, however, linked with the second one which is: what am I good at? And if you don't think you're particularly good at anything, where amongst my many inadequacies am I a little more capable than in other respects? You might find that this tallies with what you wish.

3) But if you are a dedicated person, which is the type of person I am addressing (because that is the hallmark of spirituality, and that is what I am about), then you will only feel good about your motivation if it is of service to others. This gregarious motivation is founded upon a deep feeling: really caring for others.

4) It is by aligning the three above-mentioned considerations that you develop the makings of a leader.

5) Many people out there entertain wishes, even motivations, in resonance with yours, but remain in the never-never realm of wishful thinking, or the legendary *mañana.* So if you answer the call of the Seraphim to dedication in service by saying "send me," then you will have to make those people's dreams, which are also your dreams, come true.

6) It is an observation that most people do not like to take responsibility; and also an observation that people paradoxically both want to be told what to do and do not want to be told what to do. So much for the rational mind! But if you embody their aspirations and yourself prove that these can be materialized, then people will gain enough confidence in you to trust your judgment.

7) This means that you have to go out on a limb and make it happen. This entails that you have to work out every detail, program the steps leading to the target set for accomplishment, watch for the pitfalls, bear in mind the security measures to protect the project and the people involved, and guard people's pride because you can damage their psyche by dealing unfairly with them or undermining their self esteem. On the other hand if you give in to a person because he or she is more pushy, you might jeopardize the project that so many have been looking forward to or have invested their energy into.

8) This is where both your insight and your mastery are at stake, and what is more, you are being tested in your love. If you trip over just one mistake, others not only lose confidence in you but you have blown all their hopes in themselves.

9) There are good reasons why people procrastinate or demur at going out on a limb, and that is caution regarding their own judgment or that of another. This is generally based upon past failures due to faulty judgment. Also it is so difficult to foresee the consequences of a move. The success of the chess player is in the ability to envision the consequences of a large number of moves ahead, and those consequences of all the alternatives which are somewhat of the nature of a logarithmic exponential progression coasting on towards infinity. The other reason for procrastination and inaction is, of course, sheer laziness, lethargy, timorousness, and a lack of self confidence which is grounded in poor self esteem.

10) This is where one needs to cast an in-depth look at human judgment, and where the things I have been saying about the limitation and therefore unreliability of judgment, based upon our fallacious interpretations of situations, prove to be relevant. Our opinion cannot but be limited by our personal vantage point, which is just one vantage point in an infinity. A further limitation is our middle range

thinking. This is where complementing one's point of view with the hunch of intuition proves to be the hallmark of the successful leader. Note: this means reconciling the two poles of the antinomy of cognizance—and not simply dismissing one's personal assessment either.

11) But how do I develop intuition? And how do I gauge if it is reliable? No doubt learning how to turn within will shift consciousness into the intuitive mode. However one cannot integrate the "input processing" type of judgment with the intuitive mode if one totally dismisses the judgmental.

Consequently, rather than "placing a sentinel at the doors of perception" *alone*, one places a sentinel at the doors of perception *and* at the doors of the speculative mind. One grasps the issues behind the situations or facts as one turns within. Admittedly the intuitive mode is in stark contrast to the speculative mode. One does not set oneself up as the subject passing judgment on an object, but one tunes oneself to a state of resonance, so that one discovers in oneself that which one was experiencing as other than oneself.

12) How does one know if one's intuition rings true? By one's scruple about truthfulness, one develops a sense of authenticity about one's own inner subliminal feelings and promptings.

13) One might rightly ask: where is the spirituality in all of this? Yes, the spiritual dimension requires of one a whole other quantum leap. It allies divine insight with divine power.

14) We started with looking at things from a very personal view point. Now if we wish to crown our actions with this infinite dimension offered to us as our divine inheritance (but hardly ever availed of), we will need to have the courage to make a complete about-turn of our vantage point and look at things as they would appear from the cosmic vantage point.

15) One may well ask: But how do you know you are not fooling yourself? How do you know it is the divine vantage point? The answer is that we are programmed with a built-in

sense of infinity; otherwise we could not envision infinity in numbers or space or eternity in time. This intuitive inherent knowledge is evidenced in our ability to envision that there can always be a larger number than any number that we conceive etc. But to transpose our consciousness into the infinity of consciousness is a tour de force that few, mainly the mystics and sometimes the scientists, achieve. A clue to our ability to do so may be found in our ability to transpose our consciousness into that of another human or animal or plant or even mineral or angel, and by analogy in infinite steps, to God.

16) The same applies to power, discovering the divine heritage that is the infinity of potentialities invested in one's being. To all intents and purposes it looks as though there were some magic in this: the dervish reaches a point where what is wished for materializes.

17) If one's motivation is limited by personal interest, one's power to achieve is limited by one's personal axe to grind. The same applies to understanding: one's personal motivation sets up constraints on one's insight and hence one's sagacity. Where the motivation is totally disinterested, both one's insight and the power one wields are limitless, overwhelming, magical, and inspiring. But we must be clear that what we mean by being disinterested does not mean indifference, but espousing the aspirations of others and indeed of the nostalgia moving the universe; which means not just caring for others, but caring for others more than oneself.

18) At this stage the leader is a catalyst, inspiring and emboldening people to follow their bliss and actualize their incentive for the fulfillment of their purpose, in the context of the overall purpose of life, which like the horizon, "recedes as one advances."

The Guru Syndrome

To become conscious of inner contradictions, he must perforce act out the conflict and be torn into opposite halves.

C. G. Jung

It has become clear to me that, because I have been emphasizing the idealistic dimension of people and the environment while underplaying the "shadow," mureeds have been lulled into a high-flown image of themselves and of myself, which matches neither the reality of their being nor of mine and leads to difficulties in how they handle situations.

The ideal is the means, but its breaking is the goal.

Pir-o-Murshid Inayat Khan

Here, my own idealistic temperament carries over into others. Firstly, because my ideal of the sublime mirrors an archetype and aspiration latent and pressing as a nostalgia in those coming to me for spiritual nourishment, and furthermore, because of the impact that the "guru image" has on those in contact with him or her. Nourishing this splendid dimension is so important for so many people in helping them to overcome their disenchantment in the sordidness of much of our society, and to overcome their inadequate self image. But if one fails to make the connection between this level of reality and the existential conditions, one runs the risk of escaping from real situations into wishful thinking, and also in thinking of oneself as special. Everyone is special in their own way.

Great people have great faults; it is their greatness that is their greatest fault.

Pir-o-Murshid Inayat Khan

Living up to that image to nurture the need of the guru image in people (although I have consistently disavowed such a status) forces me, and indeed all those in a leadership position, into a role in which one runs the danger of neglecting to confront one's own defects, weaknesses or inadequacies. Because of a pupil's awe in the face of the aura of eminence of the guru, it is sometimes difficult to unmask the justifying faculty of the mind resorted to by a person who is looked upon as an example. The arguments offered often scramble the issue by flaunting contradictions, ascribing them, for example, to the "reconciliation of the irreconcilables" instead of striking a balance between clearly defined choices. This is a typical guru syndrome which we are witnessing in our time: masking contradictions, instead of recognizing their incongruity and correcting them.

Those who try to make virtues out of their faults grope further and further into darkness. The way to overcome error is first to admit one's fault, and next to refrain from repeating it.

Pir-o-Murshid Inayat Khan

The consequence of masking contradictions is the conflict and confusion that these ambiguities arouse in oneself and in others. Since in the drama of real life one senses how important the image is for people "out there," those in a leadership position fear that, should they admit criticism, they would spoil that image. However, by justifying oneself, one deprives oneself of the opportunity of ever progressing. The image cannot hold long unless matched by the reality of one's personality, so that in the end, one's scruple to uphold one's image to help people defeats its own end.

It is no use trying to prove what you are not. If you begin at the end, you will end at the beginning.

Pir-o-Murshid Inayat Khan

Anybody volunteering to embody the archetype representing people's higher self will have to choose between artfully concealing one's shadow, and when discovered, stand on one's high horse, justifying it hypocritically; or alternatively, by putting oneself on the line, be open to be exposed to scrutiny and criticism by all. Should one have the honesty and courage to confront one's shortcomings, one will in addition better understand people's problems through seeing oneself in others and others in oneself, thus affording real help to those who also need to transmute their shadow. Clearly, how could one expect to help another if one has not experienced their problems oneself and dealt with them constructively?

By justifying oneself, one blunts one's ability to earmark one's defects.

The human personality acts as a lens distorting the divine impulse. For example, wrath facing injustice gets distorted into hatred, or mastery into an ego trip; love into possessiveness or nobility into vanity; compassion into indulgence and condoning, or truth into callousness; cautious responsibility into fear or timorousness. If one is not extremely scrupulous about being honest to oneself, one tends to fail to recognize this distortion and firmly believes that one is acting under the higher impulse.

Our personality acts as a lens, distorting our divine inheritance, as in the picture of Dorian Gray. However, this distortion can be redressed by confronting it with its archetype, just like light distorted by a concave lens can be reconstituted to its original pattern by a convex lens. Caruso's voice distorted by the recording machines can be restored to its original beauty just as if we were able to reverse the arrow of time. Similarly, our divine nature, suffering from defilement like a distorted exemplar of a perfect archetype, can be reinstated in its pristine glory.

This requires one to match a divine quality latent in divine inheritance with its distortion in our personality, without slipping into a guilt complex or a state of despondent self denigration. The role played by the ideal becomes evident when one realizes that one cannot compensate for the distortion we have inflicted upon our divine inheritance without referring back to the divine model. Conversely, the ideal can only be known in and by means of its exemplification which is perforce distorted.

It is only if one is able to recognize one's inadequacies as a distortion of that very ideal to which one pays lip service that this ideal can operate in transmuting the "shadow," thereby realizing the divine legacy in our being so that it may become a reality in our personality. To know what one's defects are, all one needs is to recognize one's qualities and earmark the distortions of those qualities in one's personality. It is this distortion of a quality that stands as an obstacle to developing that same quality. Should one fail to admit and confront the defect, that very defect will, by the synchronistic interplay in our relationships with people, call up a situation in which we are placed before the choice either of applying the defective idiosyncrasy in handling the situation, or the divine quality of which the former was a distortion.

Pir-o-Murshid was very aware of the hazards of the transference syndrome and warned people about role playing.

> **Every soul has its own way of life; if you wish to follow another's way, you must borrow his eyes to see.**
>
> **Pir-o-Murshid Inayat Khan**

A further disadvantage of the guru image strikes clearly: if mureeds think of me as the image they have projected upon me rather than the real person, they run the risk of going wrong if they assume that my advice is absolute.

Much as I make it clear that neither I or the representatives in the Sufi Order are entitled to give advice to mureeds as to what to do, some still try to read, in the inflections of my voice, how I feel about a situation. Failing this, they think that, assuming I must have higher guidance, they need to try to capture this guidance, whereas they run the risk of wishful thinking!

Representatives, particularly, and those active in spreading the Sufi Message tend to model themselves upon my own life pattern which is practically 99% dedicated to service at the cost of my private life. In this instance, genetic traces of my ancestry of sannyasins and dervishes, and my own temperament that prioritizes service above anything else sets a challenge that people tend to emulate. Here once more, the guru transference image acts adversely, though I warn people not to consider me as a guru or even as an example. People get burnt out, while I go on striding ahead apparently unscathed. This accounts for increasing stress incurred by accumulating the responsibility of service with the need of matching up their job and the care of their families.

In as much as I am fully aware of this issue in my life, my choice is involved. Assuredly I am becoming increasingly sensitive to the need for balance here, yet I must follow my conscience.

Pir-o-Murshid saw the need for people to give some satisfaction to their personal emotions. In the following quotes, the wisdom of Pir-o-Murshid comes through with clear evidence:

> **The way you choose is the way for you.**
>
> **Pir-o-Murshid Inayat Khan**

> **Balance is the keynote of spiritual attainment. A virtue carried too far may become a sin. The fulfillment of life is by being human.**
>
> **Pir-o-Murshid Inayat Khan**

Christ had already warned:

> **Give to Caesar what belongs to Caesar and to God what belongs to God.**

Pir-o-Murshid gave space to people's need for love, for recognition, for self esteem, for fulfillment in achievement, and for security, while equally giving satisfaction to the need for ecstasy, for freedom, for glorification, for the discovery of the divine in one, for sacredness.

I have to shatter your image of me so that I may make my ideal a reality and you will have to shatter it also, and what is more, any replication of that image in you, especially if a representative in The Sufi Order. Since we are so inextricably intermeshed I will have to recognize myself in both your ideal and your idiosyncrasies, as you may recognize yourself in my ideal and in my failures without the screen of your image of me or my image of you confusing the issue.

May our ideals resonate like the multiple projections of mirrors placed face to face, cross-pollinating each other, while we strive in our interconnectedness to make these ideals a reality in our lives. Restored to their pristine splendor, our ideals may fertilize our personalities.

Chapter 10

Death and Life

Death and Resurrection

"Die before death and resurrect now."

Sufi saying

People are beginning to ask more questions about death and its process. This is because today people are more bent on confronting feelings honestly, rather than dismissing them out of fear. While neither the investigations on spiritism of our forefathers in the beginning of this century, nor the testimonies of people who have lived to recount their experiences in a "clinical death," are considered by many as evidence of survival after death, it doesn't make sense to our minds to assume that a person has achieved and attained in a lifetime can be wiped out in a moment of utter annihilation. The programming of the universe, while often paradoxical and not altogether consistent to our way of thinking, still must make more sense than that!

Admittedly, if one has left works of art or inspiring thoughts of pioneered breakthroughs in science or technology, one survives indirectly through one's creativity, which may indeed seed further achievements relayed by others. Besides, one's personality does indeed spill over onto those who love us by an uncanny osmosis, which links humanity by dint of a kind of interdependence in a network like that of the terms of an equation. Yet the individual—individuality—does it not mean something irreplaceable in its uniqueness? Mutations in nature are triggered by individuals; the forward march of civilization is impelled by the genius of a few exceptional beings. If, indeed, their incentive has meant so much to so many, how could one say that their special contribution is now finished?

Nature optimizes its chances of progress, of beating its own records. Perhaps our misconceptions about death are due to our preconceptions about our body, or matter in general. In as much as the body acts as a scaffold for the superstructure of our being, one might infer that if it collapses while the building is being is built, the completion of the building would be halted. Who can claim that the building is ever complete? What sense would it make for nature to leave a building half built? If we consider the body as the support system, then perhaps our being would collapse when the body does. But then what sense in all that went into it in the beginning? Is it tenable that the programming works that way? No, this doesn't make sense.

Matter never dies: it undergoes changes, gradual ones as in radiation, osmosis, and aging, and also sudden ones, as in a quantum leap such as water into steam, the jump of an electron from one orbital of the atom to another, and what we call death.

In the evolutionary leap from the inorganic to the organic, the electrons within the atom rearrange themselves more meaningfully and efficiently as a support system for the advance of intelligence and consciousness than in the previous arrangement. Hastily observed, the devastating eclipse in the in-between stage could easily be misconstrued as a falling apart. Never does the same water flow under the same bridge, yet the river remains. Judged from the point of view of the particular drops, it looks as though they have eluded one's gaze.

If a magnetic field structuring metal filings into a pattern were to undergo a momentary depolarization and then get repolarized, perhaps with different orientation, the metal filings would disperse, and then re-form again, no doubt differently. The magnetic power is the more essential element of the system; the outer pattern of the metal filings is secondary. The reality of our body is not visible structure, but what Dr. Rupert Sheldrake calls the "morphic resonance," which is more basic than the building blocks and survives their demise, while itself mutating over the aeons of time. If you take a computer apart, just examining the chips, it would be difficult to figure out the software. If you know the software, however, you are in possession of the key that would enable you to make any number of computers. Grasp the software of the universe and even the intention behind that software. If after death you have freed yourself from the support system, you don't need the hardware anymore.

After the quantum leap we call death, the protons and electrons of the body get scattered in the universe. Owing to the limitation in the speed of light, this cannot be communicated by the kind of signaling that we encounter in the universe in its explicate state. They are still interconnected, say the physicists, in a "non-local" state, the implicate state. Since each subatomic particle stores some information in its spin, they still are interconnected, forming together the network that acts as a support system for our minds and consciousness. If you have experienced even a flash of out-of-body travel, you will realized that, indeed, one can continue to see without eyes, hear without ears, displace yourself without wings, and communicate without language signals and understanding, without involving the brain.

While one may grasp splendor as it transpires through a scene of beauty, one can, moreover, grasp splendor directly, irrespective of, or bereft of, its physical support system. While one's understanding is usually based upon the assessment of a situation, one may, moreover, grasp meaningfulness directly, a kind of feed-forward instead of a feedback. Although the stress of a challenge will mobilize one's latent power to achieve, one gains a still greater power by renouncing the fruit of action; this is the epitome of unconditional love.

Information is built up at the cost of the expenditure of its support system, energy. This is called negentropy. We also need to distinguish between the knowledge that we attain by processing and interpreting the input from outside (that is, reacting to circumstances and adapting ourselves to conditions), and a kind of pre-cognizance irrespective of the feedback of experience. In philosophy it is called proto-critical knowledge. Imagine the mind, having built its constructs on experiencing other than itself, now discovering meaningfulness within itself, because our minds are isomorphic, homologous with (that is, of the same nature as) the mind of the universe and co-extensive with that global mind which we call the mind of God. Even as the global mind is self-generating, so our mind, which actuates that mind, is self-generating. A good example in Greek mythology is Bellerophon abandoning his steed, Pegasus (the support system of the mind), who could reach no further. Bellerophon then proceeded on his way to Olympus!

"The tendency of the soul is to reach to the highest spheres to which it belongs, but it cannot rise from the lower regions until is has left behind all earthy attachments," said Pir-o-Murshid Inayat Khan. Do you ever feel that your body cannot contain you or constrain you, or live up to the thrust of your mind, or withstand the exhilaration of your soul? These are the vistas attained in farther reaches of the mind where illumination flashes as realization. Here meditation will help one have a foretaste of life after life.

Imagine that you have awakened from your commonplace perspective, having shaken off that perspective like a snake shedding its skin, and you remember having been caught in that bind in the mind. For one who values splendor, the software of the universe is more thrilling than the hardware. I have a hunch that after death, instead of getting flashes of the manifestation of the divine intention transpiring from a distant perspective, one grasps that intention directly, so that its manifestation is secondary and is in the twilight of consciousness. You may prepare yourself for this in meditation with open eyes by, as the Sufis say, always looking for the hallmark of the divine intention behind all occurrences.

Imagine that you are attuned to the splendor that manifests as and through the forms of the universe. You will not be satisfied with its inadequate expression in the forms you perceive in the universe, however beautiful. Suppose you have been cultivating mastery and now touch upon the magic that mobilizes the marvel of existence. You will exult in that power and not try to appropriate it for your self in a spirit of covetousness. Suppose that you are dancing with joy, despite all the frustrations and wounds wreaked upon you by the limitation whereby the divine perfection in your being suffers in the existential condition. You will demur from building your joy upon precarious circumstantial conditions.

Suppose that you have reached a peace, not the peace of withdrawal from strife, but the peace in the vacuum of the existential realm out of which all activity emerges. You won't have to seek the cave or escape life. Suppose you are shattered by the ecstasy of unconditional love. You will love those who make themselves unlovable by acting loathesomely and obnoxiously, even though you do not approve of their behavior or their intentions or their attunement. The children of the world will spit at your face and tear your hair, poke out your eyes and trip you over, and you will still love them, for "they know not what they do."

According to some testimonies, at the eleventh hour, at the moment of death, one's life on the Planet comes to a head. That which was accomplished, that which one failed at, one's assets and one's defects or foibles, the harm one did to others, one's resentments for those who offended one, the ruthless and inexorable unexpected we call fate, one's loves and enmities, hopes and disappointments, struggles and satisfactions, all interweave into a kaleidoscopic pattern upon the screen of the mind.

The interfacing and interacting of the plethora of elements flashing over the threshold between the unconscious and the conscious issues enacted in one's life pattern, and the challenges met or not met by our resourcefulness, or what we made of our resourcefulness, suddenly zooms into perspective. As Dr. Kubler-Ross once pointed out, one is assailed with the remorse of not having done those things one could have done, but more desperately, for not having become what one might have become. I like to add "how one could have been if one would have been what one might have been." Here lie the crucial issues, particularly the latter. Obviously, it would have been wiser to have dealt with this earlier. Let us deal with the paramount issue now: our personality. Three parameters strike us:

1) Unfurling the resourcefulness lying dormant in our heritage from the whole universe, as much in its enormous compass as at all its levels;

2) Customizing these levels creatively, according to our own bent or peculiar genius, by rearranging them, fluctuating them like variations on a theme, and confronting and sharpening them by the encounter with the challenge of our lives;

3) Transmuting them so as to extract the essence of them, like the perfume out of flowers.

In the early stages of one's life, the first seems to prevail; in the middle of life's struggle, the second; at the autumn of one's life, the third. One needs to learn to resurrect before death. This requires pruning, assessing priorities, freeing oneself from a lot of ballast, and, most importantly, identifying oneself with the perfume extracted from that flower that was our personality, with its many idiosyncrasies. Petals will need to fall apart so that perfume may prevail.

Preparing for Resurrection

Our notion of death is perhaps the most nonsensical of all our notions! Exploring the software of the universe, physicists never cease to be amazed by the intelligence of the planning. How could we possibly believe that all that has been gained, not only by our know-how but by the uniqueness of each of our personalities, should get lost from the bounty of the universe?

If we are unaware of our immortality, we will think that we die. It is all in our way of looking at things. Our fear of death is linked with our failure to grasp more advanced paradigms of thinking: the first step in learning how to resurrect consists in widening our sense of identity which eventually avers itself to be co-extensive with the universe.

We commonly think of ourselves as a distinct individual but if we are updated with the holistic view of our day and age, we realize that every fraction of the totality carries virtually the entire code.

If you envision yourself as the keyboard of a piano, most of whose keys are taped so you can only play a simple melody, and should you then realize that you could tear away more and more of the tape and awaken many-splendored features of the investiture of the universe latent in you, you will exult in self validation.

In addition to the holistic paradigm, we need to consider the transcendental one. Our commonplace thinking thinks in terms of categories: mind, body, perhaps the soul, that mysterious unknown. The consequence is that our thinking breaks up in a dualistic or pluralistic view: the body dies; hopefully the soul continues to live—two categories.

The advanced way of thinking is in terms of polarity: I am also my body. In our spiritual beliefs, we are so old-fashioned! We still think in terms of one time dimension. If we shift into the new paradigms, and are able to shift between two or more dimensions of time, then we may envision ourselves as a pendulum of which one pole, the lower end, is moving in space-time and the other remains unchanged. In between these two poles there are numberless transitional stages. Information input from our perceptual interface with the physical environment is processed upwards so that ultimately the quintessence is recycled into that level of our being where meaningfulness prevails over perception—eventually into the software of the universe.

As we shift our sense of identity upwards, our feeling of the process of becoming merges into a sense of being continuity in change. Indeed the very cellular structure of our bodies—particularly our faces—that is configured by our emotional attunements and insight will imprint the fabric of the subtler levels of our being. These subtle levels would include our electromagnetic field, the sparkling of our aura, the morphogenetic field that acts as a template of our body, and further upwards in infinite degrees of subtlety. Thus our bodies will outlive the dispersal of the building blocks of our body, the electrons and protons that survive and carry some imprint of memory. This could be illustrated by the fact that not one cell of our body is today the same cell as a few years ago, yet we think it is the same body. This is because its basic structure survives the disruption of the cells.

Consequently we can consciously and willfully fashion our bodies of resurrection as a sculptor does, in a creative way. Our bodies of resurrection are our celestial bodies that maintain the gist of the countenance that sometimes transpires through our face when we are aware of the bounty and thinking of the universe coming through us.

By identifying with our self image, a fallible notion of ourselves, we are obstructing the shift in our thinking that enables us to bypass our transiency (the condition of our learning how to resurrect). The resulting mis-assessment of our involvement in our problems stands in the way of our realization, because we ultimately are our realization and it is this transcendent dimension of our being that survives its support system.

This would then require that we stretch our minds beyond their middle range. We would see the implications of our problems from the point of view of those involved in them, and while surveying ourselves with a bird's eye view in the context of the cosmic drama in all its compass, grasp the dovetailing of our lives and beings.

In this perspective, our way of looking at ourselves and our participation in the human drama will aver itself to be just the kind of thinking that will prepare us for the experience of resurrection. We cease to limit our assessment of our problems to causation in a linear fashion in the arrow of time, and we cease to succumb to the conditioning of our personality. Rather, we grasp a pre-causal stage out of which the programming of the universe arises behind the apparent universe of our own self image. Then we see ourselves in the universe, not just on Planet Earth or in our personal dramas (the storms in our teacups), and we interrogate ourselves: what are we doing on Planet Earth, what is our place in the universe?

The body, then, rather than being our spacesuit on Planet Earth that we will discard at death, is seen as a support system. Truly enough, Pegasus could not reach Olympus, but he imprinted upon his rider Bellerophon the thrust that hoisted him aloft. The bodiness of Pegasus was transmuted into energy.

Although it might be that many of the recollections in Dr. Moody's *Life After Death* and sequels could be accounted for by the residual exercise of brain functions, the out-of-body overview of the physical shroud gives us some clues as to the aftermath of this episode: Life after life.

I quote Shams Tabrizi, the mentor of Mevlana Jelal Ud Din Rumi:

> **I walk without feet and fly without wings, and see without eyes and hear without ears...**

and may I add:

> **and think beyond the mind.**

However, we cannot be creative, be it of a work or art or of ourselves, just by willing it. We have to be moved and shattered, bemused and filled with wonder.

Chapter 11
The Divine Banquet

The Banquet

Do we realize yet that we all participate in the delights of the cosmic feast only to the degree of our nostalgia? What a gift is ours: sharing in the cosmic celebration, in the cosmic banquet!

From our personal vantage point, we feed on the fabric of the Planet—in fact on the fabric of the galaxies; yet does it ever occur to us that by ingesting food, by breathing, by thinking, by feeling, by suffering, by rejoicing, by experiencing, by discovering our Planet, by exploring stars in outer space, by espying the thinking materializing as the cosmos, we are transforming the Planet (the galaxies) into humans—into ourselves?

Brahman is food, according to the Taitiriya Upanishad.

This sacrament becomes holy when we realize that the universe is a Being traditionally called God from whose very nature we inherit, if we recognize our host.

There are grades, of course, between the fast food snack, the rustic *pot au feu*, or the refined banquet; and we have a choice between chatter, elegant conversations, or participating in holy communion, notwithstanding those starving souls who crawl to pick up the crumbs from the floor. Pride of place is given to the privileged ones who have earned their official invitation at the behest of the "powers that be," the spiritual VIPs who legislate the do's and don'ts of our spiritual lives, and who organize the faithful into "the institutionalization of spirituality," to those adepts who, owing to their assiduity in spiritual practice, by dint of asceticism and piety, are *personae grata.*

But is there room for the noninvited at the banquet, for those who feel they do not deserve that privilege, for those with tears yet sunshine in their eyes? Does divine love stay the hand of the sentinel? Would the divine host refuse admission to those who solicit his/her grace?

Al Hallaj was certainly not welcomed by those who arrogated to themselves the right to legislate for the prevailing religious authority which condemned him. Al Hallaj said: "I have been invited to the banquet by the divine host, who offered me to drink from his chalice. His drink is poison. How could I refuse?"* Could we conjecture that, in his case, bureaucracy was bypassed by the divine host him/herself? But at the cost of what suffering!

Those who venture closer to the divine host are either awed (*haybat*) by his/her divine majesty, or moved by divine love by his/her proximity (*uns*).

Hujwiri, in the *Kashf ul Mahjub*, said: "God annihilates the souls of those who love him by revealing his majesty and endows their hearts with everlasting life by revealing his beauty... When God manifests his glory to a man's heart so that his majesty (*jelal*) predominates, he feels awe (*haybat*), but when God's beauty (*jemal*) predominates, he feels intimacy (*uns*)... There is a difference between one who is burned by his majesty in the fire of glorification, and one who is illuminated by his beauty in the light of contemplation."

The lover, desperately longing for the presence of the beloved, runs the risk of encountering opposition from the world. In traditional lore, he/she needs to proceed by stealth, incognito, to evade the threat of punishment

*paraphrased from quotation given in *In Search of the Hidden Treasure: A Conference of Sufis*. New York, Tarcher/Putnam (2003), page 153.

wreaked upon him/her by authority. Protected by the darkness, in the night of unknowing, St. John found freedom from the prison that our societies have built for the unconventional, the rebels.

On a dark night,
Kindled in love with yearnings
—oh, happy chance! ...

... In darkness and concealment,
My house being now at rest.

... In secret, when none saw me,
Nor I beheld aught,
Without light or guide,
save that which burned in my heart,

This light guided me
More surely than the light of noonday
To the place where he (well I knew who!)
was awaiting me—
A place where none appeared.

Oh, night that guided me,
Oh, night more lovely than the dawn,
Oh, night that joined Beloved with lover,
Lover transformed in the Beloved!

St. John of the Cross*

If we feel we have not earned the divine grace, we may invite the divine joy of giving.

* from *The Ascent of Mount Carmel*, tr. David Lewis (1909).

~

A Final Message to his Mureeds from Pir Vilayat Inayat Khan

Pir Vilayat's final message was given in Suresnes, France, on January 27, 2004, six months before his death. It was published in *Heart and Wings*, a publication of the Sufi Order International Secretariat, New Lebanon, New York.

I must say, it has been such a joy to share with you the encounter of our thoughts sparking each other. The mission—the meaning of the Message of the future, all of it has been exciting and overwhelming, and I am very grateful for your sharing with me. From the moment that one has broken bread at the same table, one is linked by a special link, and that's the reason for the Mass. The Mass is the ritual of eating at the same table together, and we have been sharing this wonderful bread and wine at the same table, and that establishes a link between us that can never be broken, so that we can always find each other. So, I will just say that you can find yourself—you can find me in your heart; and I can say, I can find you in my heart. God bless you.

~

Index

C

H

N

Pir Vilayat Inayat Khan with his cello

Biographical Note

Pir Vilayat Inayat Khan (1916–2004) was the son of the Indian Sufi master Pir-o-Murshid Hazrat Inayat Khan and an American mother, Ora Ray Baker. As his father's successor, Pir Vilayat served as head of the Sufi Order International for fifty years and became an internationally recognized spiritual teacher and master of meditation.

Born in London and raised in France, Pir Vilayat studied music under Nadia Boulanger at L'Ecole Normal de Musique de Paris, and read philosophy and psychology at Oxford University and the Sorbonne. During World War II he served as an officer on a British mine sweeper and participated in the invasion of Normandy. His sister Noor Inayat Khan was executed at Dachau for her role in the Resistance.

After the war, Pir Vilayat pursued his spiritual training, studying with masters of many different religious traditions in India and the Middle East. He incorporated the rich mystical heritage of both East and West into his teachings, adding the scholarship of the West in music, science, and psychology. Pir Vilayat brought together both spiritual and scientific leaders for public dialogues and initiated dozens of international interfaith conferences.

For more information on Sufism contact
the Sufi Order International Secretariat for North America
PO Box 480, New Lebanon NY 12125
www.sufiorder.org